The Boundaries of Genre

The Boundaries of Genre

Dostoevsky's *Diary of a Writer*
and the Traditions of Literary Utopia

BY GARY SAUL MORSON

NORTHWESTERN UNIVERSITY PRESS, EVANSTON, IL

NORTHWESTERN UNIVERSITY PRESS
PAPERBACK EDITION
Northwestern University Press, Evanston, Illinois 60201

Printed in the United States of America

For my parents, David and Shirley Morson,
and to the memory of my grandmother, Minnie Estrin

Contents

Preface

Faced with centuries of contradictory genre theories, some have despaired, others synthesized. From Giordano Bruno to Croce (and after), generic skeptics have held that the particularities of texts defy the generalities of classification systems, that it is in principle possible to classify texts in an indefinitely large number of ways, and that new works (or the rediscovery of old ones) inevitably render obsolete all existing or conceivable systems. To these objections it has been answered that innovation is identifiable as such only if norms are presumed, that even the frustration of expectations depends on their presence, and that interpretation itself is inconceivable without prior experience of works similar in some respects. For a text to be truly *sui generis*, it has been suggested, its readers (and author) would have to lack a biography. The variability of genres, it is concluded, argues not for the abandonment of genre theory, but for the formulation of a theory that would describe and account for that variability.[1]

In contrast to the generic skeptics, Paul Hernadi has advocated a dubious generic tolerance. Hernadi argues persuasively that no single generic system has yet been, or could ever be, adequate to the exclusion of all others; but his alternative, a "polycentric" synthesis of systems, does not seem helpful. In Hernadi's view, "the discerning critic" should reject "the monistic principle of classification" in favor of one that includes "several systems of coordinates" and can consequently help us find our way "in the more-than-three-dimensional universe of verbal art. . . . Given the slow interaction between most critical approaches of our day, it is an important task of future theories of literature to explore how the best generic concepts propounded in the last few decades may become integrated into a set of interlocking 'systems,'"[2] which is to say, systems of systems. But as one reviewer of Hernadi's book observes, it is difficult to see how such an all-embracing synthesis could be *used* (except as an introduction to genre theories themselves). Whereas each particular generic system may be "interesting from some point of view or serviceable for some purpose,"[3] the reviewer reasons, their mixture would seem to be adapted to no purpose at all.

The key word here, it seems to me, is purpose. No doubt, one can classify a set of texts in any number of ways, each of which is arbitrary in the sense that there could be another. But the choice of one or another classification system is not necessarily arbitrary when there is a reason for classifying: given a particular purpose that a generic system may be expected to serve, some may serve it better or worse than others. There is no absolutely "privileged" generic system without respect to purpose, but purposes themselves confer a relative privilege. A system well-suited to information retrieval may be poorly suited to understanding how a particular culture or period classified and responded to texts;[4] a system adapted to studying literary history or influence within a single tradition is unlikely to be helpful for cross-cultural studies of forms of discourse (say, narrative or brief meditative soliloquy).[5] Confusion or untenable claims result from the assumption that if one examines enough texts with sufficient attention one will discover the classes into which they naturally fall, or from the no less problematic assumption that one can deduce the one true generic system *a priori*, without reference to any texts. It is always possible to show how, to another observer with different interests, the texts would group themselves (and the categories would suggest themselves) differently. *For genre does not belong to texts alone, but to the interaction between texts and a classifier.*

To put this another way, there are two sources of variation in generic classification: there are differences among texts and there are also differences in the purposes of classifiers. Indeed, the same person may divide a group of texts differently from day to day or hour to hour depending on the questions of interest and the reasons for doing the dividing. At the beginning of each semester, I reshelve the books in my office according to what course I am teaching. Sometimes *Notes from Underground* is placed with the "novels," other times with the "anti-utopias," and still other times with the "self-referential monologues," such as *The Praise of Folly* and "The Diary of a Madman." And each time I contemplate Dostoevsky's work among different neighbors, features that I had previously ignored or regarded as unimportant appear central to me: and so I give myself the work anew. I see no compelling reason to decide, once and for all, what the work "really is." Nor does it seem necessary to insist that the word "novel" be used in all discussions to refer to the same class of texts—only to those long prose narratives, let us say, written in the West during a given period; or only to those narratives dealing primarily with character; or only to those that exhibit certain formal features. In one discussion it may be convenient to speak of the novel so as to exclude *The Tale of Genji* and Socialist Realist fiction, in another to speak of the "Socialist Realist *novel*."[6] Conversely, it is pointless to ask whether Gladkov's *Cement* is a novel (or *War and Peace* an epic, or an Indian poem about death an elegy) unless one first specifies the particular function to be served by the classification one has in mind.[7]

The genre theory outlined in this study is designed to contribute to a broader theory of literary interpretation. Texts are therefore classified according to what I shall call their "semiotic nature," which is to say, the conventions acknowledged to be appropriate for interpreting them. Acknowledged by whom, under what circumstances, and for how long, are questions we shall have occasion to ask. It will be seen that, because in this system interpretive conventions rather than formal features determine a work's genre, genre is not manifest in the work itself. Readers can and do disagree about conventions for interpreting a work; when they do, I shall say they disagree about its genre. Strictly speaking, therefore, I shall not be stating that given works belong to certain genres. I shall, rather, describe the herme-neutic consequences entailed by classifying a work as one of a particular semiotic type.

I should like to stress at the outset that in my discussion of "literature," "fiction," "novel," "utopia," "anti-utopia," "parody," and so forth, I shall *not* be concerned with defining or regulating the proper use of those *terms*, which may, as I have suggested, be properly used in different senses in differ-ent contexts. I shall rather be concerned with identifying and characterizing classes of *texts*—classes which, to be sure, more or less coincide with some uses of those terms, but for which it would in principle be possible to use other names or to coin new ones. For example, when I specify the criteria a text must satisfy to be called a parody *in this study*, my purpose is not to account for the often inconsistent usage of that term, but rather to identify unambiguously the texts to be characterized in the subsequent discussion. In general, I have preferred the risk of using old terms in a special and speci-fied sense to that of making my text impenetrable with neologisms, and, when it has been necessary to coin new terms, I have tried to make the terms self-explanatory and the principles of their coinage clear.

* * *

An account of how this book came to be written will be useful in under-standing its organization. Before I was interested in genre theory, I became fascinated with Dostoevsky's *Diary of a Writer*, which, it seemed to me, would reward reading as an integral (if idiosyncratic) literary work rather than as an amorphous collection of unrelated pieces. Statements by Dostoev-sky (especially in his correspondence) confirmed my suspicion that the work was designed to be so read. Nevertheless, neither in the *Diary* itself nor in the immediate external evidence was I able to discover to my satisfaction the basis of the work's unity or the way in which it was designed to be under-stood. My first approach was to consider the *Diary* in relation to Dostoev-sky's thinking about literary form and to other of his experimental works that are apparently similar to the *Diary*. The results of this investigation are presented in chapter 1 of this study, "Dostoevsky's Icon of Chaos." Subse-quently, I decided to consider the *Diary* not only in the line of development of Dostoevsky's own works, but also in the line (or rather, lines) of other works that, in one way or another, it resembled most closely. That is, I de-cided to explore the generic traditions to which the *Diary* might belong, beginning with works that combine fiction with nonfiction and that also contain heterogeneous embedded works. Inasmuch as the principal concern of the *Diary* appeared to be the possibility of a utopian society, I also exam-ined the tradition of works concerned with that theme, works which I even-tually decided to distinguish as utopias, anti-utopias, and meta-utopias.

In exploring the *Diary*'s combination of fiction with nonfiction and its relation to "traditions" and "genres," I became increasingly interested in the more general issues raised by these concepts, particularly where I found they were employed in questionable ways in recent critical studies. As a result, the *Diary* proved interesting in a new way: namely, as a touchstone for, and illustration of, certain problems in literary theory. For this reason, each of the central three chapters, 2 ("Threshold Art"), 3 ("Utopia as a Literary Genre"), and 4 ("Recontextualizations"), begins with a theoretical issue, which is then illustrated by an examination of particular works or genres—the last of which is, in each chapter, *The Diary of a Writer*. In chapter 2, I first consider what I call "threshold art," that is, works designed to be interpreted according to contradictory sets of conventions; then I examine a number of threshold works in which this kind of ambivalence serves to foreground interpretive conventions usually taken for granted; finally I discuss those sections of the *Diary* which clearly function in this way, especially those related to its periodical form. In chapter 3, a discussion of literary utopias exemplifies how other genres might be identified and characterized on the basis of their semiotic nature; those sections of the *Diary* indebted to literary utopias are then placed in that generic context. The final chapter turns to parodies of utopia (and, more generally, to parodies of other works or genres). The "Theory of Parody" presented in the first part of chapter 4 lays the groundwork for considering both "Anti-utopia as a Parodic Genre" (part 2) and what I call *metaparodic* works and genres, that is, a specific type of threshold literature that alternates inconclusively between "original" and parody, and between parody and parody of parody (part 3). Finally, I treat the *Diary* as a member of one particular metaparodic genre, namely *meta-utopia*. That is, I examine Dostoevsky's literary experiment as one of a number of works in which utopia *and* its parody enter into an inconclusive dialogue. In the *Diary*, as in some other works of this complex genre, utopia usually seems to have the upper hand, but not definitively so. An ironic shadow threatens to embrace the utopian passages in its uncertain penumbra.

My reading of the *Diary*, in short, is intended as an illustration and exemplification of my theoretical arguments, but emphatically not as their justification or "payoff." Although literary theory and literary criticism may be written by the same people, taught in the same departments, and co-exist within the covers of a single book, it is nevertheless a mistake to confuse their objectives. Whereas literary criticism (in the sense in which I use the term) is concerned with the interpretation and evaluation of particular works, the objective of literary theory—what the Russian Formalists hoped to make into a "science of literature"[8]—is, in my view, the systematic and progressive study of literature, including not only what has often been regarded as specific to literature (as the Formalists at first proposed), but also what literature shares with other cultural institutions and activities (in their later formulations). Literary theory seeks to formulate or disconfirm falsifiable propositions where that is possible; and where it is not possible, to indicate the reasons why. The reasons advanced may themselves be shown to be true or false; it is, in other words, necessary to be clear about the level of abstraction, and the kind of problem, to which one's theory is addressed. For reasons which I shall specify, I regard the theory of literary interpretation (a part of literary theory) to be properly concerned not with producing new (or re-affirming old) readings of particular works, but with accounting for how readings are produced. In those cases where interpretations of a work have differed, the theory of literary interpretation attempts not to adjudicate but to explain that difference. In addition to theory and critical readings of particular works, therefore, this study also contains what I call *metareadings*, that is, accounts of, and accountings for, how works have been interpreted.[9]

I might note, in conclusion, that I am not concerned in this study with demonstrating that *The Diary of a Writer* is an undervalued work, yet another "neglected masterpiece." The value one ascribes to the *Diary* (or any other work) is likely to depend on what one takes it *as*. What the present study does attempt to demonstrate is that the *Diary is* a work, that it may be *taken* as a number of different *kinds* of work—and that it clarifies a set of problems in the nature of literary kinds.

* * *

This study was completed under grants from the George and Eliza Gardner Howard Foundation, the National Endowment for the Humanities, the National Humanities Center, and the University of Pennsylvania. I am also grateful to Dan Ben-Amos, Caryl Emerson, Aron Katsenelinboigen, Barbara Kirshenblatt-Gimblett, Vadim Liapunov, Martin Price, Gerald Prince, Madeline Stone, Robert Whittaker, Tatyana Whittaker, and Harry Willetts for their encouragement and suggestions over the years, and to Robert Belknap and Wayne Booth for their extensive and valuable criticisms of my penultimate draft. Special thanks are due to Elliott Mossman, for his generosity of mind and wholeness of spirit; to Michael Holquist, my constant inspiration; and to Barbara Herrnstein Smith, my most demanding reader. I do not know how to express how much this book and its author owe to Robert Louis Jackson.

* * *

Addressed to readers who do not know Russian as well as to those who do, this study uses a double system for rendering Russian names. For convenience in locating Russian sources, all references to them in the notes use a standard, letter-for-letter transliteration system (š, ž, c, j, x, è, ',"). In all other cases, I have followed the most common, and hence most recognizable, spelling of Russian names. Thus, whereas the text and discursive notes consider Bakhtin, Tolstoy, Chekhov, and Herzen, the note giving the original source transliterates Baxtin, Tolstoj, Čexov, and Gercen. Like generic classification systems, systems for rendering names and terms in other alphabets are properly judged with regard to the purposes to be served—and different or multiple purposes may require different or multiple systems.

University press policy is to try "to avoid language that implies that the male is the norm and the female a special case." I am largely in sympathy with the spirit and purpose of this policy and so have, as a rule, chosen plural rather than masculine singular forms ("the readers ... they" rather than "the reader ... he or she") even when I felt this was stylistically cumbersome. It is my hope that the necessity for such cumbersomeness will prove temporary and that the time will soon come when readers routinely assume that a chairman is as likely to be a woman as a man. Only social changes can change the implications of such phrases and forms; as I argue in this study and elsewhere, meaning does not lie in texts alone but in the interaction between texts and readers, readers who think, speak, and interpret in a given community with given values pervading language to its core.

It has not been possible, however, for me to follow this policy mechanically or to find nonsexist substitutes for every sexist phrase. For, inasmuch as language is idealogical and evaluative in *many* ways, one cannot always eliminate a sexist phrase without losing other, desired implications carried by the phrase's history and frequent contexts of usage. More than sexism is lost by current substitutes for "one man's meat is another man's poison," "man and nature," or "the brotherhood of man." This is especially so when such expressions appear in contexts where substitutes would be anachronistic: one cannot change a reference to the hero of a Victorian novel and his *lady* to a hero and his woman without also changing the nature of their connection. In such contexts, I ask my readers to assume that I do not mean to imply that the male is the norm and the female a special case. The special case is language itself.

The Boundaries of Genre

1. Dostoevsky's Icon of Chaos

Is it possible to perceive as an image that which has no image?
—Ippolit Terentiev, in *The Idiot* [1]

A Work of Paradoxes

At the beginning of *Moby-Dick*, Ishmael notices an unusual painting in The Spouter-Inn.

> On one side hung a very large oil-painting so thoroughly besmoked, and every way defaced, that in the unequal cross-lights by which you view it, it was only by diligent study and a series of systematic visits to it, and careful inquiry of the neighbors, that you could any way arrive at an understanding of its purpose. Such unaccountable masses of shades and shadows, that at first you almost thought some ambitious young artist, in the time of the New England hags, had endeavored to delineate chaos bewitched. But by dint of much and earnest contemplation, and oft repeated ponderings, and especially by throwing open the little window towards the back of the entry, you at last come to the conclusion that such an idea, however wild, might not be altogether unwarranted. [2]

The fact that it is a painting seems to invite the search for design, but its apparent formlessness, its invitation no sooner extended than withdrawn, "puzzled and confounded" the viewer. For Ishmael, the puzzle itself becomes a source of interest. Standing in the semidarkness that blurs the already indistinct lines of the canvas, he finds "a sort of indefinite, half-attained, unimaginable sublimity about it that fairly froze you to it, till you involuntarily took an oath with yourself to find out what that marvelous painting meant." He concedes, however, that the elusive shape he ponders with such fascination was "enough to drive a nervous man distracted" (36); and one may imagine that other viewers, not having thought it worthwhile to make so careful an inquiry, left its mystery unraveled and, perhaps, scarcely noticed.

Like this obscure painting, Dostoevsky's *Diary of a Writer* has gone largely unexamined. So formless has the *Diary* appeared to most modern readers, and so meagerly does it seem to reward investigation of its structure, that it has often not been taken as a literary work at all. As a result, its great popularity with its many original subscribers has not lasted and has been largely attributed to the purely topical interest of its political articles. [3] To be sure, a number of Soviet critics have, over the past half-century, tried to identify a hidden pattern in the work and to clarify what Dostoevsky had in mind when, for instance, he wrote that "the *Diary* has at last matured to the point where even the slightest change in its form is impossible" (*Pis'ma*, III, 284). Aware that systematic defiance of generic norms is quite common in Russian literature and that, as Tolstoy wrote in defense of *War and Peace*, "not a single work of Russian literature at all rising above mediocrity has quite fitted into the form of a novel, a poem, or a tale,"[4] these critics have looked for precedents for Dostoevsky's experiment and urged the formulation of a poetics capable of explaining both the *Diary* and these other formal anomalies. Most recently, I. L. Volgin, speculating on the reasons for the failure to find such a poetics, suggested that it may be impossible either to describe or to interpret the *Diary* as "a literary phenomenon" until it has been properly classified. "*The Diary of a Writer*," Volgin's programmatic article begins, "is a literary work of a special type. Until now, however, not only has the literary nature of Dostoevsky's one-man journal gone unstudied, even its genre has not been convincingly defined."[5] Volgin implicitly proposes that an examination of the *Diary* be based on a more general theory of generically ambiguous works. I would add that a principal source of the *Diary*'s interest may be its capacity to raise and exemplify problems of genre theory, and to serve as the occasion for exploring the relation of classification to interpretation.

If the *Diary* is taken as a literary work, it is Dostoevsky's longest—about as long as *Crime and Punishment* and *The Brothers Karamazov* combined. It began as an erratic series of feuilletons in the *Citizen*, a politically conservative journal that Dostoevsky edited in 1873 and the first part of 1874. Under the title *F. M. Dostoevsky's Diary of a Writer*, the column appeared first in every number (1, 2, 3, 4) of the *Citizen*, then in every other number (6, 8, 10), and progressively less frequently after that. The next twenty-five issues of the *Citizen* contain as many installments of the *Diary* as the first ten, and after that only one more contribution appeared (50). After a two-year hiatus, during which Dostoevsky wrote *The Raw Youth*, the *Diary* resumed in 1876 with an amended title to describe its revised form: *The Diary of a Writer: A Monthly Publication*. Now an independent, one-man journal rather than a contribution to another publication, the *Diary* appeared twenty-one times in 1876 and 1877 (with combined issues for July–August, 1876, May–June, 1877, and July–August, 1877) until a second interruption during which Dostoevsky wrote *The Brothers Karamazov*. A single issue appeared in 1880, its designation as the "August" number (when there was none for any other month) suggesting that the monthly form was central to the author's design. Intending to resume the *Diary* on a regular basis in 1881, Dostoevsky did not live to publish anything more than the January issue.

This arbitrary ending was apparently the only kind the *Diary* was designed to have. Lacking a plot, and drawing its material from ongoing stories in the daily press, the *Diary* is, in principle, as endless as history. Thus, in contrast to a number of Russian novels that appeared *in* periodicals, the *Diary* *is* a periodical. When read in book form, as Dostoevsky intended it to be republished,[6] it directs its readers to reconstruct its original appearance as a

monthly journal. The seams are, so to speak, designed to show, as they are
not, for example, in *Anna Karenina*. Or to put it somewhat differently,
whereas novels and plays often indicate that time has elapsed in the characters' lives between chapters or acts, the *Diary* indicates that time has elapsed
in the *author's* and original readers' lives. In this respect, the *Diary* resembles
Eugene Onegin, which also takes the time between installments and the aging
of the author as themes and plays on the arbitrariness of starting and stopping
points. Another form on which Dostoevsky's generic experiment obviously
draws—namely, the diary—is also like the periodical, potentially endless.

Those who have taken the *Diary* as a literary work have been especially
puzzled by its thematic and formal heterogeneity. Commenting on the work
of the Roman satirist Lucian, Mikhail Bakhtin once observed that when all of
Lucian's dialogues, diatribes, narratives, and other menippean satires are conceived as a single work, the result is "a sort of *Diary of a Writer*" making up
"an entire encyclopedia of the contemporary life of his time: they are full of
both open and hidden polemics with the various philosophical, religious, ideological and scientific schools, tendencies and currents of the time; full of the
images of contemporary or recently deceased public figures, the 'masters of
thought' in all spheres of social and ideological life (under their own names or
disguised); full of allusions to the great and small events of the epoch. . . ."[7]
Dostoevsky's *Diary* embraces all this, and more. Designed, as its first monthly
issue tells us, as a record of all its author "has seen, heard, or read" ("Announcement," January, 76) and as a chronicle of the current spiritual development of Russia, the *Diary*'s concerns range from metaphysics to military
strategy, literary theory to foreign policy, aesthetics to the apocalypse (which
the diarist describes as imminent). Denunciations of Jewish capitalists and
Polish papists alternate with articles advocating greater educational opportunities for women and reports of ongoing trials (which Dostoevsky attended)
of domestic brutality cases. There are also predictions, in the form of fictional sketches, of the likely consequences of the verdict in those cases; a model
philosophical suicide note; discussions with a "paradoxicalist" about the advantages of war, the benefits of hypocrisy, and the approaching end of history; a dialogue with a second paradoxicalist, the "witty bureaucrat," about the
positive contributions of waste to progress; two contradictory reviews of
Anna Karenina (favorable after book 7 of the novel appeared, unfavorable
after book 8; reminiscences of recently deceased Russian writers and a eulogy
to George Sand; the text of Dostoevsky's Pushkin speech and an account of
its reception; considerations of techniques for speaking through a censor and
for detecting a forgery; an extract, perhaps genuine, "From the Book of Predictions by Johann Lichtenberger, in the Year 1528"; "The Plan for a Satirical Story from Contemporary Life"; "The History of the Verb 'Stuševat'sja'";
"A Turkish Proverb" and "An Old Krylov Fable about a Certain Pig"; articles
on spiritualism and one on "The Extraordinary Shrewdness of Devils, If Only
They are Devils"; and numerous meditations on *Don Quixote*. The January,
1876, *Diary*, the first monthly issue, begins with an article "Instead of a Preface about the Great and the Small Bears, about the Prayer of the Great

Goethe and, Generally, about Bad Habits"; and the subsequent three articles of the issue's first (of three) chapters concern, or profess to concern:

2. A Future Novel. Again, an "Accidental Family."
3. The Christmas Tree at the Artists' Club. Thinking Children and Spoiled Children. "Gluttonous Youth." "Oui-girls." Jostling Raw Youths. The Hurrying Moscow Captain.
4. The Golden Age in the Pocket.

The titles of articles in other issues are as lengthy and as enigmatic as these. Generally speaking, the *Diary*'s tables of contents seem designed not to indicate their unifying concerns, but rather to challenge the reader to discover them—that is, if there are any to discover.

A generic as well as a thematic encyclopedia, the January, 1876, issue, which is about forty pages long in most editions, contains fiction (the story "A Boy at Christ's Christmas Party"), nonfiction, and entries that may be taken as either; a description of the experience that apparently inspired the story and of the author's first intimation of its plot; "A Word Apropos of My Biography"; and a number of ironic characterizations of the new work's perplexing form. Later issues also include, as part of the text, advertisements and letters to the editor (from both real and fictitious readers), all carefully noted in the table of contents and sometimes parodied months later. Monologues often break into dialogues with imagined readers who, having acquired a personality and biography, may return in subsequent articles and stories. Nor is it clear what relation the *Diary*'s stories—"The Dream of a Ridiculous Man," "Bobok," "The Meek One," "The Peasant Marey," and "The Boy at Christ's Christmas Party"—bear to the polemical journalism in the midst of which they appear and to which they sometimes refer, or how the reader is to interpret a work that includes its own notebooks and chronicles the composition of its embedded fictions.

In tone, also, the *Diary* is radically inconsistent and heterogeneous. While some articles proclaim that "War Is Not Always a Scourge, Sometimes It Is Salvation" and defend a "Utopian Understanding of History," others wryly comment on these quixotic ideas. Irony alternates with contempt for irony, humorless polemics with satires on humorless polemicists, dogmatic ideology with metaliterary play. Rapid shifts, often many times in a few pages, make it hard to determine what is satiric and what is the object of satire, or where—if anywhere—"Dostoevsky" is speaking directly. The article on Lichtenberger, for instance, seems sometimes to endorse and sometimes to parody oracular pronouncements, and "The Dream of a Ridiculous Man" has been read as both utopia and anti-utopia. Setting the tone for the work it introduces, the article "Instead of a Preface" first grimly contrasts the meaningless suicides of contemporary youth with Werther's final "regret that he would never more behold 'the beautiful constellation of the Great Bear'" and then switches to self-referential play. Just as the diarist observes that modern Werthers would be ashamed to bid farewell "not only to the Great, but even to the Small, Bear," he is "interrupted."

"What have you begun speaking about?" an amazed reader will ask me.

I was about to write a preface, since it would not be customary to have no preface at all.

"In that case you had better explain your orientation and your convictions; and explain what kind of man you are and how you presumed to announce *The Diary of a Writer*."

But this is very difficult, and I see that I am no master of writing prefaces.

After some not entirely inconclusive indications of the work's political orientation, the diarist observes, "With this I am ending my preface. Besides I only wrote it for form."

It is, in fact, quite common for the diarist's statements to be qualified in this way, and for his diatribes to be "interrupted" by "amazed readers"—or by Dostoevsky himself in his role as page-conscious editor. "But having finished my first chapter, I shall interrupt my article on finances because I feel that what I am writing is quite boring," he introduces his conversation with the "witty bureaucrat" (January, 81, II, 1):

I am also interrupting it because I would be unable to get it all in the two signatures of the *Diary*, and so I would have to postpone it for future issues anyway . . . [ellipsis in original]

"There's no reason, no need to resume it in coming issues," voices will interrupt me with distaste (I already anticipate these voices). This isn't an article on finances, it's—self-indulgence. . . . In future issues give us a story.

Digressive author and critical editor, "private" diarist and public journalist, dreamer and satirist, prophet and self-parodist, Dostoevsky seems constantly poised between opposites, between vision and self-conscious revision. Indeed, the conflict between his roles and the inconsistency of his tones are themselves discussed—inconsistently, to be sure—in a number of the work's self-referential articles.

What sort of unity, we may ask, can obtain in a work so encyclopedic in theme, diverse in form, and contradictory in tone? Bakhtin considered these questions, and in discussing the synthesis of topical polemic with narrative fiction in menippean satire, he alluded confidently to "the organic unity of all these seemingly very heterogeneous traits and the profound internal integrity of this genre" (97), but he did not explain the nature of that "organic unity." Does it consist, for instance, in a reconciliation of antitheses or, on the contrary, in their constant and intensified dialectical opposition? Could there not, moreover, be several kinds of genres composed of antithetical genres, and if so, would it not be useful to explain their different kinds of coherence? To be sure, there are, as Bakhtin observes, many encyclopedic or generically contradictory works—in addition to ancient menippean satire, a number of more recent works, such as Burton's *Anatomy of Melancholy*,[8] Pushkin's *Eugene Onegin, A Novel in Verse*, and Shklovsky's *Zoo* raise similar problems—but to identify a literary tradition is not yet to describe the poetics of any particular work or of such works in general.

Poetics of the Underground

Before considering these more general questions, I would like to discuss Dostoevsky's own views regarding a number of his generically problematic and formally anomalous works. As Dostoevsky was well aware, his novels were likely to appear shapeless to most readers—"loose and baggy monsters," as Henry James was to call them—and he therefore outlined a theory of realistic art to justify, and to aid in the development of, his aesthetic practice. Like the novels themselves, which have had such great influence on twentieth-century European literature, this theory seems remarkably modern. Briefly put, Dostoevsky increasingly came to view the concept of "realistic art" as bordering on self-contradiction. For art, he reasoned, strives for coherence and order, but reality, as the principal narrator of *The House of the Dead* observes, "strives toward fragmentation."[9] What art represents, it misrepresents. Moreover, by the mid-1870s Dostoevsky had come to believe that social "disintegration," "fragmentation," and "dissociation"—terms frequently used and discussed in the *Diary*—were, in all probability, literally apocalyptic in extent and, therefore, that the divergence between art and reality was particularly extreme, perhaps absolute. Can there be art at Armageddon? Or as Ippolit Terentiev (in *The Idiot*) poses the central question of Dostoevsky's aesthetic thought: "Is it possible to perceive as an image that which has no image?"

Dostoevsky's contemporary Goncharov believed it was not possible. "Art, a serious and strict one, cannot depict chaos, disintegration," Goncharov wrote in 1871; and in a letter to Dostoevsky three years later, the author of *Oblomov* criticized the author of *The Possessed* for being concerned with the disfigured world of the underground and the formless life of contemporary "accidental families." "A work of art (I mean the work of art of an objective artist such as you, for example)," Goncharov advised, "can only appear, in my opinion, after life has been fixed. . . . "[10] Their dispute can be taken as emblematic of that between nineteenth-century realism and twentieth-century modernism. For his part, Dostoevsky prided himself on his refusal to retreat from a difficult artistic problem into what he regarded as other writers' conventional descriptions of a beautiful past (e.g., *War and Peace*) or the already "insignificant and isolated" (*Diary*, January, 77, II, 5) life of the nobility (in *Anna Karenina* and *Oblomov*). "Our talented writers, who have been depicting in highly artistic form the life of the middle-upper circle (familial)—Tolstoy, Goncharov—thought that they were depicting the life of the majority," Dostoevsky observed in the notebooks for his most "fragmented" novel, *The Raw Youth*.

> On the contrary, their life is the life of exceptions, while mine is the life of the general rule. . . . I am proud to have portrayed for the first time the

real man of *the Russian majority*, and for the first time to have exposed his tragic and misshapen side. . . . Underground, underground, *poet of the underground*, our fueilletonists have been repeating as if this were something derogatory to me. Fools, this is my glory, for that's where the truth lies.[11]

But the poetry of the underground, Dostoevsky believed, requires a poetics of the underground, a poetics that he tried to exemplify in his formally anomalous fictions and that he explicitly argued for in his most experimental work, *The Diary of a Writer*. In an article in the opening issue of the 1877 *Diary* (II, 5), Dostoevsky first contrasts the description of a contemplated suicide in Tolstoy's *Boyhood* with an account of an actual child's suicide in a letter Dostoevsky has just received. The explanation for why a boy of Tolstoy's time might dream of, but not commit, suicide whereas a contemporary boy "*dreamed and then acted*," Dostoevsky contends, is to be found in the advent of "some new social reality, completely different from that which existed in the tranquil and stable, long-established Moscow landowner's family of the upper-middle circle, of which Count Leo Tolstoy was our *historian*." Here the word "*historian*," italicized in the original, is used pejoratively to describe Tolstoy's unwillingness to grapple with urgent but intractable problems of the day. At the close of his article, Dostoevsky turns from his consideration of the "new reality" to a plea for a new art ("The Boy Celebrating His Name Day," January, 77, II, 5):

And who will be the *historian* of all those left-over corners of Russian life which, it seems, are now so terribly numerous? And if in this chaos—in which already for a long time, but especially now, social life is taking place —if in this chaos it is still impossible even for an artist of Shakespearean dimensions to seek out a normal law and a guiding thread, then who, at the very least, will illuminate just a part of this chaos, even without dreaming of a guiding thread? The main point is that no one is yet concerned with the matter, as if it is still too early for our greatest artists. Without a doubt, we have among us a disintegrating life and, therefore, a disintegrating family. . . . Who even in the smallest degree can define and express the laws of this decomposition . . . ?

To "define and express the laws of decomposition"—that is the goal of the Dostoevskian novel and, indeed, of the very work in which this passage appears.

Stories That Cannot Be Told

Dostoevsky tried a number of experiments to "delineate chaos." One technique he used especially frequently was to tell the story of a failure to tell a coherent story, a failure that is itself the best index to a world beyond the reach of ordered vision. The narrator of such a story is, as a rule, a man whose disfigured personality reflects the disintegration of Russian society; who writes in order to make sense of his life by arriving, in the process of composition, at a coherent account of it; but who, unable to comprehend either himself or his world, creates not a finished work but "notes" and fragments that end as uncertainly and abruptly as they begin. Whatever order there is is often attributed to an "editor" who has shaped the text just enough to make it readable at all. For example, the narrator of *Notes from Underground*, whom the editor describes as the sort of person who "not only may, but positively must, exist in our society, considering those circumstances under which our society was in general formed,"[12] decides to write his autobiography as a form of therapy—to comprehend his life by learning how to tell its story. "There is a whole psychological system in this [experiment]," he explains to the readers whom, he says, he will never have (36):

> What precisely is my object in writing? If it is not for the public, then after all, why should I not simply recall these incidents in my own mind without putting them down on paper? . . . perhaps I will really get relief from writing. Today, for instance, I am particularly oppressed by a certain memory from the distant past. . . . I have hundreds of such memories, but at times some single one stands out from the hundreds and oppresses me. For some reason I believe that if I write it down I will get rid of it. Why not try?

Part 2 of *Notes from Underground* is his attempt, which ends in failure—a failure marked by his inability to reach either a logical or a formal conclusion. "But enough," he interrupts his endless circles of self-justification. "I don't want to write more from 'underground' . . . " (ellipsis in original). The fragment is then concluded by the editor: "The 'notes' of this paradoxicalist do not end here, however. He could not resist and continued them. But it seems to me that we may stop here" (115).

Essentially the same technique is used in Dostoevsky's earlier work *Notes from the House of the Dead*. A description of life in a Siberian prison camp, this collection of sketches, narratives, and philosophical meditations may also be taken—as Goryanchikov, the fictive author, occasionally implies—as a description of Russia in microcosm. The "editor" of Goryanchikov's notes stresses both their fragmentary quality and their intended function as therapy—a function which, judging from Goryanchikov's nearly insane behavior to the moment of his lonely death, they did not fulfill. The relatively coherent version that follows, the editor explains, is the product of his own selection and ordering of random writings that the unsociable author apparently never intended to publish. Three-fourths of the papers that Goryanchikov's landlady had not yet destroyed turned out to consist of "trifling, insignificant scraps," says the editor in introducing his abridgment,

> But among them was one rather thick volume of finely written manuscript, unfinished, perhaps thrown aside and forgotten by the writer. It was a disconnected description of the ten years spent by Alexandr Petrovitch [Goryanchikov] in penal servitude. In parts this account broke off and was interspersed by passages from another story, some strange and

terrible reminiscences, jotted down irregularly, spasmodically, as though by some overpowering impulse. I read these fragments over several times, and was almost convinced that they were written in a state of insanity. But his reminiscences of penal servitude—"Scenes from the House of the Dead" as he calls them himself somewhere in his manuscript—seemed to me not devoid of interest. . . . To begin with I am picking out two or three chapters as an experiment. . . . [13]

In order to understand his psychological disfigurement, Arkady Dolgoruky, the hero of Dostoevsky's *Raw Youth*, also sets out to tell his life story completely truthfully—which means for him, first, not to consider the possible reactions of an audience, and, second, to avoid the ready-made forms and conventional expressions of traditional narrative art. "I shall simply record all the incidents, doing my utmost to exclude all literary graces," he explains at the beginning of the manuscript that he, too, does not intend to publish. Like the underground man, however, he rapidly discovers that the forms of speech and writing he uses already acknowledge a public and narrative traditions he would ignore. "I foresee, however, that it will be impossible to avoid [artistic] descriptions of feelings altogether," he concedes, "so corrupting is every sort of literary pursuit in its effect, even if it is undertaken for one's own satisfaction" (14). No sooner does he begin his narrative than, "reading over what I have just written," he interrupts himself (ellipsis in original):

> I am beginning—or rather, I should like to begin—these notes from the 19th of September of last year, that is, from the very day I first met . . .
> But to explain so prematurely who it was I met before anything else is known would be cheap; in fact, I believe my tone is cheap. I vowed I would eschew all literary graces, and here at the first sentence I am being seduced by them. It seems as if writing sensibly can't be done by simply wanting to. [14]

At the end of his novel, Arkady submits his manuscript to his former tutor, Nikolay Semenovich, for evaluation. The tutor, many of whose views seem to echo Goncharov's, takes the opportunity to comment not only on "the general lawlessness and chaos" that has produced so many "accidental families" and their brooding raw youths, but also on the insurmountable difficulties contemporary novelists face in creating "beautiful forms" from such recalcitrant material. Inasmuch as Arkady has no literary aspirations, and claims not to intend to publish his manuscript, these comments seem less applicable to his novel than to Dostoevsky's. In any case, believing that there can be no finished work of art unless there are "fine finished forms of social life," Nikolay Semenovich suggests that Arkady's narrative can at best be described as "material for a future work of art" (606-607), for a historical novel to be written in a distant and orderly future. Contemporary novelists, he writes, should avoid "inharmonious" forms by choosing different material. "If I had been a Russian novelist and had talent," he observes (604-605),

> I should certainly have chosen my heroes from the old nobility, because only in that type of cultivated Russian is it possible to find at least that

outward semblance of fine order and aesthetic beauty so necessary in a novel to produce an artistic effect on the reader. . . . Pushkin selected the subject for his future novels from the "Traditions of the Russian Family," and believe me that everything beautiful we have had so far is to be found therein. Everything that has been brought to some sort of perfection, anyway, . . . completely worked out forms of honour and duty which have never existed anywhere in Russia except among the nobility, even in the most rudimentary shape. I speak as a calm man seeking calm.

Whether that honour was a good thing, and whether that duty was a true one—is a secondary question. What to my mind is of most consequence is the finality of the forms. . . . instead of this everlasting destruction, instead of chips flying in all directions, rubbish and disorder. . . .

In a passage usually taken as an allusion to *War and Peace*, Nikolay Semenovich advises Arkady that "our supposed contemporary novelist . . . would be unable to write in any other form but the historical, for there is no fine type in our day. . . . Oh! and in the historical form it is possible to depict a multitude of extremely attractive and consolatory details! It is possible so to fascinate the reader indeed that he will take the historical picture for the possible and the actual." By contrast, he continues, the only possible contemporary hero would be the "grandson of heroes"—a probable allusion to Levin in *Anna Karenina* as the "grandson" of Pierre and Andrey in *War and Peace*— but even he is bound to appear "a somewhat strange figure, so that the reader might from the first glance recognise . . . there was no field of action left for him." Soon even this misanthropic kind of hero will disappear, Nikolay Semenovich observes sadly, which means that "the Russian novel is impossible in the future" (605-606). *The Raw Youth* then concludes with its most explicit justification of its raw form. "I must say I should not like to be a novelist whose hero comes from an accidental family!" Nikolay Semenovich writes (607; ellipsis in original):

> To describe him is an ungrateful task and can have no beauty of form. Moreover, these types are in any case transitional, and so a novel about them cannot have artistic finish. One may make serious mistakes, exaggerations, misjudgments. In any case one would have to guess too much. But what is the writer to do who doesn't want to confine himself to the historical form, and is possessed by a longing for the present? To guess . . . and make mistakes.

Dostoevsky's most accomplished story about a failure to tell one's own story is probably "The Meek One: A Fantastic Story," which occupies almost the entire November, 1876, issue of the *Diary*. Characteristically for that heterogeneous work, the fiction is introduced by a nonfictional preface outlining the plot of the story in advance and explaining its unusual form—so that the story is offered and becomes interesting, in part, as an exemplification of the technical problems solved in the course of writing it. That remarkable preface, which I quote in full, seems both to recall the formal self-characterizations of *Notes from Underground, Notes from the House of the Dead,* and *The Raw Youth* and to look forward to the *Diary*'s own self characterization in "The Boy Celebrating His Name Day":

> I apologize to my readers that this time, instead of the *Diary* in its usual form, I am printing only a story. But I was really busy with this story most of the month. In any case, I ask my readers' indulgence.
>
> Now about the story itself. I have entitled it fantastic even though I consider it to be realistic in the highest degree. But the fantastic really is here, and precisely in the form of the story, which I find it necessary to clarify in advance.
>
> The fact is, that this is neither a story nor notes. Imagine a husband: his wife, a suicide who threw herself out the window a few hours earlier, is laid out on the table before him. He is distraught and has not yet been able to collect his thoughts. He goes from room to room and tries to make sense of what has happened, "to focus his thoughts." Moreover, he is an inveterate hypochondriac, one of those who talk to themselves. And so he talks to himself, narrating the incident, trying to *make it clear* to himself. Despite the apparent coherence of the speech, he contradicts himself several times, both logically and emotionally. Now he justifies himself, now blames her, now enters into extraneous explanations; here there is both crudeness of thought and heart and also deep feeling. Gradually he does *clarify* the matter to himself and "focus his thoughts." The series of memories he has evoked irresistibly lead him to *truth*; and truth irresistibly exalts his mind and heart. By the end, even the tone of the story changes in comparison with its disordered beginning. The truth reveals itself to the unfortunate man rather clearly and definitely, or, at least, so it seems to him.
>
> That is the theme. Of course, the process of the narrative continues for several hours, in fits and starts, and in an uneven and confusing form: now he talks to himself, now addresses an invisible listener, some sort of a judge. And so it always is in reality. If a stenographer could have eavesdropped and written down everything, the result would have been rougher and less polished than what I present, but it seems to me that the psychological order would, perhaps, remain the same. This assumption of a stenographer (whose record I would then have polished) is what I call fantastic in this story. But partially similar techniques have already been admitted more than once in art. For instance, Victor Hugo, in his masterpiece "The Last Day of a Man Condemned," used almost the very same device. And although he did not introduce a stenographer, he admitted an even greater implausibility, supposing that a condemned man would be able, and would have time, to keep notes not only during his last day, but even in his last hour, and, literally, in the last minute. But if that fantasy were not admitted, then the story would not have existed—the most realistic and the truest of all he wrote.

Like so many of Dostoevsky's stories about the process of arriving at a story, this one begins with an account of the circumstances and therapeutic motives for its telling. In the opening paragraph, which begins on an ellipsis, the narrator sets out, evidently not for the first time, to come to terms with his wife's death by working out a coherent account of it (ellipses in original):

> . . . Oh, while she is still here, it is still all right; I go up and look at her every minute; but tomorrow they will take her away—and how shall I be left alone? Now she is on the table in the drawing room, they put two card tables together, the coffin will be here tomorrow—white, pure white "gros de Naples"—but that's not it . . . I keep walking about, trying to explain it to myself. I have been trying for the last six hours to get it clear, but still I cannot focus my thoughts. The fact is, that I walk to and fro, and to and fro . . . This is how it was. I will simply tell it in order. (Order!) Gentlemen, I am far from being a literary man and you will see that; but no matter. I'll narrate it as I understand it myself. The whole horror of it for me lies in the fact that I understand everything![15]

But as he soon admits, the "horror" lies in large measure in what he does *not* comprehend: "But even now I don't understand," he interrupts his narrative in the next chapter, "even now I understand nothing!" (part 1, ch. 2). Taken as a whole, "The Meek One" consists of a series of tentative tellings, no sooner formulated than rejected, of the events leading to his wife's suicide, a process that continues "in fits and starts, in an uneven and confusing form" until the end of the story. Then "truth reveals itself to the unfortunate man . . . or, at least, so it seems to him." That "truth" is, in effect, his inability ever to reach the truth, his inevitable inarticulateness before the horror and his own responsibility for it. "Men are alone, around them is silence—that is the earth," he concludes. His final sentence, like his first, begins on an ellipsis that points to the failure of expression: ". . . No, seriously, when they take her away tomorrow, what will I do?" *Seriously*, he writes, as if definitively acknowledging, before the muteness that follows, his inability to make sense of his universe of death, loneliness, and silence.

Annexing the Boundaries: Sketch and Feuilleton

Dostoevsky seems to have entertained the idea that even radical experimentation with the novel might not be adequate for the depiction of the formless— that however digressive or fragmentary one might make it, the plot of a novel necessarily imposes some kind of beginning, middle, and end on a historical continuum in which no such pattern is present. Narrative, Dostoevsky apparently reasoned, may itself be a lie. He might well have agreed with the observations of one literary "grandson" of his own underground man and raw youth, Antonin Roquentin in Sartre's *Nausea*:

> Everything changes when you tell about life; it's a change no one notices: the proof is that people talk about true stories. As if there could possibly

be true stories; things happen one way and we tell about them in the opposite sense. You seem to start at the beginning: "It was a fine autumn evening in 1922. I was a notary's clerk at Marommes." And in reality you have started at the end. It was there, invisible and present, it is the one which gives to words the pomp and value of a beginning.[16]

"Realistic art," "true stories"—both, Dostoevsky suspected, may be contradictions in terms. And so he turned to a number of forms that would be maximally open to the flux and indistinct outlines of "the current of life" (*tekuščaja žizn'*)—forms which, if they could not entirely escape the distortions of artistic structure, would at least acknowledge them. Suspicious of art, he explored its frontiers—frontiers which had only recently been claimed for the Russian literary commonwealth by its most influential geographer (and most furious realist), the critic Vissarion Belinsky. There are those, Belinsky observed,

> who wish to see in art an intellectual China, sharply separated by exact boundaries from everything that is not art in the strict sense of the word. But these boundary lines are more hypothetical than actual; at least, you cannot point them out with your finger as you can trace the boundaries of a state on the map. To the extent that art approaches one or another of its boundaries, to that extent it gradually loses something of its essence and assimilates the essence of that which it borders upon—so that instead of defining features, there exists a realm that reconciles both sides.[17]

As the Soviet scholar E. I. Zhurbina glosses this passage, Belinsky apparently had in mind not only works and genres in which the traditionally aesthetic and nonaesthetic were "reconciled," but also those in which they were set in "dialectical" opposition. It would probably be most in accord with the intentions of the authors of such works, Zhurbina argues, to imagine them as claiming the "double jurisdiction"[18] of both literature and journalism, and as enjoying extraterritorial rights in each domain. Beginning in the 1840s, Dostoevsky composed a number of boundary works of this kind, the last and most complex of which was *The Diary of a Writer*.

The most important boundary genres with which Russian writers were experimenting in the 1840s were the feuilleton and the sketch (or essay—the Russian word *očerk* being used to render both terms and appearing in the translated titles of Montaigne's *Essays* as well as Dickens' *Sketches by Boz*). Gorky was to describe the sketch as lying "somewhere between research and story"[19] and, emphasizing the word's etymological derivation from *čertit'* (to draw) and *očertit'* (to outline), was to characterize the genre as the literary equivalent of the pictorial sketch—which is to say, as a work that takes the form of a plan for a future work, but also as an outline that invites and rewards interpretation as complete. Arrested creation and inconclusive hints at unrealized form are a conventional source of interest of the genre, which, as a number of Russian theorists have pointed out, cultivates an illusion of spontaneity and excites an impression of immediate, unfinished presentation.

Zhurbina cites Korolenko's observations on the genre: "Whatever has flashed before the author in the vague outlines of a future truth, he pursues passionately, not waiting while it is formed by itself in his soul into a clear, self-finished image. . . . the reader is forced to live with him through his search, his disappointments, and all his preparatory work, as if apartments were let out when the wood for their construction had not yet been gathered."[20] Such sketches are, in short, "essays" in Montaigne's original sense of "trials" or "experiments"; and they frequently seem to echo Montaigne's self-conscious characterizations of his whimsical and digressive form:

> Observing the way a painter I employ went about his work, I had a mind to imitate him. He chooses the best place, the middle of each wall, wherein to place a picture, elaborated with his utmost art, and the empty space about it he fills with grotesques, which are fantastic paintings that have no other charm than their variety and strangeness. And, in truth, what are these things I scribble but grotesques and monstrous bodies pieced together of sundry members, without any definite shape, having no order, coherence, or proportion, except by accident? [As Horace wrote,] "A lovely woman, up above, tails off into a fish."[21]

This "unfinished" and "haphazard" quality is especially apparent in the feuilleton, a boundary genre that attracted efforts by a number of Russia's most talented writers, including Dostoevsky, Turgenev, and Goncharov as well as Panaev, Pleshcheev, and Druzhinin. Originally a journalistic miscellany in which disconnected items of news of the city's cultural life were presented, the feuilleton gradually became tied together by the loose and whimsical transitions of a digressive persona wandering from topic to topic—and sometimes, in the conventional role of flâneur, from place to place as well. The genre's subject matter was characteristically broad—so broad, indeed, that the problematic unity of the feuilleton became a theme for both feuilletonists and their critics (who sometimes attacked feuilletons in feuilletons). "It is not necessary to explain what a feuilleton is," observed one author of an article in *Fatherland Notes* (1843). "Everyone knows what it is. A feuilleton is everything: theatrical reviews, stories, anecdotes, the chatter of drawing rooms, all kinds of odds and ends, a table laid with every type of excellent little thing" (cited in Zhurbina, 252). "Everything" often included not only the author's chatter about the "news," but also documents from the daily press or from everyday life which the author had collected—or claimed to have collected—rather than composed. In 1845, the *Literary Gazette* described its new section for feuilletons ("Daguerreotype") as "Light physiological notes concerning the theater, society, and literature. Literary scenes, vaudeville songs, parodies. Noteworthy letters. Biographies of unknown persons, edifying parables for youth" (cited in Zhurbina, 257). As this heterogeneous list implies, almost the only topics excluded from the feuilleton were political ones forbidden by the censor—and so "Aesopian" hints at the censorship also came to have a place in this genre's testing of its ill-defined limits.[22]

The feuilletonist himself was generally understood to be a conventional speaker—"a chatterer," as Belinsky described him, "apparently good-natured and sincere, but in truth often malicious and evil-tongued, someone who knows everything, sees everything, keeps quiet about a good deal but definitely manages to express everything, stings with epigrams and insinuations, and amuses with a lively and clever word as well as a childish joke."[23] Also given to sentimental (and mock-sentimental) meditations, the Russian feuilletonist often resembles Yorick, the seriocomic narrator of Laurence Sterne's *Sentimental Journey* (a work that was quite well known in Russia). A succession of contradictory tones as well as of unrelated or apparently incompatible themes tended to create a sense of the grotesque and of self-parody—perhaps even of parody of self-parody. "I began my remarks about the feuilleton seriously enough," wrote the feuilletonist I. Panaev, "but then I saw that there is no way to talk seriously about the Russian feuilleton" (cited in Zhurbina, 252). Within a feuilleton of this type, indeed, there was no way to talk consistently seriously about anything.[24] So characteristic were whimsical digressions, unexplained shifts in tone, and constant self-parody, that in the 1920s Victor Shklovsky chose to parody the feuilleton (in a feuilleton) by *not* digressing and by *actually* discussing his ostensible topic (which happened to be the generic conventions of the feuilleton). "The title of this article," Shklovsky begins his feuilleton "Zorich" (the name of a Russian feuilletonist), "is a violation of the rules for constructing a feuilleton, inasmuch as in this article I am really preparing to write about Zorich."[25]

"A Petersburg Chronicle"

Probably attracted by the genre's thematic diversity and amenability to formal experimentation, Dostoevsky composed a series of four feuilletons for the ongoing column "A Petersburg Chronicle" in the *St. Petersburg News*. A mixture of impressionistic sociology and self-parody, these seriocomic pieces alternate between brief sketches of everyday life and mock-apologies for violating the genre's ill-defined rules. Setting out to discover the identity and to chronicle the spiritual development of the Russian capital—"to study its physiognomy and to read the history of the city and of our entire epoch in this mass of stones"[26]—Dostoevsky's feuilletonist soon discovers that his task is impossible because the city has neither identity nor meaningful history. A haphazard mixture of incompatible styles and a thoughtless medley of foreign borrowings, Petersburg architecture—and, implicitly, its social life—may be, the feuilletonist suspects, entirely "characterless" and lacking in "anything national." "Here all is chaos, all miscellany" (June 1), he concludes, deciding that everything is eternally unfinished and describable, if describable at all, only in caricature.

Or, perhaps, in a feuilleton. The central irony on which Dostoevsky's "Chronicle" depends is that its incoherent and unfinished portrait of Petersburg may be the most appropriate, if not, indeed, the only possible one. Moreover, these feuilletons are themselves the product of one of the city's most characteristic types, the dreamer (described at length in the "Chronicle"'s conclusion)—and so may be taken, in effect, as the city's *self*-description. Identifiable by his unpredictable shifts in mood ("sometimes too cheerful, sometimes too gloomy") and by his inability to finish anything, the Petersburg dreamer is, Dostoevsky's feuilletonist tells us, a poet who never completes a poem, a writer in whom "a whole novel or story is at once born" (June 15) but who does not work his plans through to final form. As we are likely to recognize by the time this characterization appears, it applies well to the feuilletonist himself, who also resembles a number of Dostoevsky's other poetic flâneurs. In particular, he resembles Ordynov in "The Landlady" (also written in 1847):

> ... there had never been and was not even now any order and system in his solitary studies; even now he had only the first ecstasy, the first fever, the first delirium of the artist. He was creating a system for himself, it was being evolved in him by the years; and the dim, vague, but marvelously soothing image of an idea, embodied in a new, clarified form, was gradually emerging in his soul. And this form craved expression, fretting his soul; he was still timidly aware of its originality, its truth, its independence: creative genius was already showing, it was gathering strength and taking shape. But the moment of embodiment and creation was still far off, perhaps very far off, perhaps altogether impossible![27]

The search for expression that does not finally come, the first image of arrested creation, the limning of the outlines of a work realized at most in rough drafts—that is the moment, the uncrossed threshold to art, recorded in "A Petersburg Chronicle." A half-finished product of a city where "it is as if we were somehow packing, preparing to go, bustling about" but never going anywhere or achieving anything of our own, the feuilletonist's haphazard chronicle seems emblematic of the Russian capital's own unsuccessful search for identity and form.

In each of the four feuilletons, the chronicler sets out to tell the news of the city, but almost immediately realizes that in a city with neither identity nor history "there is no news" except of the most trivial kind. In Petersburg, the feuilletonist explains in the first two pieces, inquiries about the news are as formulaic as questions about the weather—more so, in fact, because the weather changes, but there is never any news. "I have often observed that when two Petersburg friends meet in the street and, after greeting each other, ask with one accord, 'What's the news?' there is a piercing feeling of desolation in the sound of their voices, whatever the intonation they started their conversation with. Indeed, this Petersburg question conceals a feeling of utter hopelessness" (April 27).

Characteristically for the genre, therefore, the title of the series turns out to be a mistitle, and the feuilletons become a self-conscious demonstration of the impossibility of fulfilling their promise to chronicle what cannot be chronicled—"to perceive as an image that which has no image." In his search for such an image, the feuilletonist frequently repeats a pattern of inspiration and interruption, of incomplete descriptions and extended digressions. Wandering aimlessly through the streets, the flâneur falls into a reverie concerning the city or a possible way of characterizing it; he is then startled by an incident which he describes "instead of" writing his chronicle; having completed nothing, he offers the reader a piece of drawing-room gossip or theatrical news, which he immediately characterizes as trivial and boring; he then repeats the process until, at the end of the feuilleton, he postpones the promised sketch or story about the city until next time. His text is a fabric of lost threads.

In the first sketch, for instance, the feuilletonist interrupts his descriptions of the city's "types" and their conversations about the lack of news to remind himself of the generic conventions he will not fulfill (April 27; ellipsis in original):

> But, gentlemen, I am a feuilletonist, and have to tell you the news, the latest and most *burning* news—I'm afraid to use this ancient, venerable cliche, which no doubt came into being in the hope that the Petersburg reader would burn with joy on hearing some burning piece of news, such as, for example, that Jenny Lind is going to London. But then, what's Jenny Lind to the Petersburg reader! He has lots of other interesting things . . . But actually, gentlemen, he has nothing, absolutely nothing. So there I was, gentlemen, walking along the Haymarket, pondering what I could possibly write.

After a brief sketch of a personified Petersburg ("Petersburg got up bad-tempered and angry, like a malicious society woman. . . . "), the feuilletonist is interrupted again (April 27):

> At that moment I came across a funeral procession, and, in my capacity as a feuilletonist, I recalled that grippe and fever were then almost a contemporary issue in Petersburg. It was a magnificent funeral. The hero of the cortege, in a sumptuous coffin, was solemnly and decorously, feet foremost, on the way to the most comfortable apartment in the world. . . . His decorations followed after him on a cushion.

The combination of the morbid and the playful here is characteristic of these grotesque and self-conscious pieces. So is the dreamer's sudden awakening by the nip of a playful horse—who, the dreamer suspects, is accustomed to playing jokes on Petersburg flâneurs. "Poor old hack! I came home and was about to sit down to write my chronicle, but instead, not knowing how myself, I opened up a magazine and began to read a short story." And so instead of the chronicle, we are offered an account of this short story—and a justification of the "violation" of generic conventions in terms of those very conventions. "Could there, in fact, be any better news that I could tell you?" he asks. "That for instance, new omnibuses are flourishing on Nevsky Avenue, that the Neva had been the topic of discussion for a whole week, that they still go on yawning in the salons on the appointed days in expectation of summer? Is that what you want? But all this must have bored you long ago, gentlemen" (April 27).

Characteristically, the feuilletonist relates not the story, but the process of reading the story: "What's going to happen now? I was impatiently and fearfully awaiting for the arrival of Ivan Kirilovich." "He returned home drunk at midnight . . . my heart began to throb . . . what's going to happen now?" As the feuilleton is about to end, he at last recalls that "I have brought up the subject of this story because I intended to tell you a story too . . . But another time" (ellipsis in original). He closes with "the most important thing. I remembered it all the time while talking to you, and then it slipped my memory. Ernst is giving another concert. The takings will be in aid of The Society for Visiting the Poor and the German Philanthropic Society" (April 27).

Although this is a "chronicle," its only relation to time is to run out of it. Of course, this metaliterary play is itself a generic convention, as the feuilletonist occasionally implies. "You cannot imagine, gentlemen, what a pleasant duty it is to talk with you about the Petersburg news and to write a Petersburg chronicle for you!" he tells the readers of his second piece (May 11; italics mine):

> I will go further: it isn't even a duty at all, but one of the greatest of pleasures. I don't know whether you will appreciate my joy. But it really is quite pleasant to gather like this, to sit down and have a little talk about public affairs. I am sometimes even ready to burst from sheer joy when I enter some social gathering and see such very well-bred and respectable people gathered together, sitting and discussing something decorously. . . . [True,] I have so far been unable to grasp the sense, the content, of what our society people talk about. . . . it is somehow hard to understand. *It is all as though the conversation were only just starting, as thought the instruments were only just being tuned; you sit there for two hours and they are only just starting.*

This passage describes not only a conversation *in* the feuilleton but also the conversation *of* the feuilleton. The audience of *these* rambling discussions might also observe that "you occasionally get the impression that they are talking about some highly serious subjects. . . . but afterward, when you ask yourselves what it was they were talking about, you simply cannot find an answer" (May 11). In short, these feuilletons discuss Petersburg in the Petersburg style—that is, haphazardly and formlessly—and so their title does, in a sense, finally answer to the text: though not a Petersburg *chronicle*, they are a *Petersburg* chronicle.

"Petersburg Visions in Prose and Verse"

At about the same time that Dostoevsky was experimenting with the genre of the novel (*Notes from the House of the Dead*, 1860-1862, and *Notes from Underground*, 1864), he also continued to explore the formal and thematic possibilities of boundary genres. Published in 1861, his "Petersburg Visions in Prose and Verse" not only takes to an extreme the feuilleton's characteristic heterogeneity of forms, themes, and tones, but also seems to take a few cautious steps beyond that genre—perhaps even to parody its very tendency to playfulness and parody. Together with the *Winter Remarks on Summer Impressions* (1863), the "Visions" may be regarded as anticipatory of the more complex structure of *The Diary of a Writer*.

To be sure, the "Visions" contains a great deal of the self-conscious chatter and metaliterary play characteristic of the genre. Published in the same issue of Dostoevsky's journal *Time* in which the first installment of his "novel-feuilleton" *The Insulted and the Humiliated* appeared,[28] the "Visions" apparently reaches beyond its frame, across the pages of the journal, and alludes to the other work: "If I were not a casual feuilletonist, but a regular daily one, it seems to me that I should wish to turn to Eugène Sue [author of the novel-feuilleton *Mysteries of Paris*] in order to describe the mysteries of Petersburg" (*Stat'i*, 156). Moreover, the work's central passage—the feuilletonist's revelatory dream-vision of the grotesque and fantastic essence of the city—is taken almost verbatim from, and therefore seems to enter into an intertextual dialogue with, Dostoevsky's story of thirteen years earlier, "A Weak Heart."[29] Dostoevsky's readers probably recognized as conventional the introduction of each of its brief visions as rough sketches for a more complete portrait that might have been, but was not, written. Nor are they likely to have been much surprised either by the beginning about how feuilletons usually begin (*Stat'i*, 154; ellipsis in original):

> "Oh, may my obligation, my obligation as a feuilletonist, forever be accursed! . . . "
> Don't worry gentlemen, it's not I who exclaim this! I concede that such a beginning would be too eccentric for my feuilleton. No, I do not exclaim this, but until my arrival in Petersburg, I was convinced that every Petersburg feuilletonist, taking up his pen to scribble his weekly or monthly feuilleton, necessarily must so exclaim as he sits down at his desk. And, in fact, tell me, what is he to write about?

or by the ending that apologizes for not ending as planned (172):

> Oh, my God, I forgot! I wanted to relate my dream about gracious poverty. Yes, I promised to relate this dream at the end of the feuilleton. But, no! I will leave that, too, for next time. It's already better to have everything together. What kind of story it will be—I don't know, but I assure you it will be an interesting history.

The tone of this work is so ambivalent, and judgments about it so difficult to make, that any overall characterization of it is risky. But the sombre vision at the work's center—the dark epiphany in which a sudden understanding of the city's fantastic horror changes the narrator forever—does seem to stretch the bounds of the feuilleton, perhaps verging on the medieval dream-vision or other forms of literature of conversion. In the shadow of this vision, the narrator's criticism of earlier feuilletons as being "without fire, without thought, without an idea, without a desire," and as works in which everything has become "routine and repetition, repetition and routine" (155) seems different from the genre's usual self-parody and perhaps even to include the latter in its censure. When the narrator imagines the sombre conditions under which most playful feuilletons are written, the role of the parodist is itself parodied (155):

> And how much drama there may be, indeed there may even be something tragic taking place somewhere in a damp corner on the fifth floor, where an entire hungry and cold family lives in a single room, and in the next there sits a feuilletonist, who shivers in his torn housecoat and writes a feuilleton à la the New Poet [i.e., I. Panaev, the feuilletonist of the *Contemporary*] about camelias, oysters, and friends, tearing his hair, gnawing his pen, and all in circumstances not at all feuilletonistic.

The tragedy of the comic poet and parodist—here, truly, is a Dostoevskian theme, one he was to develop a number of times in *The Diary of a Writer* (e.g., in the story "Bobok"). He develops it as well in *The Brothers Karamazov*, where Ivan, whose ecclesiastical "burlesque" is discussed in the first book of the novel, begets as his double the father of all parody, the devil himself—a devil who, moreover, parodies both traditional ideas of the demonic and Ivan's own self-indulgent self-parodies.

Winter Remarks on Summer Impressions

The "Visions" seems, in short, to point to the necessity of a new boundary work in which it would be possible to treat social and political themes with greater "thought" and "fire." Dostoevsky's next attempt at such a work was his *Winter Remarks on Summer Impressions* (1863), an impressionistic account of his trip to Western Europe. Drawing on the feuilleton, the physiological sketch, and the well-established Russian tradition of travel literature (from Karamzin's *Letters of a Russian Traveler* to Herzen's *Letters from France and Italy* and *Ends and Beginnings*), the *Remarks* takes the form of a series of six sketches, written as letters to Russian friends. Though longer and more explicitly political than the "Visions," the basic structure of the *Remarks* is similar: after three generally playful sketches, there occurs a revelation of such horror and significance that it may be seen to parody and discredit retrospectively the earlier playfulness and parody.

In the first sketch, a wry foreword "Instead of a Foreword," the author begins, as the feuilletonist of the "Chronicle" usually begins, by confessing his inadequacy to the demands of his genre, in this case travel literature. "For many months, my friends, you have been urging me to hasten the writing of my foreign impressions, not suspecting that your request simply puts me at my wit's end. What shall I write for you? Is there anything original I can say, anything that is still unknown or hasn't been said?"[30]

Moreover, the conventions of travel literature call for at least minimal factual accuracy, and, the author apologizes in advance to his imagined readers, anything I write is sure to be notoriously unreliable (41-42):

> I must tell an untruth at times in spite of myself, and therefore . . . [ellipsis in original]
>
> But here you stop me. You say that for once you do not need accurate information, that you will find it when needed in the *Reichard Guide*, and that, on the contrary, it would not be at all regrettable if every traveler strove not so much for absolute accuracy (which he is almost never capable of attaining) as for sincerity; he would not be afraid to reveal a personal impression or adventure of his—even one that did him little credit. . . .
>
> "Ah!" I exclaim, "so you want mere chatter, light sketches, personal impressions registered as I rushed by." I agree to this, and shall lose no time in consulting my notebooks.

Wryly cautioning that much of what he says will be exaggerated, inconsistent, or untrue—he refers later to his warning "in the first chapter of these remarks that, perhaps, I would tell frightful lies" (88)—this self-conscious relative of the underground man adds that, nevertheless (42),

> Not everything I say will be incorrect, though. It is impossible, for instance, to be mistaken about the facts that Paris has a Notre Dame and a Bal Mabille. The latter fact especially is so well certified by all Russians who write about Paris that it is now almost impossible to doubt it. In this, perhaps, even I shall make no mistake; but I had rather not vouch for it.

He promises, at the end of the foreword, to begin with his impressions of Paris, which, "after all I did look over more thoroughly than the Cathedral of St. Paul or the ladies of Dresden. Well, I shall begin" (43). This start is a false one, however; continually digressing, and commenting on his digressions, he does not actually reach Paris for three more sketches. "Incidentally," he interrupts himself during chapter 2, "wouldn't you say that I have started discussing Russian literature instead of Paris? Am I writing an article of literary criticism? No, I was just whiling the time away" (47). He then justifies his delay in describing Paris by referring to his promise to "consult"—which turns out to mean follow the order of—his notebook, and "according to my notebook I ought now to be sitting in a railroad coach, my heart beating wildly, as I prepare for tomorrow's arrival at Eydkuhnen [the Russian border] " (47).

Like his "notebook," therefore, chapter 2, "On the Train," consists of random thoughts which, the author admits, are boring—but that, he explains, is what long train rides usually are. He ends that chapter, and begins the next, with his characteristic metaliterary play (51-52):

> And do you know what—I have an urge to impart my railroad coach meditations to you, in the name of fairness, as the train chugs toward Paris: I was bored in the train, and now it is your turn. However, it is necessary to spare the other readers [i.e., aside from the conventional "friends" he is addressing in these "letters"] , and therefore I shall purposely include all

these meditations in a separate chapter and call it *superfluous*. You will fight your way through it, but the others may ignore it as superfluous. One must be cautious and considerate in dealing with one's readers, but with one's friends one can be more curt. And so:

Chapter III
WHICH IS COMPLETELY SUPERFLUOUS

This Shandyism (or Pushkinism) of confiding to one set of readers what one is not supposed to say to another—Tristram dismisses his "female readers" so he can talk alone with the male readers, and "Pushkin" stage-whispers to his future audience about how to elude the censor—is a technique Dostoevsky was to use especially frequently in *The Diary of a Writer*.

This third, "superfluous" sketch is interrupted at several points by "readers"—apparently those who were directed to skip the chapter entirely—who complain that he is not keeping even his amended promise to discuss whatever came into his head during the train ride. Not only is the author expressing objectionable political opinions, they contend, but, apparently confusing the time he is describing with the time in which he is describing it, he is recording thoughts that could not have occurred to him before his return to Russia (56):

> "Reactionary!" someone will cry upon reading this. "To advocate the birch rod!" (For someone is bound to deduce from this that I advocate the birch rod.)
>
> "Excuse me, but what are you talking about?" another will say. "Your subject was going to be Paris, but it has been birch rods instead. Where does Paris come in?"
>
> "What's going on?" a third will add. "You yourself write that you heard all this recently, but your trip took place last summer. How could you have been thinking of all this on the train at that time?"

Switching ground once again, the author justifies his failure to keep his explicit promise by his fulfillment of the ones implicit in the titles of his chapter and book (56-57):

> "Yes, that is admittedly a good point," I answer. "But never mind; this is, after all, winter remarks on summer impressions, and this belongs to the winter component. . . . Now I myself see that all this is superfluous here. But I warned you that this whole chapter was superfluous. Now, where had I left off?"

The author's tone changes abruptly, however, in chapter 5, "Baal." Wandering the London Streets, and encountering child prostitutes before gilded cafes and desperate workers enticed by cynical Catholic propagandists, he is overwhelmed by a terrible revelation. "Here, in fact, you do not see a people," he proclaims, "but rather a systematic, submissive, fostered loss of consciousness. And you sense, as you behold these pariahs of society, that for a long time to come the prophecy [from Revelation, ch. 7] will not come to to pass for them, that for a long time to come they will be given neither palm branches nor white robes, and that for a long time yet they will appeal to the throne of the Most High, 'How Long, Oh Lord!'" (93). Here the flâneur turns prophet, and when, against the background of the city's slums, he sees the Crystal Palace exhibition he senses "that something final has taken place here, that something has come to an end. It is like a Biblical picture, something out of Babylon, a prophecy from the Apocalypse coming to pass before your eyes" (91).

What is final here, he declares, is the Western ideal—an ideal which for him is exemplified at its best by Cabet, Owen, and other Utopian Socialists to whom Dostoevsky had been attracted before his condemnation to Siberia. A cruel parody of Christianity, that ideal is destined to fail, the author proclaims, because it bases love on law and brotherhood on rational self-interest. But love and brotherhood, he argues, can be achieved only through a completely voluntary act of self-sacrifice—"I shall annihilate myself, I shall melt away, if only your brotherhood will prosper and last" (113)—answered by spontaneous communal love, no less total and uncalculated (114):

> After this, naturally, there is no partitioning to worry about, everything will be shared of itself. "Love one another and all this will come of itself."
> This is truly utopia, gentlemen! Everything is based on feelings, on nature, not on reason. Why this actually humbles the reason. What do you think, is this utopia or not?

It is the same critique of false, Western utopianism advanced about the same time—and with considerably greater subtlety—in *Notes from Underground*. The advocacy of this "true" utopia was to become the thematic center of *The Diary of a Writer*.

We may ask here, as we shall have occasion to ask in our discussion of the *Diary*, how are we expected to reconcile the playful tone of some passages in the *Remarks* with the apparently contradictory, prophetic tone of some others? What sort of whole embraces both Shandyisms and citations from the Revelation to St. John; what is the place of parody in an apocalypse? To be sure, the author has warned us that he would lie and say things which "did him little credit," but which role—the quixotic prophet or the self-conscious feuilletonist—is discredited?

It seems to me that the *Remarks* invites both readings. On the one hand, the first chapter contains what might, retrospectively, be taken as a parody of the xenophobia in later chapters. Standing before the new bridge at Cologne, the author recalls, he gave in to that characteristic Russian sense of insult and humiliation before Western achievement. "You see our bridge, miserable Russian, and you see that you are a worm before our bridge," he imagined the German toll-taker was about to say to him (41):

> You will agree that this was insulting. Naturally the German did not utter any such thought, and maybe it never entered his mind, but that makes no difference; I was so sure that he meant precisely that, that I lost my temper

altogether. "The devil take you," I thought. "We invented the samovar.
. . . We have journals . . . We do the sort of things officers do . . . We . . . "
[ellipsis in original] In short, I got angry, and having bought a vial of
Eau de Cologne, . . . I skipped off to Paris.

Moreover, when he describes the Crystal Palace in apocalyptic terms, he is
interrupted by his readers: "'But this is nonsense,' you will say, 'the raving
of an invalid, nerves, exaggeration. . . . Well-fed dilettantes on pleasure jaunts
can easily call up pictures from the Apocalypse and divert their nerves by
exaggeration" (91).

On the other hand, it may also be those very readers, who prefer to play
while Europe burns, who are the object of parody. Not prophetic indignation
but feuilletonistic chatter—and those who indulge in reading it—may be discredited. Dostoevsky's point, in other words, could be taken to be similar to
one he makes in his essay "Mr. D——bov and the Question of Art," namely
that not all kinds of art are appropriate at all times. For example, he writes in
that essay, if the day after the Lisbon earthquake the survivors should find in
the newspaper a prominent author's poem describing "whispering, timid
breathing, and the warbling of the nightingale" and "magic changes in the
face of the beloved," they would probably, and quite rightly, lynch the author. The *Remarks* may be taken to imply the inappropriateness of the chatty
feuilleton and of sentimental and confessional types of travel literature in an
age of apocalyptic disintegration; the work may, in other words, be read as a
sombre parody of what it initially announces itself to be. Apparently designed
to resonate between parody and parody of parody, the *Remarks* may, in
short, be taken as what we shall discuss in chapter 4 as a *metaparody*.

Transforming the Periodical into Literature

At about the same time that he ceased publishing the journal *Epoch*, Dostoevsky apparently conceived of the idea of transforming an entire journal, rather
than a series of brief sketches or feuilletons, into a generically encyclopedic
literary work. It is not clear whether he conceived of this projected work as
modeled on such publications as the *Spectator* or the *Rambler*,[31] but it does
seem likely that he had in mind Dickens' experimental weekly periodical,
Master Humphrey's Clock. Begun in 1840, Dickens' literary miscellany was
framed as the proceedings of a small club who met at "Master Humphrey's"
to "beguile time from the heart of time itself"[32]—that is, to read papers
placed by the members in the pendulum closet of Master Humphrey's old
clock. There was to be little or no restriction on the kind of material that
could be contributed, Master Humphrey explains: "Spirits of past times,
creatures of imagination, and people of today, are alike the objects of our
seeking, and, unlike the objects of search with most philosophers, we can
ensure their coming at our command" (*OCS*, 678). Or as Dickens himself
described his plan for the new publication in January, 1840:

> I should be willing to commence on the thirty-first of March, 1840, a new publication consisting entirely of original matter. . . . I should propose to start, as the *Spectator* does, with some pleasant fiction relative to the origin of the publication; to introduce a little club or knot of characters and to carry their personal histories and proceedings through the work; to introduce fresh characters constantly; to reintroduce Mr. Pickwick and Sam Weller, the latter of whom might furnish an occasional communication with great effect; to write amusing essays on the various foibles of the day as they arise; to take advantage of all passing events; and to vary the form of the papers by throwing them into sketches, essays, tales, adventures, letters from imaginary correspondents and so forth, and so to diversify the contents as much as possible.[33]

In 1848, Dickens described his original intention as a publication which was "to consist, for the most part, of detached papers, but was [also] to include one continuous story, to be resumed, from time to time, with such indefinite intervals between each period of resumption as might best accord with the exigencies and capabilities of the proposed Miscellany" (*OCS*, 41). That story was *The Old Curiosity Shop*, which first appeared as one of the *Personal Adventures of Master Humphrey* in the fourth number of the *Clock*, then ran parallel to other *Clock* material for a short time until, as Dickens wrote, he amended his original design and gave the whole *Clock* to the *Shop*. After "Chapter the Last" of Master Humphrey's manuscript, the *Clock* is allowed to run again as Master Humphrey reveals that he himself is the novel's unidentified "single gentleman," hears the consolation of his friends, and takes the next manuscript out of the clock, the novel *Barnaby Rudge*. Victor Shklovsky once described Dickens' experiment as a daring attempt to go beyond the novel by embedding that genre in a larger, generically heterogeneous context.[34] Given Dostoevsky's own dissatisfaction with the novel, it is possible that he viewed Dickens' miscellany in a similar light. It would, of course, be no less interesting if convergent literary evolution led Dostoevsky to a similar form independently of his English predecessor.

Dostoevsky's earliest reference to the project that was eventually to become the *Diary* occurs in a letter written in 1865 to Baron A. E. Wrangel. Many people were advising him to give up journalism and make money by writing a novel, he confided to his friend, but "I have in mind a certain periodical publication, though not a journal. Both useful and profitable. It could come into existence in a year" (*Pis'ma*, I, 424). Two years later, he wrote from Geneva to his niece, S. A. Ivanova, that he was anxious to return to Russia because "when I return I would certainly like to publish something like a newspaper (I even recall mentioning it to you in passing, but here both the form and the purpose have now become completely clear). But for this it is necessary to be home and to see and hear everything with my own eyes [*sic*]" (*Pis'ma*, II, 44). "When I return to Petersburg," he wrote two weeks later to the widow of his late brother, "I dream of beginning to publish a weekly journal of my own type, which I have invented. I hope for success, only for God's sake don't tell *anyone anything* about it in advance" (*Pis'ma*, II, 53). At the beginning of 1869, he wrote to Ivanova that he was now considering *two* new publications. One, which he barely describes, would take up all of his time and not allow him to write a novel; the other would be a special kind of "enormous useful *annual . . .* to be issued without fail in a large number of copies and to appear without fail every year in January." The work on this second publication would be mainly compilative and "editorial," he continues, but it would be editorship "with an idea, with great study" (*Pis'ma*, II, 161–162).

It is interesting to note that in *The Possessed* (written 1869–1872) Liza Drozdova tries to persuade Shatov to join her in compiling and editing a similar publication. When she first describes her projected annual as little more than a reference book, Shatov is skeptical. But he reconsiders when he understands that she has in mind a record of the development "of the moral life of the people, of the personal character of the Russian people at the present moment" so that, taken together over the years, the books would constitute a spiritual biography of Russia. "Of course, everything might be put in," she explains,

> strange incidents, fires, public subscriptions, anything good or bad, every speech or word, perhaps even floodings of the rivers, perhaps even some government decrees, but only such things to be selected as are characteristic of the period; everything would be put in with a certain view, a special significance and intention, with an idea which would illuminate the facts looked at in the aggregate, as a whole. And finally the book ought to be interesting even for light reading, apart from its value as a work of reference. It would be, so to say, a presentation of the spiritual, moral, inner life of Russia for a whole year.[35]

Stressing that the very selection and organization of the material would already imply an "idea," Shatov suggests that this plan, which he now regards as a good one, depends for its successes on careful consideration of the form of the publication. "One can't work it out on the spur of the moment," he observes. "We need experience. And when we do publish the book I doubt whether we shall find out how to do it. Perhaps after many trials. . . . " (128).

Dostoevsky's first "trial" of his idea was in the column *F. M. Dostoevsky's Diary of a Writer*, published sporadically in the *Citizen* (in 1873). His wife's reminiscences indicate that that form and locale were a compromise. "After finishing *The Possessed*," she recalls,

> Fyodor Mikhailovich was very undecided for a while as to what to take up next. He was so exhausted by his work on the novel that it seemed impossible to him to set to work right away on a new one. And yet, the realization of the idea conceived while we were still living abroad—namely, the publication of a monthly journal, *Diary of a Writer*—presented problems. Quite substantial means were needed for putting out a journal and maintaining a family, not to mention the settlement of our debts. And there

was also the question of whether such a journal would have much success, since *it was something entirely new in Russian literature at that time, both in form and in content.*[36]

It was during this period of indecision, she continues, that Prince Meshchersky offered her husband the editorship of the *Citizen*, an offer which, she observes with her characteristic concern for financial matters, would pay him separately and generously both for his editorial work and for his column. "The idea of *Diary of a Writer*," she paraphrases his thinking, "might [thus] be realized in the pages of the *Citizen*, even though in a different format from the one given it subsequently" (213).

The Soviet scholar V. V. Vinogradov has suggested that in undertaking this editorship, Dostoevsky intended to transform the entire *Citizen* into an integral work with the *Diary* as its "pivot" and "inner nucleus," a plan which, Vinogradov contends, Dostoevsky was unable to fulfill because of Meshchersky's interference.[37] Vinogradov's hypothesis seems quite plausible. It is evident, in any case, that Dostoevsky regarded this first trial of his idea as at best a mixed success and as distinct from its later reformulation.[38]

Nevertheless, the 1873 *Diary* does seem closer to the mature work than to Shatov's almanac or to the "new publication" projected in Dostoevsky's letters. For instance, unlike those early plans but like the monthly issues, the 1873 *Diary* contains fiction (the "certain person's" story, "Bobok," and his journalistic polemic, the "Half-Letter") as well as nonfiction. It now becomes clear, moreover, how great is the "unprecedented" publication's debt to the early feuilletons and sketches: even new literary forms, it would seem, may have a genealogy. Like the "Petersburg Chronicle" and the *Winter Remarks*, the *Diary* unifies its heterogeneous material as the impressions of a digressive author-flâneur, who, in this case, jots down whatever interests him in his irregular "diary." In the manner of a feuilletonist, the author wanders from topic to topic and place to place, recording "spontaneous" impressions and "apologizing" for his unconventional form and for violating vague or unstated promises. "Idle, impractical people without serious affairs have the right and may be excused if they are sometimes inclined to dream about what is to come," the article "Visions and Reveries" introduces its "digression" on politics. "After all, Poprishchin, in Gogol's 'Diary of a Madman,' dreamed about Spanish affairs." The *Diary*'s three "Little Pictures" of Petersburg, though more sombre than the earlier "Chronicle" and the "Petersburg Visions," repeat their basic themes and devices. Here, too, the author characterizes Petersburg and its architecture by their "utter lack of character" and abruptly concludes two of the pieces with self-conscious "apologies"—the first picture ending:

> However, I am not a Petersburg feuilletonist and it was not at all about this that I began to speak. I began with editorial manuscripts, and wound up with something entirely different.

and the series ending as follows:

Vacuous, entirely vacuous pictures which I am even ashamed to include in my diary. In the future, I will try to be much more serious.

Like the *Remarks'* foreword "Instead of a Foreword" and the monthly *Diary*'s preface "Instead of a Preface," the "Introduction" to the 1873 *Diary* discusses the conventions that will be observed only in the breach—a nonobservance which, the feuilletonistic narrator concedes, renders the journal's title, the *Citizen*, problematic. I would like to be a good citizen and write thoughtfully, the author muses, but nowadays if anyone claims to think,

> he is immediately deserted by everyone. Nothing remains for him but to find some sort of suitable fellow, or even to hire him, and to talk only with him; and perhaps to publish the journal only for him. It's a loathsome position, since it is tantamount to talking to oneself and to publishing a journal for one's own pleasure. I strongly suspect that for a long time to come the *Citizen* will take to talking to himself and for his own pleasure. And one may consider that according to medical science, talking to oneself is a sign of predisposition to insanity. The *Citizen* necessarily must talk with citizens, and that's the whole trouble!

Dostoevsky's playful personification of his journal recalls his first feuilleton (1845), an announcement of a projected (but never realized) journal to be called the *Banterer*; signed by the Banterer himself, this self-parodic self-advertisement described the difficulties of bantering in a humorless age. No less characteristic of the early feuilletons and sketches, the *Diary*'s "Introduction" warns the readers of this journal without readers to expect neither unity of subject matter nor coherence of presentation. "My situation is in the highest degree undefined," the author writes,

> But I will talk to myself and for my own pleasure in the form of this diary, and what will be, will be. About what will I speak? About everything that strikes me or makes me think. And if I do find a reader, and, God forbid, an opponent, then I understand that I will have to learn to converse and to know with whom and how to speak. I will try to master this, since among us this is the most important thing—that is, in literature.

Literature as Algorithm

When in 1876 Dostoevsky was at last about to realize the *Diary* as a monthly, his correspondence and notebooks reflect his intense concern over the work's form. Three problems were apparently uppermost in his mind: first, maintaining a broad variety of material, especially from "current life"; second, keeping the tone of the work—devoted in large measure, as it would be, to pressing social and political questions—sufficiently playful and feuilletonistic; and, third, finding a way to unify all of these "various varieties."[39] The solution he worked out was a special type of structure, related both to the early feuilletons and to Dickens' miscellany, and exploiting the work's periodical form.

Each individual issue was to have a plan, worked out in advance and reflected in its division into chapters and articles; but the structure of the work as a whole was to be the product not of a plan, but of what we might call an *algorithm*,[40] that is, a set of procedures and devices introduced in the opening issue and applied to whatever might be of interest to the author during any given month. Much of the *readers'* interest is therefore to be found in seeing how these procedures are applied to new and perhaps recalcitrant material, and in tracing the patterns that emerge from this *procedural* regularity. The product of a plan for particular issues and an algorithm for the whole, the *Diary*'s overall structure was designed to be maximally open to contingency while still maintaining the coherence of a literary work of art.

As the January, 1876, issue was about to appear, Dostoevsky wrote to Vsevolod Soloviev (*Pis'ma*, III, 201-202; ellipsis and italics in original):

> In issue No. 1 there will be, first of all, the very littlest *preface*, then something or other about children—about children in general, about children with fathers, especially about children without fathers, about children at Christmas parties, without Christmas parties, about child-criminals . . . Of course, these will not be strict studies or accounts, but only some hot words and indications. Then about *what has been heard and read*—anything and everything that strikes me each month. Without doubt, the Diary of a Writer will resemble a feuilleton, with the difference that a monthly feuilleton naturally cannot resemble a weekly feuilleton. Here the account will be not so much about events or news as about what from an event remains most constantly, most connected with the general, whole idea. Finally, I do not at all want to bind myself with the task of rendering an account. I am not a chronicler: this, on the contrary, will be a perfect *diary* in the full sense of the word, that is, an account of what has most interested me personally—here there will even be caprice.

Two things are especially noteworthy in this letter. First, Dostoevsky stresses the generic relation of his work to the feuilleton and, specifically, to the feuilleton's characteristic breadth of subject matter—"everything that strikes me"—and whimsical tone—"here there will even be caprice." His concern with that playful tone is also reflected in his lengthy notebook for this first issue, a notebook in which he criticizes other feuilletonists: "they want to talk playfully and simply . . . but then, to our surprise, no playfulness is visible . . . Some resemble Mr. Turgenev, who has been . . . milking the humble cow of his wit, with its dried-up teats."[41]

Second, we have here an indication of one of Dostoevsky's principles of unity: the use of common motifs (in this case, children) throughout an issue with articles of different genres and tones. Most likely, Dostoevsky intended his division of issues into chapters, in each of which articles of various kinds would be grouped together, to serve as an implicit invitation to readers to discover a hierarchy of thematic interrelations: a non-narrative connecting principle. This structure of issues, chapters, and articles may be the source of *Karamazov*'s similar structure of four parts, each divided into three books, in which are embedded works of genres as various as legend and satiric poem, saint's life and mock-theological oration, folktale and juridical "treatise." In the novel, as in the *Diary*, this hierarchy was probably designed to suggest metaphorical parallels between incidents that have no narrative or causal connection (e.g., the title of the book "Lacerations" may be taken to imply a link between Alyosha's bitten finger, Father Ferapont's disdainful mortifications of his flesh, and Katerina Ivanovna's public tearing at her wounded pride).[42]

Three months later, Dostoevsky answered at length a criticism by one of his correspondents that in the *Diary* "I am squandering my gifts on trifles" (*Pis'ma*, III, 205). Dostoevsky responds, first, that in his view, these "trifles" and details from "current life" should be a writer's main concern, and, second, that they are not only central to the design of the *Diary*, but also likely to appear in his next novel (as, in fact, they did). We also find in this letter Dostoevsky's characteristic contrast of his own work with Goncharov's (*Pis'ma*, III, 206):

> A few days ago I met Goncharov and to my sincere question: does he understand everything in current reality, or has he ceased to understand some things? he answered me directly that he has "ceased to understand" a great deal. Of course, I myself know that this *great mind* not only understands, but also teaches teachers, but in the sense in which I asked (and which he understood from a quarter of a word), he, it is clear, not only does not understand, but does not wish to understand. "My ideals and what I have loved are so dear to me," he added, "that I wish to spend with them those few years remaining to me; and to study this" (he pointed to the passing crowd on the Nevsky Avenue) "is burdensome to me, because it takes up my precious time."

But my ideal, Dostoevsky comments, is precisely a knowledge of that passing crowd, and, he continues, the *Diary* was in part designed for that very purpose. To be sure, he concedes, "I have not yet succeeded in clarifying to myself the form of the *Diary*" (*Pis'ma*, III, 206) which includes so much from current life. For contrary to his original plans, Dostoevsky writes, some theme of particular importance takes up so much space that "the issue suffers and becomes insufficiently heterogeneous" (*Pis'ma*, III, 206). One thing that the author of this encyclopedic work feared, in short, is that it would not be heterogeneous *enough*.

From one point of view, these fears were justified. Many later issues of the *Diary* do not contain so abundant a selection of material as do, let us say, the first two issues, each of which includes a broad generic sampling of feuilletons, playful prefaces or conclusions, utopian meditations, sketches, autobiography, and a short story ("The Boy at Christ's Christmas Party" in January, 1876, and "The Peasant Marey" in February). And, indeed, one later issue is entirely devoted to a story ("The Meek One" in November, 1876). I suspect that Dostoevsky gradually amended his original design, and sought generic variety not necessarily in each issue, but over the work as a whole. He seems to have felt, at any rate, that he had perfected the form; it was at the close of 1877 that he wrote to his friend Stefan Yanovsky that "the *Diary* has at last developed to the point where even the slightest change in its form is impossible." Indeed, it may someday be possible, he continues, to conduct a still more daring experiment: "I wish to try one new publication, in which the *Diary* itself would be included as a part" (*Pis'ma*, III, 284). Dostoevsky apparently entertained the idea that the *Diary*'s algorithmic and encyclopedic structure might, in principle, be infinitely repeatable!

Dostoevsky's Utopianism

It will be useful at this point to consider what is apparently the central—and certainly the most frequently repeated—theme of the monthly *Diary*, namely, the possibility that the apocalypse is literally imminent. In countless articles, the author argues that social "fragmentation," "dissociation," and "isolation" have reached such an extreme that the "final battle" is almost certainly near. And as promised in the Revelation to St. John, he contends, that battle will be followed by the millennium—which, for him, means a worldwide utopia headed by Russia and based on the Russian Orthodox faith.

Silencing his other voice as playful and digressive feuilletonist, the author usually speaks in these articles in the voice of a prophet. Time and again he announces the end of time. All European nations, he declares, are "living their last days, and they know it themselves" (March, 76, I, 4). "It is exactly as if everything [in Europe] were undermined and loaded with powder, and just awaiting the first spark . . . " (March, 76, I, 5; ellipsis in original). In his essay "Piccola Bestia" (September, 1876) he compares Europe's mood to his own during a night in Florence when he learned that somewhere in his hotel room there was a tarantula that could not be found. "Everybody is in a state of expectation," he writes (September, 76, I, 1):

> Everybody is alarmed, some kind of a nightmare hangs over everyone, everyone has bad dreams. But who or what is this *piccola bestia* [tarantula] which has produced such turmoil—it is impossible to specify, because some kind of general madness has ensued. . . . And yet it is as if all had already been stung. And this sting produces the most extraordinary fits: it is as if everyone in Europe has ceased to understand each other, as at the Tower of Babel . . .

The author further warns that Russia, too, may be in danger. Citing the passage in Matthew in which Jesus enumerates the signs of the end of the world, Dostoevsky identifies the leaders of Russia's new religious sects with the "false Christs" who will come to deceive the people in the Last Days. "Oh, the people must be guarded! For it is written: 'The time will come when they will say to you, lo, here is Christ, and there; but believe it not'" (81, I, 4; citation from Matthew 24:23). He suggests that Russia's current epidemic of suicide—"'the Russian earth seems to have lost the power to hold people on it" (May, 76, II, 2)—may be another sign of the End. But whereas Russia is destined to survive these dangers, he contends, Europe is not. "If not we, then our children will see how England will end. Now for everyone in the world 'the time is at hand.' And it is about time, too" (April, 77, I, 3; citation from Revelation 1:3). Nor will all Europe's armies and diplomats avail: "and all the wealth that Europe has accumulated will not save her from destruction, for 'in one hour so great riches is come to nought'" (80, I, 1; citation from Revelation 18:17). By the second half of 1877, the diarist awaits the apocalypse from month to month (November, 77, III, 2; italics in original):

> I repeat what was said above: Europe is changing from hour to hour . . . so that one cannot guarantee her unchangeability for even three months. The fact is that we are now on the eve of the greatest and most shocking events and upheavals in Europe, and I say this *without any exaggeration.* . . . Yes, the most immense upheavals await Europe, upheavals such as the mind refuses to believe, conceiving their realization as something fantastic.

The June, 1876, *Diary* outlines the historical process that the author believes will lead to a Russian utopia built on European ruins. In that issue's central article, "The Utopian Understanding of History," he divides Russian history into two periods: first, the time of Muscovy, in which Russia preserved the only, true Christian religion, "our treasure, Orthodoxy"; second, the time of Peter and his successors, during which Russia absorbed other cultures so well that it would some day be able to teach them the true religion and so save not just itself, but the whole world. And now, he argues, the third period, in which that saving lesson will be taught, has at last come. As soon as Russia defeats Turkey and "recaptures" Constantinople, the lost capital of Orthodoxy, we may expect "something that will *really* be exceptional and unheard-of," a new world order that "would be a genuine exaltation of the Christian truth . . . and the final word of Orthodoxy." This perfect kingdom, he concludes (June, 76, II, 4),

> would precisely constitute a temptation to all the mighty of this world who have so far triumphed in it, and have always looked on all such "expectations" with contempt and ridicule; to those who do not understand that one can seriously believe in the brotherhood of man, in the universal reconciliation of peoples, in a union founded on the principles of universal service to mankind, and at last, in the very renewal of men on the true principles of Christ. And if the belief in this "new word" to be spoken to the world by Russia, at the head of a united Orthodoxy—is a "utopia," worthy only of ridicule, then count me among the utopians, and the ridicule I accept as mine.

Another historical myth that ends with an imminent Orthodox utopia is outlined in "Three Ideas," the opening article of the 1877 *Diary.* "Three ideas are arising before the world, and it seems they are reaching their final form," the author proclaims. Those three ideas are Catholicism (represented by the pope, France, and the followers of French socialism), Protestantism (Bismarck and Germany), and Orthodoxy (Russia and the Slavic nations under Turkish rule). As V. A. Sidorov has observed, Dostoevsky's article personifies these ideas, endows them with a biography, and describes their development and destiny in terms of the character and personality of the nations in which they reside.[43] History becomes novelized and allegorized, taking on overtones of psychomachia—or, more precisely, of ideomachia: exhausted from the long struggle, the Vatican (proclaiming infallibility on the very eve of its fall) will join with the socialists in a doomed struggle against Protestantism. But Protestantism, the diarist asserts, is sustained only by the spirit of protest, and, having annihilated its enemy, is bound to succumb to the triumphant Orthodox idea, which, according to the author, contains all that is worth preserving in the other two. World war is approaching. The forthcoming election of a new pope, the maneuvers of Bismarck, the revolt of the Slavs, all indicate to the prophetic diarist that "these three enormous world ideas have come together almost at one and the same time for their final denouement. All this is . . . no war for some patrimony . . . as in the last century. Here we have something universal and final, which, though by no means solving *all* human destinies, without doubt brings with it the beginning of the end of all previous history of European mankind." The "denouement" may be expected "even—who knows?—perhaps this very year" (January, 77, I, 1):

> Europe is restless, of this there can be no doubt. But is this temporary or momentary restlessness? Not at all: it is obvious that the time has come for something eternal, millenarian, for that which has been preparing itself in the world since the very beginning of its civilization.

That "something millenarian," he explains, is a reign of brotherhood, based on spontaneous love (as in Russian Orthodoxy) rather than on law, as in Western socialism (repeating here the argument of the *Winter Remarks*). Readers will no doubt scoff at all this, Dostoevsky now turns to (or, rather, turns on) his audience. "It will be said that this 'Russian solution to the question' is the 'Kingdom of Heaven' and would be possible only in the kingdom of heaven. Yes, the Stivas [i.e., sybarites like Stiva Oblonsky in *Anna Karenina*] would be very angry if the kingdom of heaven actually came" (February, 77, II, 4).

"Everyone senses that something final has happened," he writes in the April, 1877, issue, reporting the Russian declaration of war against Turkey. All perceive, he continues (April, 77, I, 1; ellipsis in original),

> that an end is coming to former things, to the long, drawn-out former times, and that a step is being taken toward something already completely new, something which splits the past in two, and renews and resurrects it for a new life, and . . . that this step is being taken by Russia!

The "former things" (perhaps an allusion to Revelation 21:4) will surely pass away, the author observes, unless the pope with his Polish agents, and Disraeli, representing both England and the Jews, can prevent Russian conquest of Constantinople. "War. We are Stronger than Everyone" and "War Is Not Always a Scourge, Sometimes It Is Salvation" declare the titles of two articles in this issue, which also contains Dostoevsky's extraordinary utopian story, "The Dream of a Ridiculous Man." By September, the author is confident enough to specify the four steps, prepared by "Inescapable Fate," that will lead Europe from history to utopia (September, 77, I, 5; italics in original):

(1) The road begins at Rome and leads from Rome, from the Vatican, where the dying old man, the head of the crowd of Jesuits who surround him, indicated it long ago. . . . *Papal Catholicism, dying forever*, will certainly wage a war for its existence against the whole world in the very near future.

(2) This fatal struggle [between France and Germany] . . . is *inevitable and near.*

(3) As soon as the battle begins, it will be converted into an all-European one. . . .

(4) (And let this be called the most conjectural and fantastic of all my prophecies, that is agreed in advance): I am sure that the war will end in favor of the Eastern alliance. . . .

Now someone is knocking, some new man with a new word—wants to open the door and enter . . . [ellipsis in original] But who will enter—that is the question; will he be an entirely new man, or, once again, one resembling all of us old homunculi?

When these predictions were not fulfilled, the *Diary* was suspended, to be resumed only when new utopian hopes were entertained. (The 1880 *Diary* anticipated that Dostoevsky's own Pushkin speech might inaugurate the reign of brotherhood; in 1881, Russian conquest of Asia was apparently expected to be the apocalyptic catalyst.) Ceasing when prophecy fails, the *Diary* implicitly renders its very interruptions thematically significant: they may, in effect, be taken as the prophet's silence in the face of disconfirmation—Jonah's regret at the reprieve of Nineveh.

But so long as the *Diary* was in the process of publication, it dramatized a dialogue of utopian faith with anti-utopian skepticism—the skepticism not only of readers who interrupt in scoffing, "caustic voices" but also of the diarist himself in moments of wry self-reflection on his own and other quixotic beliefs in the incredible. The voice of the utopian prophet usually predominates, but that predominance is always precarious, and prophecy is never free from the threat of parody: the *Diary*'s dialogue of utopia with anti-utopia—and of anti-utopia with anti-anti-utopia—is ultimately inconclusive.

The diarist, like Shatov in *The Possessed*, seems forever poised on the verge of a faith he cannot quite attain. That, of course, was Dostoevsky's own most profound dilemma; and the *Diary*'s unresolved "pro and contra," like that of a number of Dostoevsky's other works, seems to recapitulate his complex and contradictory thinking about the possibility of realizing Christ's truth on earth. The author of two of the most influential anti-utopias in European literature, *Notes from Underground* and *The Possessed*, remained uncertain whether he wished to deny not only the desirability of Western socialism, but also the possibility of *any* kingdom of God on earth. During the period in which he wrote *Notes from Underground* and the *Winter Remarks*, he apparently believed that the promise of the millennium must be understood only in a figurative sense. In his truly private notebooks (as opposed to the public and literary "notebooks" of the *Diary*), Dostoevsky began a long meditation on resurrection, brotherhood, and the millennium:

> NB. The antichrists are mistaken, refuting Christianity by the following chief point of refutation: (1) "Why does Christianity not reign on earth if it is true, why does man suffer to this day and not join in brotherhood?"
>
> It is very clear why: because this is an ideal of the future final life of man and on earth man is in a transitory state. . . . Christ Himself prophesied His teachings only as an ideal, Himself foretold that until the end of the world there would be struggle and development (the parable of the sword), for this is the law of nature. . . .
>
> And thus on earth man strives towards an ideal *contrary* to his nature. When a man has not fulfilled the law of striving towards the ideal, that is, has not *through love* sacrificed his *I* to people or to another person . . . he experiences suffering, and has called this condition sin. And so man must unceasingly experience suffering, which is compensated for by the heavenly joy of fulfilling the Law, that is, by sacrifice. This is earthly equilibrium. Otherwise, Earth would be senseless.[44]

But by the time he undertook the *Diary*, Dostoevsky had apparently come to believe that the millennium might be both literal and imminent. "I recall with shame," his proofreader at the *Citizen* wrote in "A Year of Work with a Famous Writer,"

> how "wild" it seemed to me when once, while reading the proofs of his article about Prussia, Bismarck, and the pope, he suddenly began to speak in a tone—well, in that same tone with which he laughed so cruelly, but wittily, at my "liberal" acquaintances . . .
>
> "*They* do not even suspect that soon there will be an end to everything . . . to all their 'progress' and talk. They do not even sense that an antichrist has already been born . . . and *is coming!*"
>
> He pronounced this with such an expression in his voice and on his face, as if he had revealed to me a terrible and great secret, and then, casting a glance at me, he asked sternly:
>
> "Do you believe me or not? I ask you, answer me! Do you believe me or not?"
>
> "I believe you, Fyodor Mikhailovich, only I think that you are carried away and so are involuntarily exaggerating . . . "
>
> He struck his hand on the table so hard that I started, and, having raised his voice, he shouted like a mullah in his minaret:

"The antichrist is coming to us! He is coming! And the end of the world is near—nearer than they think!"[45]

Dostoevsky's biographers and critics have tended to omit mention of episodes of this sort, and by obscuring or minimizing the extent of his apocalyptic mania and messianic anti-semitism, to engage in a form of negative apologetics. Still, there is an important difference between a firm conviction and a belief entertained—even seriously entertained—in the face of doubt, and Dostoevsky may well have been exaggerating in his conversations with the liberal young lady. Certainly he seems to protest too much, to speak in words with "loopholes" and "sideward glances" at expected answers, to overstate what he himself doubts but wishes to believe. The *Diary* would seem to be the shaping of that dialogue into a literary work. As we shall see, however, the shape it took was determined not only by the ambivalence of Dostoevsky's vision and by his particular quest for a suitable literary form, but also by the available generic traditions of literary utopia and its parodies. The *Diary* belongs to one of those traditions, namely what I shall call meta-utopia; and in drawing on it, Dostoevsky drew on works as remote in time as the *Republic* and as complex in form as *Don Quixote, The Praise of Folly*, and the philosophical dialogues of Diderot. Two lines of development, Dostoevsky's experiments with boundary works and the generic tradition of meta-utopia, converge in *The Diary of a Writer*. It may well be that every innovative work represents a similar convergence of a writer's quest for form and an available genre's amenability to reformulation.

2. Threshold Art

Literature

The term "literature" is used in several senses, and much fruitless discussion of its definition probably derives not only from the failure to distinguish among its senses, but also from the tacit assumption that to specify one sense is to rule out the use of all others. I shall not offer here either to account for or to regulate the use of the *word* "literature"; I shall, rather, specify the *class of texts* I have in mind when I speak of literature and indicate how the identification and characterization of this class is helpful in understanding the poetics of certain problematic texts and genres, which I shall call "boundary works" and "boundary genres."

As I shall use the term, then, "literature" refers neither to all the texts of a given field or culture, nor to texts with certain formal (e.g., stylistic, linguistic) features, nor to the canonical texts of Western culture. Used in the last way, literature is a normative category, subsuming works that are in accord with certain implicit or explicit evaluative criteria. As a normative category, literature is a different *kind* of class from fiction. To argue whether Herzen's *From the Other Shore* is literature in this sense would be to question its value —that is, its conformity to certain evaluative criteria—but not its semiotic nature. To deny the fictionality of a text, however, *is* to make a statement about its semiotic nature. And in what follows, I shall be using "literature" as a term of the same type as "fiction"—that is, to denote a class of verbal structures, including oral as well as inscribed works and works of little as well as great cultural value, the members of which are identified by the manner in which they bear meaning. To call a text literature in this sense is to make a statement about the appropriate process of arriving at its meaning (more accurately, meanings), while to call a work nonliterature is to rule out the appropriateness of certain methods of interpretation.

To be specific, to class a text as literary in this sense is to say that its semiotic interest is not limited for its readers to its original context of communication and that the determination of its meaning is not equivalent to the reconstruction of the circumstances, causes, and effects of the original exchange between speaker and listener.[1] Whenever readers treat a text as evocative of *possible* contexts and expect it to reward the process of interpretation itself (rather than simply a particular interpretation), they are treating it as what I am calling literature. In this sense, while nonliterary texts are treated as wholly "documentary," literary texts may be taken by readers as documentary but are never exhausted in being so. If readers should take a record of a particular communicative exchange as *exemplificative* instead of simply *evidentiary*,[2] they should have made it into a work of literature. Of course, readers usually take a text as literary because it has been given, or is presumed to have been given, as such. But they may also choose to take it as literary even when they do not presume it to have been so given. Literature, in other words, may be both designed and discovered; when readers discover its suitability for interpretation apart from its original communicative context, they become, in effect, its designers as literature.

As used here, therefore, the class literature is identified not by any formal properties its members may exhibit, but by the way in which they are treated. When literature does differ from nonliterature in formal properties, those differences are the signs and consequences rather than the constituent traits of literariness. Indeed, there need be no formal differences at all between literature and nonliterature: the same genre, or even the same text, can be literary in one period and nonliterary in another. Yury Tynyanov examined the evolution of Russian literature in terms of just such problematic genres and used their changing status as a method of establishing the changing boundaries of "literature." One of his examples was the familiar letter, which briefly became a literary genre in the age of Pushkin.[3] Though addressed to a particular recipient, it was understood that these letters were written in order to be read by a public with little or no interest in the relation of writer to addressee or in the information conveyed. As their authors anticipated, these literary letters were collected and published and so were treated differently from other, nonliterary letters written by the same authors in the same period. A distinctive set of conventions governing style, structure, and suitable topics of discussion came to govern literary letters, and these differences in form and content became, in turn, signs of the literariness of a letter. A literary letter, for instance, might "inform" its recipient of what he or she must already have known. A similar transformation is likely to take place in diaries in periods when they become a literary genre. They then tend to provide "unnecessary" connections between thoughts and to "remind" the diarist of what he or she could not possibly forget; these stage whispers and extended soliloquies then mark the difference between literary and truly private diaries.

A literary historian or biographer who failed to recognize the literariness of these letters and diaries would be likely to draw naive or incorrect conclusions from them. He or she might take as evidentiary what was intended as exemplificative and, in reconstructing the original context of communication, tend to overlook a key fact about that context: namely, that it defined the text in question as not designed for this kind of reconstruction.[4] The Formalist Nikolay Trubetskoy has argued the importance of such distinctions for scholars of Old Russian literature who have tended to treat all, or almost all, texts as documents rather than as "literary monuments."[5] His example of this kind of inappropriate treatment is the criticism of Afanasy Nikitin's "Voyage beyond Three Seas" for being less ethnographically informative than Vasco da Gama's accounts of his journey to India at about the same time—a criticism which, Trubetskoy contends, overlooks the possibility that Afanasy

Nikitin was not composing the same sort of work as Vasco da Gama. Carefully structured as an alternation of narrative exposition and lyrical digressions—digressions of little ethnographic value—this linguistically self-conscious text is, Trubetskoy suggests, designed to be read against the tradition of pilgrimage literature and to evoke a general picture of a man in exile from faith and fatherland. A similar point could be made about the "Appeal of Daniel the Exile." Actually composed over centuries and extant in several different versions, the "Appeal" is purportedly addressed by Daniel, a sufferer of unjust wrongs, to a prince whose protection Daniel seeks. Within this frame, scribes from various periods inserted diatribes against various kinds of injustice (for example, rulers' neglect of the learned and wives' mistreatment of their husbands). The scribes who used the text in this way and treated Daniel as a conventional (or "exemplary") sufferer were treating the work as literature. On the other hand, the contemporary scholar who tries to establish by textological means the core text that Daniel wrote (if there was a Daniel) and so to arrive at information about a particular ruler is using the text as a document. As evidence of this kind, literary texts are notoriously unreliable. What they *can* more or less reliably indicate is, in the first instance, the culture's literary conventions, which may, in turn, be more or less reliable historical evidence of other aspects of the culture.

An important corollary for the present study follows from this conception of literature: for a text to function outside its original context, it must be seen to be shaped by a "constructive principle"[6] that makes it integral. Because the text cannot rely on any particular context to achieve its meaningfulness, it must be—or appear to be—designed to be capable of meaning in manifold contexts. In short, to be multiply recontextualizable, the literary text must appear complete in itself. The boundary of the "work," therefore, will be that point at which the constructive principle stops—the point beyond which we have no right either to posit the governing power of the text's design or to expect it to be interesting outside the context of its origin. Students who read the concluding "editor's note" to *Notes from Underground* and complain that their instructor has assigned an abridged version have obviously drawn the boundary line of the "work" short of that note; they have taken the latter as nonliterary, as no different from the information supplied by the editors of this translation of *Notes*. The same point could be made about marginal glosses. When we know that a gloss has been supplied by a later editor, we do not assume it to be designed to function as a part of the text. On the other hand, if we read the glosses to "The Rime of the Ancient Mariner,"[7] like the notes to *Eugene Onegin* and *The Dunciad*, as integral parts of the work, we will not judge them by their accuracy or informativeness, but rather seek to discover their place in the structure of the work. If they are inappropriate or inaccurate, we will look for the designing principle that dictates these "mistakes."

To take a verbal text as a literary work, therefore, is to assume in principle (1) that everything in the text is potentially relevant to its design, and (2) that the design is complete in the text that we have. To read a work as literary is to read it as complete. If a work is a fragment, it can be read as a literary work only if, and to the extent that, it tolerates the assumption that the principles of its integrity are inferable from the extant part—as they largely are, let us say, for *The Fairie Queene*. When the extant part is too fragmentary to justify such an inference, it cannot be read as a literary work unless readers should themselves imagine its completion and so become co-authors of that projected "work." For these very reasons, metaliterature often explores the nature of literary integrity by *designing* "fragments." Designed fragments are, however, not incomplete works, but rather complete works that represent incomplete works. There is a radical difference between a fragment of a poem and the *genre* of the poetic fragment, between a text left incomplete by a fictive author and one unfinished by its real author.[8] The underground man's notes are unfinished, but Dostoevsky's *Notes* is not; to read *Notes from Underground* as a literary work is, indeed, to read its "non-ending" as a designed ending.

If a work is assumed to be complete, we are justified in hypothesizing the thematic and formal relevance of all of its details. This is not to say that all of its details will necessarily be equally relevant or that the transposition or omission of any of them will fundamentally change the work. That is obviously not the case. On the contrary, to identify the structure of a work is to construct a *hierarchy* of relevance that makes some of its details central and others peripheral. No detail, however, can be completely irrelevant. Even those that are the least relevant, as Martin Price has observed, "may be reminiscent of that rougher texture at the lower part of the statue or the building, at once an element of the design and yet a vestige of the resistant materials from which the work was fashioned. They are not to be put by entirely; if they contribute to the condition of illusion or testify to the real, they also budge somewhat the inner meaning or structure of the work. It must be extended, however slightly, to admit their presence."[9] It may be observed, in fact, that a large part of the pleasure of reading literature derives from the identification of that structure, from the process of ordering through which we perceive or postulate the wholeness of a text. When we have in this way "explained" (identified the structural place of) a hitherto unexplained detail, we say we have understood the work better and we take pleasure in that increased understanding. The way readers go about this process of ordering, it should be noted, is not a constant. Different genres, for instance, imply different rules for ordering, and readers in different periods may estimate importance in different ways. What will remain constant, however, is the assumption of some kind of order. So long as the work is read as literature at all, readers will seek an integral design and postulate a structure to reward their search.

The integrity of a literary work also implies that the meaning of each of its parts is dependent on its place in the structure of the whole. We construct a work's meaning from the relation of its parts and are likely to change our interpretation of a part when we alter our understanding of the whole. "If the shortsighted critics think that I merely wanted to describe what appealed to me, such as the sort of dinner Oblonsky has or what Anna's shoulders are like, then they are mistaken," wrote Tolstoy. "In everything . . . I wrote I was guided by the need of collecting ideas which, linked together, would be the expression of myself, though each individual idea, expressed separately in words, loses its meaning; is horribly debased when only one of the links, of which it forms a part, is taken by itself."[10] Our sense of the inappropriateness of excerpting passages from a literary work derives from this assumption of integrity and from our experience in finding meaning in the "linkages." We may say that the Grand Inquisitor legend, read separately, is a profound tale but not the same tale as it is in *The Brothers Karamazov*, where it enters into dialogue with other embedded narratives and is constantly qualified by allusions to its themes. In the context of the novel, moreover, not only the narrative but the fact of narration at that point becomes significant.

The way in which the assumption of integrity informs our comprehension of each part of a literary work is best illustrated by those works that contain apparently discrepant elements. Let us consider for a moment the example of the relation between a text and its summary. When summaries occur in nonliterary works, we will, unless some other signal intervenes, take that summary as the author's abstract of the text's key ideas. Whether or not we regard the summary as adequate, we take it as "authoritative"; when it is inadequate, we may say that the author did not appreciate the significance of his or her own work. When, however, a discrepant summary appears as part of a *literary* work, it necessarily functions differently. For here, if we feel that the summary does not follow from or adequately summarize the *rest of* the text, we would have to consider the possibility of irony and postulate some structure of the whole that made sense of this discrepancy. Moreover, we may note that even if there were no such discrepancy, the summary would still function differently from a summary in a nonliterary text. After the narrative portion of Tolstoy's "Sevastopol in May" ends, for instance, the text breaks and the author makes a final statement (ellipsis in original):

> There, I have said what I wished to say this time. But I am seized by an oppressive doubt. Perhaps I ought to have left it unsaid. What I have said perhaps belongs to that class of evil truths that lie unconsciously hidden in the soul of each man and should not be uttered lest they become harmful, as the dregs in a bottle must not be disturbed for fear of spoiling the wine . . . [11]

To take this passage as part of the story is to take it differently from the way we would take the same sentences in a letter about the story. We try to understand its place in the entire literary work, and to comprehend a structure that includes both fictional narrative and the author's nonfictive evaluation of his narrative. The summary necessarily becomes dramatic rather than simply informative, and we may, for instance, read the entire story as the author's account of his complex attempt to speak the truth rather than give in to the distortions of conventional descriptions. We could then go back to the text and find earlier statements that lie outside the narrative and com-

ment on the process of composing it. In light of the author's later statement
that truth may be harmful, these attempts to speak a difficult truth may now
appear naive. Having re-patterned the text in this way, we may then attribute
particular dramatic power to its concluding statement: "The hero of my tale
—whom I love with all the power of my soul, whom I have tried to portray in
all his beauty, who has been, is, and will be beautiful—is the truth" (175).

Fiction

Although the boundaries of fiction and literature only sometimes coincide,
fictionality is a concept of the same kind as literariness, in that (1) to read a
text as fiction rather than nonfiction is to make a decision or assumption
about its semiotic nature, and (2) fictionality is not a matter of formal features but rather of a set of conventions governing the grounds and consequences of that decision or assumption. No change need be made in the form
of a nonfictional statement to make it fictional. One makes it fictional by
taking it (or indicating that others should take it) as such. We usually choose
to do so because the text is "given" as fictional; but, like literariness, fictionality may be imposed as well as designed.

What is at stake, therefore, is the nature of our response to, and of the
author's responsibility for, the text. In the fictional text, both are implicitly
or explicitly governed by a "metacommunicative statement" of the type "this
is play."[12] Or, to put it somewhat differently, it is implicitly understood that
a "fictional contract"[13] is in force, a contract specifying that the veridical
conventions of nonfictive discourse are, in a particular way, suspended. To
take a text as fictional is to recognize it as the *representation* of a *possible* utterance, not as the enunciation or inscription of a real one. As Barbara Herrnstein Smith has recently argued,

> what is central to the concept of the poem as a fictive utterance is not
> that the "character" or "persona" is distinct from the poet, or that the
> audience purportedly addressed, the emotions expressed, and the events
> alluded to are fictional, but that *the speaking, addressing, expressing, and
> alluding are themselves fictive verbal acts.* . . . The essential fictiveness of
> novels . . . is not to be discovered in the unreality of the characters, ob-
> jects, and events alluded to, but in the unreality of the *alludings* them-
> selves. In other words, in a novel or tale, it is the *act* of reporting events,
> the *act* of describing persons and referring to places, that is fictive. . . . *The
> Death of Ivan Ilyich* is not the biography of a fictional character, but rath-
> er a fictive biography.[14]

Because fictive utterances are not being said but rather represented, we
do not hold their authors responsible in the same way that we might hold
them for their nonfictional statements. We *do* hold them responsible for the
act of *representing* certain statements, which is quite a different thing. The
authors do not vouch for the veracity of their fictive statements because they

are not in fact stating them; nor do we expect them to fulfill fictive promises or be sorry when they represent a possible apology. When Smerdyakov objects to Gogol's stories because they are "not true" or the judge at the Daniel trial calls the writer's stories "slanderous" because they describe events that never happened, they fail to recognize or honor a fictional contract.

On the other hand, the judge might plausibly have argued that to compose a fiction like "This Is Moscow Speaking" and to publish it abroad could, in the Soviet context, reasonably be taken as evidence of anti-Soviet opinions on the part of the author. For to say that a text is fictional is not to say that it has no propositional implications but rather to say that its propositional implications cannot be inferred in the same way as they could from a verbally identical nonfictional text. When Tolstoy argued that most novels are lies, he did not mean that they portrayed events which had not happened. It is more likely that he had in mind the implicit claim of novels to be real*istic* even though not real; what he held authors responsible for was the generic claim of *plausibility*. It followed for Tolstoy that a young lady in whose hands romantic novels were placed could well be led astray without ever believing that the author was vouching for the factual veracity of his or her description.

Each particular fictional genre, moreover, functions as a sort of secondary contract that tells how, given the suspension of the conventions of nonfictional discourse, the reader may reasonably infer the authors' beliefs and sentiments about the real world from their having composed fictional utterances of a particular kind. There may also be tertiary contracts to govern subgenres as well. Historical novels, for example, characteristically claim more than that the events alluded to are plausible. Thus, Tolstoy can state, when describing the "contract" that governs those fictional sections of *War and Peace* that deal with real historical figures: "*Whenever in my novel historical persons speak or act, I have invented nothing, but have used historical material of which I have accumulated a whole library during my work. I do not think it necessary to cite the titles of those books here, but could cite them at any time in proof of what I say.*"[15]

Despite this claim of extraordinary scrupulousness, however, Tolstoy does not seem to be setting aside the fictional contract. We might observe, for instance, that Tolstoy describes conversations between historical and fictional characters—such as those between Kutuzov and Bolkonsky—for which he could not have had, and for which it is therefore unlikely that he expected us to believe he had, documentary evidence. It would probably also be naive or literalistic to imagine that Tolstoy could have provided sources for every action, however minor, ascribed to Napoleon. More likely, Tolstoy was not suspending the fictional contract, but rather emphasizing that a special, secondary, generic contract was in force. He was, in short, not claiming in these passages to be making real utterances about historical figures, but rather to be depicting possible ones which, if they *had been* made in a nonfictional history, *would have been* more or less accurate. (These passages are thus to be distinguished from the truly nonfictional sections of *War and Peace*, namely the essays on the philosophy of history. These essays, though literature, and subject to interpretation in terms of the whole work, are not fiction—that is, no special conventions are needed to infer from the text Tolstoy's beliefs about the subjects it discusses.)

To speak of a work as fictional, therefore, is to imply (1) that certain of the conventions governing the appropriate interpretation of nonfictive discourse have been suspended in it, and (2) that there exists a corresponding set of conventions in accord with which the reader can infer certain meanings from that text. The first characteristic describes the fictionality of the text, the second specifies its genre.

It is not always easy, however, to decide whether to take a text as fictional. To be sure, texts are often marked as belonging to a specific fictional genre (e.g., they may be explicitly designated by the author—on the title page, for instance—as novels). Nevertheless, a text, or a part of a text, may be unclearly marked and hence of ambiguous status. Consider, for instance, the preface to *The Brothers Karamazov*, a preface that has been read by some as nonfiction and by others as an intrinsic part of the larger fiction. Those who regard the preface as nonfiction interpret it in much the same way that they interpret Dostoevsky's letters, that is, as more or less authoritative statements of Dostoevsky's intentions, but as not properly "part of" the novel. The preface is, in fact, omitted from some "unabridged" editions. On the other hand, its description of *Karamazov* as only the preliminary narrative for a more important, but still unwritten, second volume is used to justify interpretations of the work as a fragment and speculations on Ivan's recovery, Dmitri's imprisonment, and Alyosha's "mature life."[16] It is also possible, however, to consider the author of the preface to be not Dostoevsky himself, but the fictional narrator of *Karamazov*. In that case, one might ask not what the second volume would have contained, but why Dostoevsky chose to create this work, like *Notes from Underground*, in the form of a "fragment." The preface's self-characterization as spontaneous and "needless"—"but since it has already been written, let it stand"[17]—could then be seen as the first of the narrator's many professions of ignorance or incompetence: "I am not a doctor, but yet I feel that the moment has come when I must inevitably give the reader some account of the nature of Ivan's illness" (771). "I ought to say something of this Smerdyakov, but I am ashamed of keeping my readers' attention so long occupied with these common menials, and I will go back to my story, hoping to say more of Smerdyakov in the course of it" (118).

To class the preface to *Karamazov* as fictional is to say that its "statements" are *created* but not *stated* by Dostoevsky, and that they are to be interpreted as literature and as part of the whole work. Because novels are usually defined as a certain kind of fictional literature, the boundaries of fiction and literature in this case coincide. The "coincidence," however, is just that. As we have seen, some literary works, like *War and Peace* and "Sevastopol in May," contain both fictional and nonfictional sections. To interpret these works as literature is to try to understand how, in each case, these two kinds of prose cohere and so to identify the place of nonfictional essays and commentary in a predominantly fictional work.

There are, moreover, genres of literary prose that are entirely nonfictional. Fictional works so predominate in the literature with which we are most familiar that we sometimes forget, first, that this has not always been so, and, second, that there are modern genres of nonfictional literature—for example, literary autobiography (as distinguished both from nonliterary autobiography and from novels in the form of autobiographies). It is probably because fiction and literature are so often equated that literary autobiography (and biography) has seemed paradoxical and proven to be a difficult problem in literary theory. For so long as that equation is made, one is likely either to exclude all autobiography from literature or to extend, indeed distend, the concept of fiction so as to include it. So, at least, Northrop Frye defines the alternatives in the *Anatomy of Criticism*. The inadequacy of Frye's solution —to extend the concept of fiction—points to the advantage of not equating literature with fiction in the first place, which is to say, the advantage of recognizing two classes rather than one. Objecting to "novel-centered"[18] descriptions of prose literature, Frye correctly points out that such descriptions lead not only to the anachronistic classification of narratives from Greek romances to *Gulliver's Travels* as pre-novels but also to the neglect of other literary genres, such as what he calls "rhetorical genres" and the "anatomy" as well as autobiography. However, in order to rescue these genres from neglect as literature, Frye classes them, on dubious grounds, as fiction: "Surely the word fiction, which, like poetry, means etymologically something made for its own sake, could be applied in criticism to any work of literary art in a radically continuous form. . . . Most autobiographies are inspired by a creative, and therefore fictional, impulse to select only those events and experiences in the writer's life that go to build up an integrated pattern" (303-307). Frye further contends that autobiography and confession merge "with the novel by a series of insensible gradations" (307) that make it impossible to draw a line betweeen autobiographies of real people and "the fictional autobiography, the *Kunstler-roman*, and kindred types" (307). To be sure, Frye is wise to emphasize the importance of selection and integration in autobiography. Nevertheless, in preserving a single category where two are required, Frye's solution to the classification of autobiography would seem to correct an old mistake with a new one. For there *is* a crucial difference between a real autobiography and a representation of a possible one, and this difference is not one of insensible gradations but, on the contrary, an absolute one. The difference lies in the kind of responsibility the author takes for his or her statements. In one case, we are asked to believe, and invited to look for, outside confirmation of the speaker's statements; in the other, we are not, because in fact no one is *making* (as opposed to *representing*) statements. Although it may sometimes be hard to tell whether a particular text is given as a real or a fictive autobiography, the distinction itself is not one of degree.

To obscure this distinction, moreover, may make it easy to overlook what autobiographers themselves tend to stress as a particular source of value of their work, namely its truthfulness. The defining generic characteristic of autobiography as literature—that is, its claim to be of interest outside the context of its origin to those who are not, or are not only, interested in the author's life and milieu—may well be the author's solution to the problem of discovering difficult truths about himself or herself and revealing them to others. Rousseau's boast that his *Confessions* could serve as testimony when he appears before God overstates what most autobiographers conventionally seek: sincerity, accuracy, and freedom from the falsities that the ready-made forms of language and the familiar circles of self-justification introduce. To class such texts as fictional may therefore be to mistake how they function as a genre. Far from being fictional because of their selection and ordering, literary autobiographies may well be characterized as a genre by their struggle with the potentially distorting effects of those processes.

Not all fiction is literature, not all literature is fiction.[19] The class of non-fictional literature includes, in addition to autobiography and Frye's "rhetorical genres," Tynyanov's example of the familiar letter in the age of Pushkin and Trubetskoy's of the medieval account of a pilgrimage. It includes as well Lomonosov's poem on the techniques of glassblowing and the essays in Herzen's *From the Other Shore*—meditations on the failure of one revolution that are designed to be metaphoric of reactions to all failed ideals and emblematic of other encounters, including nonpolitical ones, of hope with experience. Each of these works or genres is designed to function outside the context of its origin and to be interpreted as an integrated whole, but none of them, I think, is designed to be taken as fictional, as the representation of possible utterances.

Nevertheless, many forms of nonfiction come under the suspicion of fictionality in an age when fiction predominates as the literary mode. Some "shadow of fictionality" falls on them, and some readers will regard them as taxonomically ambiguous. This kind of ambiguity is, in fact, the identifying characteristic of boundary genres, to which I now turn.

Boundary Works

In what I shall refer to as boundary works, it is uncertain which of two mutually exclusive sets of conventions governs a work. When this kind of ambivalence obtains, it is possible to read the work according to different hermeneutic procedures and hence, all other things being equal, to derive contradictory interpretations. Doubly decodable, the same text becomes, in effect, two different works. Because they admit of opposed meanings, boundary works may be compared to puns or homonyms on the scale of an entire discourse (rather than a single word). The conventions in question may be those of a particular genre, those of fiction, or those of literature as a whole; more than one of these classes may be doubtful simultaneously. The text's meaning will depend on the reader's classificatory choice, which is to say, on an explicit (rather than the usually implicit) act of intertextuality. A work may also be characterized by this kind of ambivalence through membership in a genre that itself admits classification fiction and nonfiction or as both literature and nonliterature. There are, in other words, boundary genres as well as boundary works.

I shall refer to boundary works only in those cases where the uncertainty of classification involves two sets of conventions that are in principle exclusive, distinct, and discontinuous—that is, only where the possibility of double classification leads to double decodability. Although not all generic distinctions are of this kind, the boundaries of fiction, literature, and some genres are as absolute as international political boundaries. It may be hard to decide whether Alsace-Lorraine is historically French or German, but at any given moment it is one or the other. One cannot cross an international boundary by "insensible gradations." A boundary genre may be compared to disputed territory over which neither side has clear sovereignty at a given moment or to a person with dual citizenship in time of war.

Boundary works are created in two ways. They may, like some provinces on the Russian-Polish frontier, be passive victims of a changing boundary line. Just as some Jewish Americans do not know whether to say their ancestors came from Russia or Poland, so later generations of readers may not know which set of literary conventions originally governed a text. Thus, it may be unclear to biographers whether a given familiar letter was designed to function as literature, and they may therefore be unsure what kind of evidence it constitutes. If they should take a generic *topos* as a statement of fact, or information intended for a public audience as news to the ostensible addressee, they may draw dubious conclusions. Ambivalent decoding may be the result both of changing *signals* of genre, fictionality, or literariness and of changes in the literary system as a whole. The more remote a literary system is, the less clear will its genres and their conventions be. Faced with this kind of uncertainty, readers may decide to read the text according to the conventions of their own (or some other) period, and so to re-encode it once again. Over time, the same text may become a palimpsest of different, but verbally identical, works.

The hermeneutic *perplexity* that characterizes boundary genres must be carefully distinguished from the hermeneutic *indeterminacy* of literature itself, that is, the fact that literature may function in unforeseen contexts and therefore be emblematic of changing concerns and exemplificative of quite different propositions to different sets of readers. The disagreements engendered by boundary works are of a different order. Strictly speaking, it is not meanings but appropriate procedures for discovering meaning that are disputable—not particular readings, but how to read. The authors' intentions are unclear—not, it should be stressed, their intentions about what the works mean, but about the sorts of work they would be read *as.*

Threshold Literature

Boundary works may not only *become* ambiguous in this way, that is, because of the chances of literary history, but they may also be originally *de-signed* as such. An author may deliberately create a text that is doubly encoded from the start and that invites contradictory classification. I refer to boundary works of this type as *threshold literature*—a class that is perhaps best described in terms of the three principal strategies its works use. First, the author of a threshold work may create an entire text of uncertain status and exploit the resonance between two kinds of reading. The reader's experience would be planned as one of "hermeneutic perplexity." That perplexity would be appropriately resolved not by choosing one kind of reading over the other, but by comprehending the work's import as the dialectic between the two.

We may observe that several of Dostoevsky's *characters* are masters of this kind of threshold art. Ivan Karamazov, for instance, describes his Grand Inquisitor "legend" as a "poem in prose," one which, moreover, resembles medieval mystery plays and narratives from folk apocrypha as well. "Even this must have a preface—that is, a literary preface" (292) Ivan wryly begins, and the next two pages are devoted to a discussion of the narrative's genre. "Well, my poem *would have been* of that kind *if it had* appeared at that time" (293; italics mine), he concludes his inconclusive preface. Unsure how to take several passages, Alyosha frequently interrupts to ask for generic clarification—interruptions which Ivan has probably planned and to which he responds evasively. In jest and with forced laughter, Ivan usually tells Alyosha to understand the text as he chooses. "'Take it as the last,' said Ivan, laughing, 'if you are so corrupted by modern realism and can't stand anything fantastic. If you like it to be a case of mistaken identity, let it be so'" (297). "Mistaken identity" is, in fact, an apt characterization of Alyosha's attempt to make the text mean one thing or the other. In similar situations, Myshkin and Tikhon, who are wiser listeners than Alyosha, understand that their hesitation before multiply encoded confessional narratives has been engineered.

A second type of threshold work creates hermeneutic perplexity not by generic ambiguity but by generic incompatibility, that is, by embedding or juxtaposing sections of radically heterogeneous material. The generic conventions governing individual sections may be clear, but the laws of their combination are not. Attempting to understand the entire text as a single literary work, the reader postulates hierarchical relations among its constituent parts, but discovers that the text sustains radically different hierarchies and therefore admits contradictory readings. Foreground and background switch places until a conclusion ostentatiously fails to solve the problem. In Gogol's stories, for example, comic anecdote and sentimental declamation, meticulous realism and Gothic supernaturalism, succeed each other with astonishing rapidity and so produce what Eichenbaum calls "an apotheosis of the grotesque"[20]—a concept that Eichenbaum in effect defines in terms of generic incompatibility. It is not surprising that the history of Gogol criticism should have been particularly full of controversy, a history that Gogol seems to plan as well as foresee when his narrator "apologizes" for his "improbable" and motley form. (Gogol owes this metaliterary *topos* to two earlier masters of inter-

generic play, Sterne and Pushkin.)[21] In a more serious vein, Tolstoy exploits
a similar technique in *War and Peace*. Part novel and part essay, *War and
Peace* is both a novel and "not a novel" as Tolstoy suggests in an essay that
explicitly dissociates his work from the traditional conception of the novel.[22]
Here the categories in question are fiction and literature, both of which
would seem to exclude polemical essays. The feuilleton, which, as we have
seen, juxtaposes the topical with the more traditionally literary and typically
apologizes for violating unstated rules for their combination, is likely to become a heterogeneous collage of this type. So, perhaps, was menippean satire,
to its ancient, as well as modern, readership.

In the third type of threshold literature, double encoding becomes neither
ambiguous nor incompatible, but deceitful encoding. The author unambiguously frames the text at the start and then, having encouraged one kind of
reading, retroactively reframes the text at some later point, usually the end.
When Tolstoy presents a fiction and then declares that "this is not a fiction"
(e.g., in "Lucerne")[23] he is making use of this technique. The reader must
*mis*take the text in order to take it correctly. As Tolstoy was aware, this strategy underlies much didactic literature, where it serves as a way of inducing—
or seducing—readers to learn moral lessons they might otherwise ignore.
Under the guise that the text is "only a story" or "only a poem," readers entertain an unorthodox or unfamiliar process of thinking, which they may
then be urged to accept in earnest. Alternatively, they may be encouraged to
engage in familiar forms of thinking and then be reproached for doing so—a
strategy that Tolstoy often used in his late works of art about the harmfulness of art. *The Kreutzer Sonata*, for example, explicitly traces the parallel
between art and seduction and then exploits it to teach the danger of both
kinds of self-indulgence. I shall argue below that utopia, as a form of didactic
literature, characteristically relies on this technique.

Framing: Shklovsky's Zoo

In their attempt to formulate a science of verbal and nonverbal art, the Russian Formalists paid particular attention to doubly encoded works. Such
works raised questions about how form is perceived and meaning implied in
the arts generally, questions of the sort that E. H. Gombrich later discussed in
Art and Illusion[24] and in other studies of the relation of the understanding of
art to the psychology of perception. The analogy between doubly encoded
works and the optical illusions that have since become classic examples in the
psychology of perception was not lost on the Formalists. In an article on
"Space in Painting" in *The Knight's Move* (1923), Shklovsky reproduces one
optical illusion, the truncated pyramid, that can be seen in two ways, and
concludes, as Gombrich does from the well-known duck-rabbit drawing, that
artistic convention and tradition play an important role in directing us to see
a particular figure and to perceive lines and paint in a given way. Shklovsky
adds that the conventions of illustration and the habits of perception are his-

torically determined and may therefore change over time. "When we see an object, we receive a sense of its form only when we have recognized the object, recognized what kind of an object it is."[25] Perception, in other words, depends on classification, classification on convention, and convention on a historically variable "pictorial system" (96). The analogy of visual art with literature implied for Shklovsky that changing literary conventions could, in effect, re-encode a work and so make it visible in a new way. For Shklovsky, this possibility (or what I have called boundary literature) was only one step from the possibility that authors could themselves doubly encode their works from the start, and so produce literary equivalents of Gestalt visual paradoxes —that is, what I have called threshold art.

Threshold works can be, and often are, used to make us aware of the conventions both of verbal art as a whole and of particular genres. By directing our attention to aspects of the interpretive process we normally take for granted, such works can be used to exemplify a theory about that process. Shklovsky regarded *Tristram Shandy* as such a work; for him it was, indeed, "the most typical novel" because he saw its themes as novelness, fictionality, and literariness themselves. Formalist interest in such texts—and in equivalents in other arts, such as suprematist painting, constructivist architecture, and the early experimental film—points to what I take to be a key idea in their work, an idea that I will have occasion to refer to many times in this study: whenever a text can be firmly classed as anomalous, the outlines of the class or classes that exclude it are themselves sharpened. A text can be recognized as a formal paradox only if we have a sense of what it is to be formally orthodox; it follows that a good way to illustrate a rule is to violate it strategically and ostentatiously.

Transgressions *mark* boundaries. In a broader sense, the Formalists described and defended literature itself as such a transgression against the perceptual and interpretative habits of everyday life. According to Shklovsky, art removes what it considers from "the sphere of habitual associations" and makes it undergo a "semantic shift" through a recontextualization that renders it "perceptible" (*Knight's Move*, 115-116). In a passage unusual for its moralism, Shklovsky cites an observation from Tolstoy's diaries on habit and unreflective adherence to social conventions: "If the whole complex lives of many people go on unconsciously, then such lives are as if they had never been."[26] Shklovsky generalizes this observation into a justification of art: "Automatization devours things, clothes, furniture, one's wife, and the fear of war. . . . And what we call art exists so that one may recover the sensation of life; it exists to make one feel things, to make the stone *stony*. The purpose of art is to impart the sensation of things as they are perceived and not as they are known. The technique of art is the technique of 'defamiliarization,' the technique of rendering forms difficult, of increasing the difficulty and length of perception" (*Theory of Prose*, 13).

The ways in which literature "defamiliarizes" (or "bestranges") the world, however, may themselves become "automatized" and so art could cease to fulfill its function. Shklovsky concluded that the highest value must therefore be placed on those works that defamiliarize the conventions of literature itself. These reflexive and self-conscious works (now often called "metaliterature") make all other works possible, the Formalists reasoned, by the technique of "baring the device," a concept that may be regarded as equivalent to "defamiliarization of the methods of defamiliarization." For the Formalists, this kind of self-conscious defamiliarization was an important engine of literary history.

While many of the concepts of Russian Formalism have become "familiar" to Western critics, it is not generally known that the Formalists *composed* as well as analyzed threshold works. Many of Shklovsky's best-known essays on the nature of literary encoding were themselves doubly encoded sections of literary works: appearing in novels, these essays describe the novelistic conventions that would seem to exclude them, and so become an exemplification of the concept of baring the device (which they also discuss). For example, one essay in Shklovsky's multiply titled novel *Zoo, or Letters Not about Love, or The Third Heloise* describes itself as "Unexpected and, in my opinion, utterly superfluous. The content of this letter obviously escaped from some other book by the same author, but perhaps the compiler of the book deemed the letter indispensable for reasons of variety"[27]—indispensable, that is, because it does *not* belong. As Tynyanov observed in his review of the book, "Shlovsky's *Zoo* is . . . a work 'on the boundaries'. . . . We are not accustomed to reading a novel which is at the same time a scientific paper. We are not accustomed to science in 'letters about love' or, for that matter, in 'letters not about love.' Our culture is built on a rigid differentiation between science and art."[28] Neither, for that matter, is it common for an epistolary novel to contain letters that were not written by the author (that is, *if* they were not written by the author). As its main title suggests, *Zoo* is a menagerie of literary species, each of which is "made strange" through location in a new context alongside unexpected neighbors. The presence of two subtitles, each of which suggests a different unity for the work, looks forward to its central theme: the nature of literary integrity itself.

It will be pertinent here to have before us an outline of the theory of literature that Shklovsky designed *Zoo* and other literary works to exemplify, the theory that is frequently and explicitly argued in the embedded essays of those very works. In Shklovsky's view, no forms or themes were intrinsically literary or nonliterary; it is not "material" but "semantic shift" that defines "literariness." This semantic shift is produced by a particular kind of "framing" (*obramlenie*) that removes the text from its "habitual sphere of associations," thus freeing it to serve as "material for metaphors" (*Zoo*, 4) in new and unforeseen contexts. The text is, in other words, decontextualized so that it may be recontextualizable. Formal changes—what Shklovsky calls creative "deformation"—*may* accompany and signal this act of framing, but in principle they need not. Although the creators of verbal artworks usually author the text of their work, it is, according to Shklovsky, not authorship but framing and design that is essential to literary creation. Shklovsky apparently had in mind what we now call "found poetry" (he may also have been thinking of collage and other Russian experimental art), the creator of which *as literature* is not, according to his reasoning, the author but the finder or "framer." The creative act that has "made" such a work, in other words, is its removal from original context and reframing *as* art. Much of the interest of such art—to Shklovsky, at least—lies in its capacity to illustrate just that theoretical lesson, in the "strangeness" of a work whose author is not its author. Shklovsky himself creates this kind of interest when he reminds the reader that the woman's letters in *Zoo* were real letters *to* Shklovsky not *by* Shklovsky. Nevertheless, he implies, the act of reframing has in effect reauthored the letters, which have consequently become interpretable in a new way. Their meaning as part of *Zoo*, rather than as records of Shklovsky's correspondence with Elsa Triolet, can now be inferred only by reference to the structure of the work as a whole. The semantic authority over Triolet's words thus shifts from her, their original author, to Shklovsky, the designer of the work in which they are embedded.

The structure of Shklovsky's literary works followed directly from this concept of the author as "framer," a concept that Shklovsky characteristically chose to exemplify by baring the device. If literary creation is essentially a matter of composition ("putting together")—or, to use the controlling metaphor of Shklovsky's *Third Factory*, of assembly—rather than authorship, then, by Formalist logic, the best way to create literature about the definition of literature is to make it as difficult as possible for the reader to discover what the structure of the work could be, or even *whether* it has a structure at all. The illusion of chance thus directs attention to the necessity of design. Shklovsky's "apologies" for the "haphazard" quality of his works take on a dadaist tone when, for instance, he describes how he composed *Zoo*. "I had to give a motivation [*motivirovka*] for the appearance of unconnected pieces ... ," he explains, "and when I placed the pieces of the already prepared book on the floor and sat down on the parquet to begin gluing the pieces together, the result was quite a different book from the one I was making."[29] In the preface to *Zoo*, he describes its composition as a search for *something* to link the separate, "already prepared," letters. "Here I needed a new detail: since the basic material of the book had nothing to do with love, I introduced a prohibition against writing about love. What emerged I expressed in the subtitle, 'Letters Not about Love'. . . . all the descriptions thus came out as metaphors for love" (3). The experience of reading *Zoo* is a repeatedly frustrated attempt, planned and remarked upon by the author, to do what one must do to read a text as literary, namely to identify a structure from which to infer meaning. *Zoo* "impedes" and "makes difficult" this very process, and thereby renders it "perceptible."

The central argument of *Zoo* is that the processes of structuring and inferring structure from literary works have become automatized. If literature is to be more than hack work, Shklovsky insists, it is necessary to experiment with new ways of linking parts into wholes. "How I want simply to describe objects as if literature had never existed!" (84) he writes, mindful of "the burden of the past" on literary creation. "I have the same attitude toward a plot of the usual type as a dentist to teeth" (4). Letter 22—the one that "obviously escaped from some other book by the same author"—contains a lecture on literary history in terms of changing types of "connective tissue," all of which, he argues, have become "scar tissue" that must be severed (80-81). It would therefore be better, he reasons, to expose the lack of viable principles of structure than to continue using dead ones. "The most vital genres in contemporary art," he concludes (81-82),

> are the collection of articles and the variety show, which depends for its interest on the individual components, not on the connective tissue. Something similar can be observed in the interpolated numbers of the vaudeville.
>
> But in theatres of this type, one already sees a new device—a device for connecting the pieces.
>
> There the master of ceremonies emerges as the hero whose fate connects the individual parts of the work. In a Czech theatre of the same variety type as the Scala, I had occasion to see one other device, which has apparently been used for a long time in circuses. At the end of the show, a clown runs through all the acts, parodying and exposing them. For example, he does magic tricks standing with his back to the audience, which sees where the missing card disappeared.
>
> In this respect, German theatres are at a very low stage of development.
>
> A more interesting case is the book which I am currently writing. It is called *Zoo, Letters Not about Love or The Third Heloise. . . .* This book is an attempt to go outside the framework of the ordinary novel.

The circus clown and the master of ceremonies in the variety show, in other words, often unify the "work" by parodying its conventions and exposing or baring its devices. *Zoo* goes one step further and bares the device of baring the device.

Shklovsky never composed vaudevilles, but he did make the "collection of essays" into a literary form by *framing* it as such. "There are many reasons for the strangeness of the knight's move," he writes in the first preface to his literary collection of that name, "and the most important reason is—the conventionality of art . . . I write about the conventionality of art."[30] In "Review of This Book," an article in *The Hamburg Score*, he draws an interesting conclusion from the presentation of the entire collection as a literary work. "It is sufficient to look over all that I have just written," he declares, "in order to be convinced that I speak in my name, but not from myself. That Victor Shklovsky for whom I write, then, is evidently not entirely myself, and if we met and began to talk there might even be misunderstandings between us" (*Hamburg Score*, 106). It is characteristic of Shklovsky that this denial of responsibility for what he writes in the first person is itself written in the first person, and so Shklovsky—or his "name"—remains as elusive as that Cretan who, the well-known Greek paradox goes, swore that all Cretans were liars. There is considerable irony in the fact that humorless critics have quoted passages from these collections without indicating their original literary context and have, moreover, proceeded to fault Shklovsky for regarding literary works as bundles of separable devices and parts! They have reclothed the device.[31]

"The Journal as a Literary Form"

Given the Formalists' interest in encyclopedic forms and their concept of the literary artist as a composer rather than a writer, it is not surprising that a number of them should have proposed turning the journalistic periodical into a literary genre. Though they did not explicitly mention *The Diary of a Writer*, Shklovsky, Tynyanov, and Eichenbaum were, in effect, advocating something like its re-creation. Their descriptions of what such a "new genre"[32] would be like apply strikingly well to the *Diary* (so well, in fact, that I believe it likely they had the *Diary* in mind, but considered it prudent not to associate themselves with a work infamous for its reactionary politics).[33] Before proceeding to a discussion of the *Diary*'s form, it will be worth our while to give some attention to their views on the possibility of a genre which, in fact, already existed.

In an impressive series of articles about how the changing boundaries of literature could make and had made facts of everyday life into "literary facts," the Formalists outlined in some detail the poetics of "The Journal as a Literary Form" (the title of one of Shklovsky's articles) and of the literary "Journal-Diary" (the title of a section of the same article). Tynyanov's programmatic essay "Journal, Critic, Reader, and Writer" argues that the way to restore the journal to the center of literary life is to make both the journal as a whole and its most important part, literary criticism, into literary genres. Literature has begun "to grope for a new genre," he declared. "It is rushing beyond the boundary of traditional 'literature'—from the novel to the chronicle, from the chronicle to the letter; it rushes from the adventure novel to the new picaresque novella; again to the story, again from the story. It wants to organize, to construct, to see a new thing" (*Poètika*, 149). Tynyanov observed, however, that the journal can become the sought-for new genre only if it is recognized that "all the material of a journal can be good but the *journal* itself as such may still be bad." It can become a *"literary* necessity" in other words, only if it interests the reader "in the journal as a journal, as a literary work of a special type" (*Poètika*, 147; italics in original).

Shklovsky was more specific about the poetics of the journal as a possible literary genre, which he compared to existing encyclopedic and composite works. Much as Tynyanov distinguished the fragment of a poem from the genre of the poetic fragment, Shklovsky contrasted the collection of poems with the genre of the poetic collection (or cycle). In the latter case, Shklovsky wrote, "the order in which poems succeed each other and their dependence upon each other" (*Hamburg Score*, 112) are essential parts of the work, which is designed to reward the processes of discovering networks of cross-references and recontextualizations and of postulating a structure for the work as a whole. The same processes would be invited in the new literary journal which, according to Shklovsky, would also "be held together not only by the interest of its separate parts, but by the interest of their linkages as well" (116). Combining radically heterogeneous and traditionally incompatible forms, the editor would create a work that would defamiliarize and renew techniques of literary structure and concepts of literary unity. "We are living through a crisis of the large literary form," the article concludes. "Perhaps we need a new journal which, having placed side by side pieces of aesthetic and extra-aesthetic material, could show us, if only incidentally, how and from what it is possible to create things of a new genre" (117).

The journal as a "new genre" of literature combining "aesthetic and extra-aesthetic material"—this would, of course, be an excellent description of *The Diary of a Writer*. Shklovsky's "new genre" also resembles Dostoevsky's in its projected use of an encyclopedic composite form incorporating, and suggesting thematic relations between, several fictions that could, if excerpted, stand as discrete and self-contained works. Such an encyclopedic work, Shklovsky argued, could be an alternative to the (to him) outmoded genre of the novel. To be sure, Shklovsky's reasons for regarding the novel as being in a moment of "crisis" were quite different from Dostoevsky's. Nevertheless, both writers did share a belief that, in Shklovsky's words, "the novel is not the ultimate [long] literary form" (*Hamburg Score*, 112). The passage in which Shklovsky draws this conclusion about possible alternatives or successors to the novel does not mention the *Diary* as a model, but it does cite as predecessors some works that Dostoevsky probably had in mind when he conceived of the *Diary*. In addition to Russian journals that may have been designed but not recognized as literary works (*"The Library for Reading,"* Shklovsky formulates one of his characteristic *mots*, "is a still undescribed Russian classic" [*Hamburg Score*, 11]), Shklovsky also discusses Dickens' experiments with *Master Humphrey's Clock* and *The Old Curiosity Shop* (*Hamburg Score*, 112):

> Dickens once wanted to create a new prose form: a "super novel." This new form was to consist of several novels interrupting each other.
>
> All this was to have been published in the form of a journal.
>
> The connection between the novels was to lie in their narration by a company of gentlemen and a company of their servants in the kitchen. This connection would have been strengthened by the fact that the narrators would themselves be either the heroes or the relatives of the heroes of the novels.
>
> This "super novel" never succeeded, and only pieces of it appeared, among them *The Old Curiosity Shop*.
>
> We can see from this that the novel is not the ultimate literary form, nor the only literary form that allows for extensive development.

As its title suggests, the essay's second section, "The Journal-Diary," applies especially well to Dostoevsky's work. In his somewhat oblique way, Shklovsky here seems to be suggesting that the combination of a maximally private form such as a diary with a maximally public form such as a periodical journal lends itself to the exploration of the differing relationships that various genres set up between author and reader. Shklovsky also seems to be suggesting that the fact that the editor rather than the author would be this journal's source of unity would make it suitable for examining the nature of literary unity. In such a publication, it would only be necessary for the editor to allow someone else to author some sections of the work—as Shklovsky does in *Zoo*—to raise interesting theoretical questions or to defamiliarize his or her own style and methods of presentation. Heine, Shklovsky states (*Hamburg Score*, 113), once asked another writer

> to insert two pages—no matter of what sort—into one of his prose works. ... It is possible that he felt here the need of a combination of styles resembling that which is created in Persian "motley verses" by the succession of Persian and Arabic lines. Including in his own prose the prose of another, Heine was, of course, working as an artist, but his device—was the device of the journal.

We shall see that it is also one of the devices of Dostoevsky's "Journal-Diary," which uses letters from readers (both real and fictional) and quotations from rival publications for some of the same metaliterary purposes Shklovsky discusses.

Although the Formalists were never able to create their new genre, one attempt at something like it was successful. In 1929, Boris Eichenbaum published a collection of theoretical pieces and reminiscences, similar in composition and tone to *The Knight's Move* and *The Hamburg Score*, but wryly presented as the first—and only—issue of a journal designed as a literary work. *My Periodical: Literature, Science, Criticism, Miscellany* self-consciously plays on the paradox of a periodical that has no subscribers and does not appear periodically. Like Shklovsky, Eichenbaum makes the statement of his work's conventions a part of its form. "The cover of this book," he writes in his preface,

> indicates that the book is conceived as a type of journal. The reader has a right to expect a preface from the editor.
>
> I am neither announcing subscriptions nor preparing to publish my periodical periodically. I simply wanted to issue my material in the form of a journal. ... In the eighteenth century, several writers issued journals of this type, filling them with their own works.
>
> The journal is a particular genre, to be distinguished from the almanac, the collection, and so forth. It was pleasant and interesting for me to write and gather material, imagining this genre. Call it the play of imagination. Life without play sometimes becomes too boring.[34]

Reading between the Genres: The Diary *as Metaliterature*

No less anomalous than the Formalists' realized or projected experimental works, Dostoevsky's *Diary* also juxtaposes traditionally literary and non-literary material, combines apparently incompatible genres, and frustrates the search for the pattern it intimates in order to examine the nature of literary unity and structure. That is, the *Diary* "impedes," "defamiliarizes," and so renders "perceptible" the ways in which readers usually identify structure and infer meaning. Like its metaliterary predecessors, from the *Quixote* (which it often cites) to "The Nose," and from Dostoevsky's own early feuilletons to *The Raw Youth*, the *Diary* is not lawless, but systematically unlawful, a sort of negative exemplification of the conventions it ostentatiously defies. And like *Zoo* and *My Periodical*, the *Diary* was undertaken as an attempt "to go outside the framework of the ordinary novel" and to explore "how and from what it is possible to create things of a new genre."

In short, Dostoevsky conceived of the *Diary* not as a collection of articles and stories, but rather as a literary work *in the form of* a collection. Thus, the reader of this encyclopedic "composition" is invited to infer meaning not only from the parts, but also from their "linkages," their place in the work's total structure. It follows that readers who do not consider that structure, or who know particular articles and stories only from anthologies, are likely to be unaware of or insensitive to contextual ironies, to imagine neat beginnings and endings where they are lacking, and to overlook allusions to other articles and stories. They are also likely to interpret fictive passages as if they were nonfictive, and to take as authoritative without qualification articles that lie under a shadow of irony cast by other sections of the work. As the diarist himself occasionally suggests, in order to understand an author's intentions regarding a work one must first understand his intentions regarding the *kind* of work he was writing. In "The Peasant Marey," for instance, he observes that many readers of *The House of the Dead* mistook the fictive narrator for the author and "are even now asserting that I was exiled for the murder of my wife." It is characteristic of the *Diary* that this very observation occurs in a narrative that invites (and has received) reading both as fiction and as nonfictive autobiography.

In his classic study of Dostoevsky's life and work, Konstantin Mochulsky apparently overlooked the importance of these classificatory distinctions. "The unprecedented originality of *The Diary of a Writer*," he wrote,

> lies in its revelation of the author's personality, in its singular tone of intimacy, the candidness and truthfulness of its communication. The literary work is not presented in its finished form; the writer was not partitioned off by the walls of his study; we penetrate the very laboratory of his creative activity, we see how his plans arose, grew and took form. Dostoevsky's work is inseparable from his life.[35]

To be sure, much of the interest of the *Diary* lies in its depiction of the process by which random observations suggest and gradually become ordered into a work of art. And Mochulsky is also right to stress both the importance of the *Diary*'s orientation to its readers and its role as a source of material for Dostoevsky's next work, *Karamazov*. Nevertheless, the *Diary* is by no means so candid, nor the author's laboratory so penetrable, as Mochulsky supposes. *The Diary of a Writer* is not simply a diary of a writer. It is, again, not a writer's notebook, but a literary work in the form of a writer's notebook—a distinction no less hermeneutically significant than that between nonliterary and literary familiar letters. We need only glance at the real notebooks for this literary notebook to see the difference between real and scripted spontaneity, between ellipticality to the point of incoherence and digressiveness or disconnectedness recognizable as metaliterary *topoi*. We may also find in these truly private notebooks the plans for some of the *Diary*'s "unplanned" digressions and the preparations for its "impromptu" self-characterizations.[36] The *Diary* resembles a theatrical soliloquy more closely than a private meditation; and what it offers its readers is not so much an occasion to eavesdrop as a series of envoys and stage whispers.

For the modern reader, this aspect of the *Diary* may recall Gide's *Counterfeiters* (1925), which, indeed, was probably modeled after it. One of the early popularizers of Dostoevsky in the West, Gide discussed *Journal d'un Écrivain* (the French translation of the *Diary*) as well as the novels in his well-known *Dostoevsky* lectures (1922).[37] A sharpening of Dostoevsky's self-referential paradoxes, *The Counterfeiters* is, in Harry Levin's phrase, "the diary of a novelist who is writing a novel about a novelist who is keeping a diary about the novel he is writing,"[38] the novel within the novel also being called *The Counterfeiters* and its fictive author, Edouard, developing a "Theory of the Novel" that applies as well to Gide's work as to his own. Edouard's theories of realism and the novel are also remarkably similar to those outlined in the *Diary* (e.g., in "The Boy Celebrating His Name Day"). Like Dostoevsky's diarist, Gide's novelist would "like to put everything into my novel. . . . everything I see, everything I know, everything that other people's lives and my own teach me. . . . "[39] When asked how he could possibly shape such an encyclopedic work into an artistic whole, Edouard gives Dostoevsky's characteristic answer: by showing the act of shaping itself. "What I want is to represent reality on the one hand, and on the other that effort to stylize it into art of which I have just been speaking," Edouard explains to his skeptical audience. "In order to arrive at this effect—do you follow me?—I invent the character of a novelist, whom I make my central figure; and the subject of the book, if you must have one, is just that very struggle between what reality offers him and what he himself desires to make of it. . . . the struggle between the [disordered] facts presented by reality and the ideal reality" (187-188) of art. As he describes his plans for this peculiar work—a work for which "it's essentially out of the question . . . to have a plan" (188)—Edouard discovers the form it will have to take, namely, the form of notebooks for such a work. In other words, his *Counterfeiters* will *be* notebooks for *The Counterfeiters*, notebooks that discuss not only the work they already are, but also the genre to which that work belongs (189; ellipses in original):

> My note-book contains, as it were, a running criticism of my novel—or rather of the novel in general. Just think how interesting such a note-book

kept by Dickens or Balzac would be; if we had the diary of the *Education Sentimentale* or of *The Brothers Karamazof!*—the story of the work—of its gestation! How thrilling it would be . . . more interesting than the work itself . . .

As Gide was no doubt aware, the first issue of the monthly *Diary* does contain the outline for Dostoevsky's "Future Novel," *Karamazov*, the writing of which was also the reason (given in the December, 1877, issue) for the periodical's suspension. Moreover, the *Diary* frequently depicts the "gestation" and birth of its own embedded stories—the "activity of his mind engaged in the construction of a narrative" (*Dostoevsky*, 93) as Gide himself described the *Diary*'s principal theme. Both Gide and Dostoevsky, in short, created works that self-consciously depict the process of immediate creation—a depiction that is itself far from immediate.[40]

Like the early feuilletons and the *Winter Remarks*, the *Diary* creates (and exposes) the *illusion* of spontaneity, the sense that the work is being made on the spot from the events it records and their first impression on the author's mind. In the manner of Sterne, Byron,[41] and Pushkin, the author alternately justifies and apologizes for the consequences of this "immediate" creation, namely the work's frequent self-contradictions, abrupt transitions, and labyrinthine structure. After all, he explains in one travel sketch especially reminiscent of the *Winter Remarks*, whimsicality and digressiveness are to be expected in a diary, a form which—he warns his readers—is not addressed primarily to readers ("Departure Abroad," July–August, 76, I, 1):

> The point is that I sometimes write my *Diary* not only for the public, but for myself as well (in all likelihood, that is why there is so much that is uneven and unexpected in it, that is, thoughts which are perfectly familiar to me, and which have long been worked out within me, but which seem to the reader to have suddenly leaped out of somewhere with no connection to what precedes them).

Perhaps the most explicit baring of these familiar metaliterary devices occurs in the January, 1881, issue. After the three-year interruption of its regular publication, the *Diary* resumed with a chapter of digressions from its ostensible topic, "Finances" (the first of the opening article's four titles). Inasmuch as most readers have developed an overriding interest in financial matters, the author explains, "along with everyone else I am setting out to write an economic article" (January, 81, I, 1) even though he admits to knowing nothing about economics. As his "readers" soon have occasion to observe, however, this topic is promised and introduced, but never quite reached (January, 81, I, 2):

> "And what about finances? Where is that financial article?" they will say to me. But again, what sort of economist am I, what kind of financial expert? I do not even dare to write anything at all about financial matters. Why then did I dare to, why do I set out to write about them? Precisely because I was sure that having begun to write about finances, I would

switch to something completely different, and what would come from me would be not a financial, but some completely different, sort of article. And this alone encourages me.

In the rest of the chapter, baring of the device occurs in the very titles of the articles, titles which announce what will *not* be discussed—"Instead of a Firm Financial Tone I Am Lapsing into Old Words"—or "apologize" for what somehow turned out to be the main topic: "Because of Incompetence I Now Lapse into Something Spiritual."

Unfulfilled plans, apologies, self-justifications, and revised plans—this is the pattern of much of the *Diary*, which, like so many metaliterary works, makes literature from the statement of literature's conventions and of its own broken rules. In addition to the opening preface "Instead of a Preface," for instance, the first issue of the monthly *Diary* (January, 1876) concludes with an equally inconclusive promise that is not a promise—a promise which, characteristically, relates to the author's strained relations with his readers and with other journalists:

A Turkish Proverb
By the way and in any case, I will insert here a certain Turkish proverb (a real one, not one I made up):
"If you have set out to reach a goal and stop along the way to throw stones at every dog that barks at you, you will never reach the goal."
As much as possible, I shall observe this very wise proverb in my *Diary*, although I should nevertheless not like to bind myself in advance with promises. [complete article]

Introductory phrases such as "by the way and in any case," "apropos," and "incidentally" are characteristic of the diarist's presentation of thoughts which are ostensibly "formulated directly without preparation, without preliminary proofs" (January, 81, I, 3) and which therefore appear "to have suddenly leaped out of somewhere with no connection to what precedes them." No less characteristic are his somewhat doubtful assurance that the proverb was "not made up," his retraction of a rule just formulated, and his discussion with his readers about how the text is likely to be read (or misread). Taking up where this article leaves off, the next issue of the *Diary* begins by expressing surprise that, in fact, the "dogs" did not bark at the January *Diary*—surprise, that is, that his work has been *well* received. "But one question *does* interest me," he muses. "Is it good or not good that I have pleased everyone? Perhaps it's even bad? But on the other hand, no, why should it be, let it be a good, not a bad sign, and at this point I will stop." Like the underground man, the diarist is a master of the self-cancelling self-cancellation, the potentially endless series of negations and negations of the negation.

Implicitly or explicitly, the *Diary*'s many envoys and self-characterizations recall the "announcement" of the new publication in the January, 1876, issue. The "announcement" states, or professes to state, the rules that are to govern this unusual work, the "contract" that obtains between the author and his readers: "This will be a diary in the literal sense of the word, an account of the impressions I have really lived through each month, an account of what I have seen, heard, and read. Stories and tales may of course be included, but it will be preeminently about real events." All that "I have seen, heard, and read"; real events and also stories—it would be hard to say what these "rules" prohibit. Like Rabelais' *Abbey of Thélème*, the work seems to be governed by only one "rule": "Do as you wish." The only positive information in this contract filled with loopholes is the price of a subscription.

The most interesting of the *Diary*'s self-characterizations (and of its apologies for violating even a Thelemite command) occur in the transition passages linking its fiction with its nonfiction, or embedded works of one genre with those of another. Characteristically, these transition passages not only call attention to the different conventions that govern two heterogeneous texts, but also imply the participation of both—and of the transition passages themselves—in the larger structure of the work. The passage that leads from "The Centenarian" (a fictional continuation of an ostensibly nonfictional narrative) to the journalistic article on "Dissociation," for instance, explicitly cites the January "announcement" (March, 76, I, 2–3; ellipsis in original):

> However, this is such a frivolous and pointless little picture. Really, you set out to relate something interesting out of all you have heard during the month, and as soon as you begin, it turns out to be either impossible, or irrelevant, or the sort of thing about which "you don't tell all you know"; and what is left in the end are only the most pointless things . . .

> ### III
> ## "Dissociation"

> And yet I happen to be writing about things which I have "seen, heard, and read." And it's a good thing I did not bind myself with the promise to write *about everything* I have "seen, heard, and read." For in fact I am increasingly hearing strange things. How is one to convey them if everything of its own accord falls apart, and will not for anything form itself into a whole? Really, I keep thinking that an epoch of universal "dissociation" has set in.

Linking the fragmentedness of his work with the fragmentation ("dissociation") of the world, the author, like Edouard, poses his characteristic problem— how can one create a form to represent formlessness—and, in the very process of posing it, implies the work's solution: to depict the *quest* for such a form.

The frame to "The Boy at Christ's Christmas Party" also refers directly to the "announcement" (both occur in the same issue) as it apologizes, and then retracts its apology, for violating the promise to write "preeminently about real events." "And why did I make up such a story," the diarist archly asks at the close of his narrative (January, 76, II, 2), one that conforms so little to an ordinary, reasonable diary, and still less to a diary of a writer? And after I have promised to write preeminently about real events! But that is precisely the point, it still seems to me, I still keep imagining that all this could really have happened—that is, what occurred in the basement and behind the woodpile; but as for Christ's Christmas Party, I really don't know what to tell you, could that have happened or not? But that is *why* I am a novelist, in order to invent things.

A threshold work within a threshold work, this fiction retroactively reframes itself as perhaps—but only perhaps—not a fiction after all.

The story's opening frame also plays on the narrative's problematic fictionality and on the place of fiction in the structure of a work containing nonfiction as well. Like the close of "The Centenarian," the opening to "The Boy" implicitly stresses the continuity of the story with its nonfictional context, in this case with the preceding sketch on child beggars, "The Boy with an Outstretched Hand." "Such wild creatures," the author concludes the sketch (January, 76, II, 1-2),

> sometimes understand nothing, neither where they live, nor to what nation they belong, nor whether there is a God or sovereign; things are told about them which are incredible to hear, and yet they are really all facts.

II
The Boy at Christ's Christmas Party

> But I am a novelist, and it seems that I did make up one "story" myself. But why do I write "it seems" when I know for sure that I did make it up? But I keep imagining that it did happen somewhere, at some time, precisely on Christmas Eve, in *some* huge city during a terrible frost.

These lines not only comment on the boundary between fiction and nonfiction, they exist on it. Beginning on a conjunction, the story's opening paragraph responds to the preceding article; and as that article's closing sentence insists that everything the author says is true, the story's beginning leads into a fiction in which he constantly reminds us that he is "making it up" as he goes along. The frame, in other words, self-consciously places itself between fact and artifact. Here we watch the diarist in the process of shifting genres, ceasing to speak according to the conventions of journalism and just taking up those of fiction. "Reality is transfigured, *passing through art*,"[42] Dostoevsky wrote in an early essay: the *Diary* characteristically dramatizes the paradoxes of the moment of "passing through."

The transition passages, in short, invite consideration of their own problematic status. Are they to be taken, we may ask, as part of the story, and is their denial of fictionality itself a conventional fictional device? At what point may we safely assume that statements belong not to the author but to his fictional persona—that the speaker is "not me," as Dostoevsky introduces the narrator of the story "Bobok"? These questions have apparently troubled anthologizers, who have created radically different texts. On the one hand, the editors of the Soviet ten-volume *Collected Works of Dostoevsky* (1956–1958), an edition that includes only extracts from the *Diary*, reprint both "The Boy with an Outstretched Hand" and "The Boy at Christ's Christmas Party" under the general title "The Boy at Christ's Christmas Party," the title of the story thus appearing twice. On the other hand, Constance Garnett leaves off the conjunction on which the story begins and the last sentence of its closing frame in an attempt to remove text from context without leaving a scar.[43] And whereas the Soviet editors indicate the reasons for their textological choices, readers of the English version are unlikely to be aware either that the story's beginning and end have been rounded off by the translator or even that it has been excerpted from a larger work.

In each case, the editor, in part, has *made*, not just reproduced, the text, which is shaped by his or her understanding of the *Diary*. Inasmuch as the *Diary* itself has rarely been reprinted, and was not translated into English until 1948, these versions are the best-known ones and have developed a tradition of interpretations without reference to the *Diary*. Not surprisingly, those interpretations have made little of the frame of "The Boy" (and the frames of other stories) and of its reference to the *Diary*'s "announcement." Indeed, the "announcement" itself has been omitted from most "complete" editions of the *Diary* (including the editions of the only English translation), an omission that transforms the close of "The Boy" and the opening of "Dissociation" (as well as other passages) into references to a nonexistent text.

When the stories are read in context, the transition passages play a key role in the *Diary*'s defamiliarization of generic conventions and in its dramatization of the creative process. Threshold art foregrounds its thresholds, makes the peripheries of the stories the work's center. It is unlikely, for instance, that the closing line of the story "Bobok: A Certain Person's Notes" would seem as important or interesting to readers of anthologies as to readers of the *Diary*. An insane writer's account of a conversation between corpses in a graveyard, "Bobok" concludes with the narrator's abrupt statement that "I'll submit this to the *Citizen*; they've also exhibited the editor's portrait over there. Perhaps he'll print this." Of course, the story did appear in the *Citizen*, and the editor in question was Dostoevsky himself—that is, the fictional character breaks the story's frame and confronts his maker. We see such a confrontation in a later issue, in which the "certain person" insists that Dostoevsky publish his other works as well. At last Dostoevsky agrees to publish one of them, first explaining to his readers that he is doing so

> solely to get rid of him. The editor's office is literally stuffed with his articles. In the first place, this "person" resolutely assumes the role of my defender against my literary "enemies." For me and on my behalf he has already written three "anticriticisms," two "remarks," three "casual remarks," one "apropos," and, finally, an "Admonition on How to Behave." In this last polemical composition, which ostensibly admonishes my "enemies," he attacks me in a tone so energetic and frenzied as I never encountered in "my enemies." And he wants me to print it all! I resolutely informed him that first of all, I have no enemies . . . and in the second

place, that he was too late, inasmuch as all that journalistic uproar which greeted the appearance of the first number of the *Citizen* for 1873 with such unheard-of literary frenzy . . . has suddenly ceased for no apparent reason, just as it began. . . . He grew angry, and having quarreled with me, walked out. . . . But only three days after our quarrel, he appeared again with his "last attempt," and brought this "Letter of a Certain Person." There was nothing to do, I took it and now must print it.

Like similar sections of other metaliterary works, this "letter" not only appears against (or ostensibly against) the author's will, but also is printed in a physically mangled form. The beginning of this attack on journalistic vituperation was itself so vituperative, Dostoevsky explains, that "I simply snipped off with a pair of scissors the entire first part of the letter." The result is that the "Letter"—or "Half-Letter," as the "certain person" insists it be called— begins on an ellipsis, followed by the conjunction "and": " . . . and can it be that the word 'swine' contains such a magical and alluring meaning that you immediately and unfailingly take it as referring to yourself?" ("Half-Letter," 1873).

Abusive letter writers were also a common theme of the monthly *Diary*, which contains a "Plan" for another story about them and, indeed, Dostoevsky's own answers to abusive letters complaining about combined issues or unreceived copies. In this way, Dostoevsky motivates the mechanics of the publication, thematically integrating information necessary to subscribers with the rest of the text. It was a device he had first used in his early feuilletons, a device which, like the *Diary*'s play with chapter titles, reflects that genre's characteristic metaliterary appropriation of its frames. His announcement for the *Banterer* (1845), for instance, presents the new almanac's price as the conclusion to a discussion of the age's financial and materialistic spirit. "The *Banterer* so loves, so respects, so highly values his readers . . . his future readers (he will certainly have readers!) that he would like to give the book away free" (ellipsis in original) the feuilletonist confides; but that would surely offend the "*positive, mercantile, iron, financial*" tastes of potential readers. And so, "in consideration of the expenses of publication, and with a feeling of personal dignity, the *Banterer* reluctantly announces that it will be sold for one silver ruble an issue in the bookstores of M. Olkhin, A. Ivanov, P. Ratykov and Co., A. Sorokin and other Petersburg booksellers" (*Stat'i*, 7-8).

In short, one reason that the *Diary* includes advertisements, information about the mechanics of publication, and replies to particular readers in the text itself is that this material is not expected to be there. These passages work in much the same way that the ironic footnotes to *Eugene Onegin* (or *The Dunciad*) do. By including material that is usually not part of the work, Dostoevsky plays on the perplexing problem of the boundaries of art. We are presented with the indeterminate boundaries of a work about literary boundaries, margins which turn out not to be marginal. And once we have recognized the possible interconnections of margins from previous issues with the text, we may not know how to take new ones. Thus, we are made to experience the lack of—and therefore, the need for—literary conventions and rules for reading.

We learn to read between the genres. It is in this context that we may understand a perplexing class of works which reappear in—and perhaps epitomize—the *Diary*. I am referring to pieces which, like the *Diary* itself, seem to pause deliberately between fiction and nonfiction: its threshold fictions. "A 'Certain Person's' Half-Letter," "The Plan for a Satirical Novel," "The Centenarian," and a number of other embedded works all insist that they are not finished stories, but only plans for stories. They present themselves, as the *Diary* presents itself, as notebooks, works in progress—works which, if they should ever be completed, might appear in the *Diary* in that form, too.

But we may recognize this mode of narration as a frequently used literary convention; and to do so, we need only recall that Ivan Karamazov narrates the Grand Inquisitor legend in the same way. Ostensibly the prose draft of an unwritten "poem," the legend is narrated in the subjunctive: "that would have been one of the finest passages of the poem"; "I meant to end it like this." Subjunctive narration is characteristic of a number of the *Diary*'s threshold fictions as well: "In short, it seems to me that the anonymous curser, as a type, is not at all a bad theme for a story," Dostoevsky concludes his biography of that type. "Here, of course, Gogol would be needed, but . . . I am glad, at least, that I have happened upon this idea. Perhaps I really will try to include it in a novel" ("Plan for a Satirical Story from Contemporary Life," May-June, 77, I, 3; ellipsis in original). Both Ivan and the diarist have it both ways: this story, they seem to say, is not a story—much as the early feuilletons describe themselves as unfinished feuilletons.

It is, in fact, often quite difficult to determine whether a particular article is offered as fictional and, therefore, what kind of responsibility Dostoevsky takes for it. Has Dostoevsky really received this document, we may ask, or is he using the literary convention of the found manuscript? The author seems to plan classificatory errors and, indeed, includes irate letters from quixotic readers—Cervantes' misreader being frequently discussed—who have evidently made such errors. And to extend the point, while some of these letters clearly appear to be from real readers, others appear to be from fictitious ones (such as the narrator of "Bobok"), and the status of a third group is almost impossible to determine. To avoid making mistakes, we may try to look for clues in the text, signs of conventionality; and this search also becomes part of our lesson about the experience of reading. It is probably no accident that one of the *Diary*'s earliest articles, "Mummer," is a case study in detecting a forgery, a process that parallels our own attempt to detect fictionality. Indeed, many of the *Diary*'s threshold fictions are about the kind of framing problems they dramatize, situations where it is possible to mistake fiction for nonfiction or to confuse action with enactment. Themselves duplicitous, these articles describe conspiracies, forgeries, fabrications, hallucinations, seances, and, to be sure, the composition of stories.

In a work about the creative process, the threshold fictions dramatize the mysterious moment when reality is just "passing through" to art—a moment when, in Dmitri Karamazov's words, "all shores meet, and all contradictions stand side by side." They are the central chapters of the story of the making of stories, and much of their interest lies in their depiction of the usually private "struggle" by which recalcitrant material is shaped into art. "Do you know what it means *to compose*?" Dostoevsky once asked his friend Maykov in a letter about the creative process.

> No, thank God, you don't know! . . . At the beginning of the year I fully hoped that poetry would not leave me, that the poetic thought would flash and develop artistically to the end of the year. . . . This seemed all the more likely, inasmuch as many embryos of artistic thought always flash and make themselves felt in my head and soul. But they only flash, and what is necessary is a full embodiment, which always takes place unexpectedly and suddenly, but it is impossible to calculate precisely when it will take place; and then, having received in one's heart a complete image, one can proceed to artistic fulfillment.[44]

The *Diary* presents an "artistic image" of this very process, from the first "flashes" through successive stages of "development" to the moment when— "unexpectedly and suddenly"—the artist creates a finished work. We see the diarist scan the press and wander the streets in search of a theme; observe him limn the outlines of a story; then a "plan" or rough sketch presents its tentative embodiment in literary form; and, at last, a finished fiction may follow. For "The Meek One," this process extends over many months; the composition of "The Boy at Christ's Christmas Party" takes place within a single issue of the *Diary*.

It should be evident that the threshold fictions cannot be excerpted without losing their effect of dramatizing the midpoint of the creative process. A similar point, however, may also be made about the finished stories. Encountered in the course of reading the *Diary*, they acquire considerable dramatic power as the results of the creative process we have witnessed, as a few "unexpected" instances in which a first flash has developed into a finished work. Much of the stories' interest, in other words, derives from our awareness of the problems the author has solved before our very eyes. When we read "The Boy at Christ's Christmas Party," we not only read it as a story; we also recognize the motifs and fragments in the articles and sketches immediately preceding the story reassembled in an artistic structure. We read vertically as well as horizontally. Art is made from the making of art, and what the reader experiences is the experience of reading.

3. Utopia as a Literary Genre

Identifying a Class

Few studies of literary utopias have been responsible to a more general theory of literary genres. Concerned less with the identification and characterization of a class of texts than with a defense of that vaguely conceived class's right to serious critical attention, these studies have tended to formulate what might be called "imperialist" definitions of the genre—that is, definitions which annex as much territory as possible in order to protect the designated capital, the "classic" utopias. Given the usually low evaluation of these utopias as literature, this defensive strategy is perhaps understandable; but it has led to carelessness in specifying how terms are used and in clarifying how interpretations of particular works are arrived at.[1]

Most frequently, utopian literature is read as a simple embodiment of utopian ideology, to which the principal attention is given. A description of "the other [ideal] half of the history of mankind," Lewis Mumford's *The Story of Utopias*[2] is representative of this approach in its essentially identical treatment of literary and nonliterary utopias. Without denying that there is a distinction between utopian literature and utopian tracts, Mumford dismisses that distinction as unimportant for an understanding of the meaning of the works. His method of interpreting literary utopias, which occupy most of his attention, is first to separate the sections of the work that deal with utopian institutions from those devoted to form and plot, and then, having set aside the latter as hermeneutically irrelevant packaging, to criticize and evaluate the former in the same way that he criticizes and evaluates tracts. Other versions of this approach describe the literariness or fictionality of the work as camouflage for eluding a censor or, quite the opposite, as a technique to intensify the sense of reality of the work's descriptions and so to make them more effective as propaganda. It may be observed, however, that although fictionality and literary "form" may indeed render a text problematic to a censor—who may equally well decide to proscribe it for that very reason—and palatable to a frivolous reader, their significance for an understanding of the work does not stop there. For to design a text as literature is to make a statement about how its meaning is and is not to be determined, about what procedures for deriving propositional value are appropriate. Even if one's primary interest is in the history of ideas rather than in literature, it is necessary to know whether a text *is* literature, and if so, what semiotic consequences its literariness entails, in order to interpret it according to its original design.

The history of utopian ideology raises the problem of the use of literary works as historical documents with special clarity because so much of that ideology is to be found in literary works. The problem itself, however, is a more general one, and essentially the same methodological questions are involved, for instance, in histories of Russian philosophy that include (as most do) readings of Tolstoy's and Dostoevsky's novels. No doubt, Shklovsky's whimsical assertion that nothing can be learned from a work of literature represents an unacceptable position. For it may be observed that all literature does exemplify propositions—even if only, as in some dadaist works, the proposition that literature need not exemplify propositions—and quite frequently those propositions are about something other than literature. That, indeed, is one reason why literature is read. Moreover, since everything is, in some sense, a "product of its times," it can therefore, in some way, be used as historical evidence. Nevertheless, it does not follow that all "documents" are of the same sort and that there are no important distinctions to be made between texts that were created to be read as literature and those that were not. On the contrary, one's responsibility as a historian would seem to require that the putative decoder of a text inquire into its original encoding, which means, in the case of literary works, that he or she try to determine the literary and generic conventions that the author intended to govern the work's interpretation.

The kind of oversimplification and outright error to which this "documentary" approach leads is particularly evident in studies of individual utopian works. Despite its erudition and lucidity, J. H. Hexter's well-known study *More's "Utopia": The Biography of an Idea*[3] can stand as an object lesson in the dangers inherent in readings of literary works that fail to consider literary conventions. Because Hexter does not make such elementary distinctions as that between fiction and nonfiction and does not recognize that the context of a statement in a literary work is not the evidentiary equivalent of the context of the work itself either in the author's life or in the extraliterary world, it matters little how detailed his evidence or how rigorous his textology. Regarding *Utopia*'s form as "the literary mould" (51) into which its content was poured (with, he notes, some inevitable spillage), Hexter sets out to discover what More's intentions were. In Hexter's view, those intentions do not include literary ones, but they are nevertheless identical for Hexter to what the work really means. Hexter's method of discovery is to trace the embryonic development of the idea of *Utopia* in "the mind of Thomas More *between the summer of 1515 and the fall of 1516*," that is, from the work's conception to its "birth date" (3). The work itself is for Hexter neither more nor less than a generally reliable document of what was passing through More's mind, and its final form a necessary but unfortunate impoverishment of the wealth of his social thought, which is Hexter's main concern. "To establish the lineaments of the idea for *Utopia*," he writes in his methodological preface (4),

we shall perforce, for lack of better sources of information, rely on the book called *Utopia*. But let us not deceive ourselves. The laying out into cold print of what began as a warm living idea always has about it a touch of the mortician's art. Convention requires that the dead letter conform to certain established proprieties, and quite unconsciously an author preparing his idea for interment between covers may impart to it an appearance that it did not wear in life. This, as we shall see, is precisely what the author did with his idea for *Utopia*, and unwary physiognomists examining the corpse have thus read into the living idea lineaments of character which it did not possess. We ourselves shall have to look very closely to separate the thinker's thought from the literary trick of trade.

It is hard to say which is more misguided, Hexter's conception of literary conventions as distorting "established proprieties" or his identification of the text of a work with the corpse of an idea (and its birth with its embalming), but it is clear that both conceptions are fundamental to his interpretive procedure. Hexter's method for reviving the "warm living idea" from the text's dead letter is to reconstruct the idea's "biography" (or ontogeny). For Hexter, textology recapitulates ideology. On the assumption that the earlier a passage was conceived, the more central it is to the work's meaning, he refutes other readings of *Utopia* by arguing that the passages on which they rely were composed after those on which he relies.[4] The dubious nature of Hexter's textology— almost the only evidence for it being the text itself—is disturbing; his naive identification of order of composition with structural and hermeneutic importance is still more so. Needless to say, other textologists have no less (or more) plausibly argued the opposite, namely that passages conceived last represent the most mature and therefore most authoritative ideas.

Hexter needs *some* certain and unambiguous procedure not only because he claims to have arrived at the determinate meaning of the work, but also because he believes that the work's meaning is itself unambiguous. All apparent ambiguities, he reasons, can and should be resolved by consulting the textological record rather than regarded as essential to the work or, still worse, as a source of its value. "The one point of unanimous agreement about *Utopia*," he writes (11; italics mine),

> is that it is a work of social comment; and while ambiguity may enhance the value of certain special kinds of poetry, it does not enhance the value of social comment. We should think rather poorly of any present-day social thinker whose intention was inscrutable or mysterious, and unintelligibility is no more a virtue in a criticism of society written four hundred years ago than it is in current social criticism. *If it is impossible to know what More means, it is hard to justify the favor that "Utopia" has enjoyed in the past four centuries.*

For these very reasons, Hexter does find it "hard to justify" the popularity of Erasmus' *Praise of Folly*, which he faults for lacking the "intelligibility" he attributes to *Utopia*. Having ignored the form of "ancient and traditional social criticism," Erasmus, according to Hexter, created a work that is "in-

coherent and invertebrate, lacking in the structural form which that framework provided for the writings of his predecessors." As a result, *The Praise of
Folly* is, in Hexter's judgment, "inadequate as social criticism" and its prescriptions, " in the rare instances when anything so specific is suggested, are
mere analgesics and plasters, not radical remedies" (63-64). The possibility
that More and Erasmus might have intended their works to be read as one of
those "certain special [!] kinds of poetry" that are essentially ambiguous
does not seem to have been seriously considered by Hexter, who, like a number of other writers on *Utopia*, is impatient with distinctions between kinds
of texts. Apparently equating hermeneutic monism with scientific precision,
he treats all utopian works, literary and nonliterary, as if they were of the
same semiotic type.

Whereas Hexter obscures important distinctions between litarary and tractarian utopias, Richard Gerber's *Utopian Fantasy*,[5] which we may take as
representative of a second approach to the genre, avoids or rejects distinctions
between utopia and several other forms of fantastic or "extraordinary" fiction. In a curious but common circularity, Gerber, who is primarily concerned with demonstrating that utopia has at last become "an adequate literary genre" (xiv) deserving of serious study, first insists on the advantage of
broad and flexible criteria for identifying utopias, then claims the large number of texts that fit these criteria as evidence for the importance of the genre.
His description of how he compiled the lengthy (twenty-one-page) list of
twentieth-century English utopias that appears in the appendix is characteristic of his methodology. After first "collecting every book that could possibly
be called utopian," Gerber and his assistant eliminated those in which "the
main interest was concerned with a sensational tale of adventure" rather than
with "social problems."[6] That is the only principle of elimination mentioned.
Like the main text of Gerber's study, in which "not only socially constructive
utopias are considered, but also various other kinds of imaginary commonwealths and fantastical countries" (xiii), the list in the appendix includes, or
attempts to include, all fiction from 1901 to 1971 about unreal societies,
whether perfect or imperfect, human or nonhuman, prophetic or allegorical.
The "classical" utopias that describe perfect societies occupy only a small
part of his discussion, which repeatedly refutes criticisms of the genre by expanding the category of texts it embraces to include those to which the criticism does not apply.

Gerber plays fast and loose with the concept of genre—fast when he observes that it is unfair to fault utopias for being unrealistic or burdened with
philosophical discussion inasmuch as these characteristics are given in the
genre[7]; loose when he nevertheless claims that the best utopias are those with
the closest "degree of approximation" (122) to the realistic novel! It is generally unclear whether Gerber regards utopia as a kind of fiction, literature, or
novel and what distinctions he makes between these three concepts; whether
utopia is antithetical to the novel or, on the contrary, one of the novel's possible modes; and, if it is a kind of novel, how utopias written before the novel
(e.g., Plato's *Republic*) are to be classed. Most problematic of all is Gerber's

final chapter, which advances a theory of progressive generic evolution similar to the progressive theory of history he attributes to many of the utopias themselves. That chapter's opening sentence reads: "The development towards the novel is part of the logical evolution of the myth-creating utopian imagination, which impatiently proceeds from the general idea to ever greater actualization" (120). Gerber's perplexing conclusion from this "logical evolution" is, in effect, that the best utopias are those that are most realistic and least utopian. "Utopia is no longer perfect," he writes, "it is put in doubt, it is full of the social and moral conflicts which have been considered earlier in this study. Utopia is nearer our own imperfect world. At last the utopian writer's aim has been achieved. . . . The claims of hypothesis and reality are reconciled, the utopian's impatient desire for creating a new world has found the ideal short cut to the independent realm of full-grown utopian fiction" (120). It is not explained, however, why a work that describes an imperfect society, contains "diversified and individualized" (120) characters, and narrates a story that turns on social conflict should be called a utopia at all. Or if such works are to be classed as utopias, it is not clear why numerous earlier works describing imperfect imaginary worlds, from Lucian's *Icaromenippus* and Seneca's *Pumpkinization* to Swift's *Gulliver's Travels* and Voltaire's *Micromegas*, are not; and if *those* works, too, are utopian, then how can one say that utopia is "no longer" perfect? Gerber's evolutionary conclusions seem to derive from his inconsistent system of classification.

The problematic nature of Gerber's way of handling these points becomes most clear when he declares that *Brave New World* and *1984* are the "most successful" (122-123) English *utopian* novels. He is far from unique, however, in citing *anti*-utopias as evidence for generalizations about utopias. No doubt, one can sharpen one's perception of utopia from a consideration of its parody, inversion, or exaggeration in anti-utopia—for much the same reasons that one can sharpen one's perception of epic from mock-epic. Nevertheless, one would, I think, be skeptical of a critic who claimed that scabrous humor was characteristic of epics and cited as his examples Pope's *Dunciad* and Pushkin's *Gabrieliad*. For the same reasons that a parody is not to be confused with its target, a parodic (anti- or mock-) genre is not to be confused with the genre it parodies.

There may well be an interesting and consistent way of classifying literary works in which a genre of "utopian fantasy" that included both utopias and anti-utopias would have a place. But inasmuch as Gerber neither specifies the general principles of that classification system nor indicates what other genres it might include, it is hard to avoid the impression of an *ad hoc* class constructed for purposes of special pleading. This failure to recognize that it is either senseless or useless to speak of a genre without, at least implicitly, relating it to a *system* of genres is a problem common to theorists of other genres as well. For example, the reason why the question "What is the novel?" has proven so intractable may be not—or not only—because the nature of the novel is so elusive, but rather because the nature of the question itself is problematic. What, we may ask, is the content of *is* in "What is the novel?"

(or, similarly, in "What is tragedy?" or "What is a lyric?"). Is one asking for an account of the usage of a word or for a description of a class of texts? If the latter is what is wanted, on what basis has the class been identified *as* a class? What more general objectives is that procedure for identifying classes of texts intended to serve, and into what theoretical framework is it designed to fit? Unless such prior questions are answered, the attempt to characterize or define the genre is likely to prove inconsistent, circular, obscure, and otherwise of limited value.

Criteria for Literary Utopias

In this study, the class of texts called "literary utopias" are identified as are all other classes of texts, that is, on the basis of their semiotic nature: the conventions that govern, or are assumed to govern, how the meanings of such texts are to be inferred. The identity of the class of literary utopias is best appreciated when its members are distinguished from a number of other works with which they may share thematic or formal features (and with which they might consequently be classed in *another* system—but not the *present* system). Specifically, we shall distinguish literary utopias from (1) nonliterary, or tractarian, utopias; (2) other "fantastic" or "extraordinary" narratives; and (3) their parodies, anti-utopias, which we shall discuss in a later chapter.

A work is a literary utopia if and only if it satisfies each of the following criteria: (1) it was written (or presumed to have been written) in the tradition of previous utopian literary works; (2) it depicts (or is taken to depict) an ideal society; and (3) regarded as a whole, it advocates (or is taken to advocate) the realization of that society. It will be useful to consider each of these criteria in turn.

(1) The work must be presumed to have been designed to be interpreted in the tradition of previous utopian literary works, especially the exemplars of the genre, Plato's *Republic* and More's *Utopia*. This criterion, it will be noted, would obtain in semiotic identifications of other genres as well, insofar as readers' presumptions of a tradition sustain their confidence that the way in which they derive meaning corresponds to the work's encoding, and encourages their discovery of a network of allusions and responses to other works in the same genre. It makes possible, in short, the governance of a generic contract, the assumption by both reader and author that the other shares the same understanding regarding the work's semiotic nature and ruling conventions.

It is necessary to make one important qualification of this description of the generic contract. It follows from the relation of contractual assumptions to familiarity with a tradition that the exemplars of a genre occupy a unique status. For a genre's first works cannot have been designed to be read in the tradition of previous works, nor can they have been designed to be interpreted according to the conventions of a generic tradition that began only with them. Except in those rare cases when a work is intended as a generic exemplar (e.g., *The Knight's Move*), works become exemplars only through the unforeseen creation of later works and the unanticipated emergence of a common hermeneutic approach to the entire class. History makes the exemplar; and tradition, insofar as it directs readers to take the exemplar *as a member of the genre* that it fathers, changes its semiotic nature: the original text is, in effect, re-created by its own progeny. It follows that generic exemplars are usually read according to an anachronistic set of conventions. For example, the reader who regards the *Republic* as a utopia makes hermeneutic assumptions that Plato did not make, assumptions that are likely to yield interpretations different from, and perhaps even incompatible with, the original set of possible interpretations. The same point could be made about the difference between reading the *Iliad* as an epic and reading the *Aeneid* and *Paradise Lost* as epics. In an important sense, it is really the *second* work of a genre that creates the genre by defining conventions and *topoi* for the class.[8] Read in the context of the second and subsequent works, the style of the first becomes the grammar of the class, and its idiosyncratic themes and rhetorical devices are rediscovered as the motifs and tropes of a tradition. And the exemplar or exemplars of a tradition will continue to be rediscovered in this way so long as new members of the genre are created and new readers come to see in the exemplar the germ of passages and works to which it unknowingly gave birth. Traditions are made by retrodiction.

The general point is that the tradition that constitutes a work as a member of a genre consists as much of what the work has been *taken to be* as what it has been *designed to be*. Authorship should be distinguished from generic re-creation. I do not wish to suggest that either one is hermeneutically privileged; but I do think that much fruitless controversy could be avoided if interpreters specified the assumptions on which their readings depend. Any work can, of course, be "re-authored" by being interpreted as a member of a genre to which it was not originally designed to belong, but that kind of interpretation *characteristically* takes place with generic exemplars. The distinction between authorship and generic re-creation is particularly important with regard to Thomas More's eponymous work. I shall discuss later the suggestion by a number of readers (with whom I am largely in agreement) that *Utopia* was designed by its author to be read in a tradition of deeply ambiguous works, such as Erasmus' *Praise of Folly*, and that it was intended to offer only a qualified endorsement to Hythloday's views about "the best state of a commonwealth." But when read, as it usually has been, as a member of the genre that appropriated its title, its generic relatives are no longer the ironic fictions of Erasmus and Lucian, but the dogmatic ones of Campanella and Andreae. Like other boundary works, *Utopia* has thus led a double life, and one reason for the extraordinary amount of disagreement as to its meaning is probably this generic doubling. As *a* utopia, *Utopia* is understood to have an authoritative speaker whose social prescriptions the reader is asked to accept; that authority, however, comes not from the author but from the generic tradition. More's *Utopia* is not the same kind of work as utopia's *Utopia*.

(2) The work as a whole must depict, or be taken to depict, an ideal society. Utopian society is, in Thomas More's phrase, "the best state of a commonwealth,"[9] one which is organized, as Socrates describes his *Republic*, "to secure the greatest possible happiness for the community as a whole."[10] Literary utopia is not equivalent, then, to the literature of imaginary journeys and unreal societies. Not every "nowhere" is locatable in utopia, nor is every *ou-topia*, or no place, also an *eu-topia*, or good place (as Thomas More doubly derives his neologism). This criterion excludes a number of works that often figure in characterizations of utopia—for example, Eugene Zamyatin's *We*, which depicts a maximally imperfect society, and Samuel Butler's *Erewhon*, which, despite its title's allusion to More, describes not the elimination but a satiric *inversion* of European vices. It excludes as well many fantastic narratives, such as the *Icaromenippus* and *Pumpkinization*, which may have contributed motifs and plots to utopia, but which do not themselves describe society's "best state."

(3) It must advocate, or be taken to advocate, the realization of that society. This criterion distinguishes utopias, as they frequently distinguish themselves, from eclogues, folktales of a land of Cockaigne, myths of Eden, and legends of a golden age. "*Looking Backward*," asserts Edward Bellamy at the close of that work's postscript, "was written in belief that the Golden Age lies before us and not behind us, and is not far away. Our children will surely see it, and we, too, who are already men and women, if we deserve it by our faith and by our works."[11] Anticipation and planning, not nostalgia and resignation, characterize the mood of literary utopias, which often invoke myths of a lost Eden or a past golden age in much the same spirit that *Paradise Lost* cites pagan philosophy and pre-Christian religious narratives—namely, as intimations of a truth now revealed and, in the case of many utopias, soon to be realized.

Inasmuch as literary utopias are either entirely or mostly fictional,[12] and the "fictional contract" suspends authorial responsibility for statements represented rather than made, it may be asked how it is possible to say what the author advocates. The answer, as we suggested in the previous chapter, is that a secondary generic contract specifies a number of ways in which it is possible to infer the author's beliefs and sentiments. The conventions of utopia provide, first of all, that if the work contains a nonfictional section, like the postscript to *Looking Backward* just cited, its statements are to be taken as authoritative. Moreover, utopias characteristically contain a fictional character—henceforth called the "delineator"—who explains the ideal society to an audience unfamiliar with it. Generic conventions entitle the reader to assume that even though the author cannot be identified with the delineator, the author does *endorse* the delineator's values and statements of what is socially desirable. That assumption may be made whether the utopia takes the form of a narrative, like *News from Nowhere*, or a dialogue, like Campanella's *City of the Sun*; whether it is set in the past, present, or future; and whether the delineator, like Socrates in the *Republic*, speculates on what the ideal society would be like or, like Campanella's sea captain, claims to have seen it. As authoritative as the statements of Virgil and Beatrice in *The Divine Comedy*, the delineator's social observations are designed not to portray the complex psychological ambiguities of a personal opinion, but rather to exploit the dramatic power of a truth revealed.[13]

The interpretive conventions of utopias are radically different from those of novels—a difference which, as we shall see, reflects the two genres' antithetical philosophical assumptions. First, in the novel, unlike the utopia, the narrative is to be taken as representing a plausible sequence of events (i.e., as designed to be "realistic"). Second, in a novel, the statements, actions, and beliefs of any principal character (or the narrator) are to be understood as a reflection of his or her personality, and of the biographical events and social milieu that have shaped it.[14] An important corollary for our discussion of utopias follows from this second interpretive convention. The sort of unqualified, absolute truths about morality and society that constantly occur in utopias have no place in novels. To be sure, a novelistic character may make such categorical statements (as, for example, Bazarov does in *Fathers and Children* and Levin does in *Anna Karenina*). But insofar as we interpret the work *as a novel*, we will take such statements differently from the way we would take them if they were made by the delineator of a utopia. Thus, we may find Bazarov's and Levin's philosophical pronouncements interesting and thematically central, but we will not take them as expressions of beliefs that Turgenev or Tolstoy would have us accept, without irony or qualification, as the Truth. We are rather invited to refer these statements to the fictive circumstances that occasioned them and to the fictive consequences to which they are likely to lead. In novels, but not in utopias, each truth is *someone's* truth, qualified by what might be called an "irony of origins"—that is, by our knowledge that it reflects a particular person's (or character's) experience and a given set of personal and contextual circumstances. They are consequently understood to be *partial*—that is, both limited and biased—even if we (or the author) are inclined to share that partiality.[15]

Novels are thus well suited to convey a skeptical or ironic point of view; utopias, by contrast, are used to make the sort of categorical claims about ethics, values, and knowledge that novels do not admit. Indeed, the very concept of an ideal society implies timeless and absolute standards—standards which, as Socrates argues in the *Republic*, could be used not only as a guide to building a new society but also as a sure measure of the justice of existing ones. Utopia, in short, surveys and describes a world that is not as complex as it has been thought to be, a world where psychology, history, and social problems are a Gordian knot to be immediately cut rather than laboriously untied. Tolstoy's utopian and apocalyptic dreamer, Pierre Bezukhov, to whom it seemed "that he was chosen to give a new direction to the whole of Russian society and to the whole world," expresses the characteristic prejudice of utopia when he explains to Natasha his reasons for joining a secret political society. "I only wanted to say that all ideas that have great consequences are always simple. My whole idea is that if vicious men are united and constitute a power, then honest men must do the same. You see, it's so sim-

ple."[16] A kind of counter-*Bildungsroman*, utopia usually tells the story of a
hero who discovers that the world is *not* as complex as he had thought, and
often concludes with the hero's attainment at last of the simple wisdom that
there could be heaven on earth, if only . . . [17]

The meaning of a literary utopia is not *limited* to the propositional assertions immediately derivable from the author's or delineator's pronouncements. Insofar as such works are designed or read as literature—which is to
say, as meaningful in manifold and unforeseen contexts—their meaning includes as well a more general commendation of a *kind* of thinking that these
particular assertions instantiate and exemplify but do not exhaust. (That, indeed, is also the case with other didactic literary genres, such as Socialist
Realism, and didactic works, such as *The Divine Comedy* and *The Death of
Ivan Ilyich*.) Much of the interest and reward of reading the *Republic*, even
for those who are uninterested in or antagonistic to its politics and philosophy, lies in the *process* by which Socrates recognizes, formulates, works out,
and finally solves philosophic problems. The *Republic*, in other words, does
not simply offer solutions, but represents the activity of finding them—an
activity which, in Plato's rendition, attains considerable dramatic power. As
the work progresses, we watch Socrates initiating Glaucon to philosophic
exploration, which for Socrates is, like justice, a thing of the highest sort
"which anyone who is to gain happiness must value both for itself and for its
results" (43). The *Republic* concludes with Socrates' praise of the philosophic
activity itself, and, as he addresses Glaucon by name, with his declaration of
that love of wisdom he hopes Glaucon will share. It should be stressed that
this passage provides the literary work, not just the philosophic argument,
with strong and rhetorically effective closure. Drawing on imagery developed
throughout their dialogue, Socrates promises Glaucon that as philosophers
"we shall be at peace with Heaven and with ourselves, both during our so-
journ here and when, like victors in the Games collecting gifts from their
friends, we receive the prize of justice; and so, not here only, but in the journey of a thousand years of which I have told you, we shall fare well" (359).

The Literary Significance of Nonliterary Utopias

To begin with, nonliterary (tractarian) utopias have been important in establishing the conventions according to which utopian literary works have been
interpreted, and so have helped to constitute generic tradition. We have already had occasion to remark upon the effect this tradition has had on readings of More's *Utopia*. Analogous relations probably obtain between other
literary genres and a specific critical or philosophical tradition; for example,
the philosophy of tragedy, from Aristotle on, has been influential in the interpretation, and hence in the composition, of particular tragedies.

Tractarian utopias have also served as a source of ideological and terminological *topoi* with which the reader is presumed or encouraged to become
familiar. As European historical novels depend on a basic knowledge of Euro-

pean history, so literary utopias depend on a measure of familiarity with the social and political issues they traditionally address. It is likely, indeed, that all genres require some distinctive "extraliterary" knowledge, the possession of which is part of the special competence that the genre both requires and also promises to reward with, among other things, the acquisition of more. A principal self-referential paradox of such metaliterary works as Shklovsky's *Zoo* is that the "extraliterary" knowledge they require and reward is knowledge about literature itself.

When readers first encounter a genre that requires an unfamiliar body of knowledge, they may judge that body of knowledge to be intrinsically non-literary. The perceived "literariness" of subject matter, styles, or extraliterary allusions varies with the readership and its sense of literary tradition: Socialist Realist narrative fiction, for example, may presume an acquaintance with Marxism-Leninism and describe not rivals in love, but rival plans for the centrifugal casting of sewerage pipes. Rather than acquire a new body of knowledge, readers familiar primarily with European novels may abandon such works to political scientists and economic historians, who may, in turn, lack the necessary competence to read the works as literature—that is, an understanding of the special semiotic nature of literature, fiction, or particular genres. Utopia, as a literary genre that is especially closely connected with a particular tradition of nonliterary writing, has suffered from both kinds of semi-competence.

An Intra-generic Dialogue: The Status of Women

I have stated that for a work to belong to a given genre, it must be presumed to have been designed to be read in the tradition of earlier works of the genre, and to be interpreted with reference to received ideological and terminological *topoi*. This presumption encourages the discovery of a network of allusions to those earlier works and to the genre's related philosophical or critical tradition. Generic tradition, in other words, includes the specification of issues and problems that are regarded as important, but about which different positions may exist; and readers may find the interest of a given work to be its particular response to a traditional question. Works may thus enter into what might be called "intra-generic dialogues" with their predecessors, and subtraditions may be established by recurrent positions on those issues. Utopias, for example, have implicitly and explicitly criticized each other's understanding of the proper status of women. Generic tradition may also be constituted by *inter*-generic dialogues with neighboring genres regarded as hostile to its core philosophical assumptions. Each of the opposing genres may then include parodies of key works and characteristic forms of the other, parodies designed to convince readers of the untenability of the antagonistic set of assumptions. Utopia and the novel have engaged in such a dialogue concerning, for instance, the malleability of human psychology and the nature and proper function of literature.

Always a concern of utopias, the status of women has become a particularly controversial one in the nineteenth and twentieth centuries. All, or almost all, utopias of the past century and a half include passionate criticisms of the status of European women, but very few have been willing to go as far as the *Republic*, which contains a classic defense of their complete equality and advocates a system of communal wives and husbands.[18] It is, indeed, remarkable how conservative utopian writers, willing to abolish private property, prisons, and police, become when they consider family life and the occupations of women outside the home. The delineator of *Looking Backward*, for instance, explicitly criticizes nineteenth-century feminists who overlooked the "distinct individuality" of the sexes: "It is in giving full play to the differences of sex rather than in seeking to obliterate them, as was apparently the effort of some reformers in your day, that the enjoyment of each by itself and the piquancy which each has for the other, are alike enhanced. In your day there was no career for women except in an unnatural rivalry with men. We have given them a world of their own, with its emulations, ambitions, and careers, and I assure you they are very happy in it" (174). ("We" may have become more important than "I," but women, it seems, are still "they.") That "world of their own" restricts them to special, less demanding occupations and to conditions of work that neither compromise their femininity nor unduly limit their time in the home. "Under no circumstances is a woman permitted to follow any employment not perfectly adapted, both as to kind and degree of labor, to her sex," Doctor Leete, Bellamy's delineator, explains. "The men of this day so well appreciate that they owe to the beauty and grace of women the chief zest of their lives and their main incentive to effort, that they permit them to work at all only because it is fully understood that a certain regular requirement of labor, of a sort adapted to their powers, is well for body and mind. . . . " (173).

In the utopian community of B. F. Skinner's *Walden Two*, the delineator of which cites Bellamy with approval, the status of women is improved, in part, by more efficient methods of housework. "Some of our women are still engaged in activities which would have been part of their jobs as housewives," Frazier explains, "but they work more efficiently and happily. And at least half of them are available for other work."[19] Still more domestically conservative, William Morris' "romance" *News from Nowhere*, in which the citizens of the future explicitly prefer medieval social ideals to those of the industrial age in which Morris lived, is uncompromising in its rejection of nineteenth-century feminism. The principal improvement in women's status in this utopia is greater public recognition of the importance of housework and childrearing. "'Come now, my friend,' quoth he, 'don't you know that it is a great pleasure to a clever woman to manage a house skillfully, and to do it so that all the house-mates about her look pleased, and are grateful to her? And then, you know, everybody likes to be ordered about by a pretty woman: why, it is one of the pleasantest forms of flirtation.'"[20] It seems that Morris, too, has a taste for the "piquant." His delineator is especially antagonistic to nineteenth-century feminist suggestions that intelligent women be liberated from childrearing, a suggestion he calls a "strange piece of baseless folly, the result, like all other follies of the period, of the hideous class tyranny which then obtained" (67).

All this is a long way from Socrates' argument in the *Republic* that inasmuch as the only difference between the sexes is that "the male begets and the female brings forth, we shall conclude that no difference between man and woman has yet been produced that is relevant to our purpose. We shall continue to think it proper for our Guardians and their wives to share in the same pursuits" (152). Socrates' argument *was* generally accepted among Russian revolutionaries and utopists, who, indeed, frequently characterized the centrality and radicalism of their feminist concerns as a sign of their tradition's superiority to European counterparts. Some of the most eloquent and thoughtful passages of Alexander Herzen's autobiography, for instance, contrast Russian appreciation of the importance and complexity of the "woman question" with the tendency Herzen finds even among the most enlightened Europeans to combine their political radicalism with domestic conservatism and complacency. "We are bold in denial and always ready to fling any of our Peruns [pagan idols] into the river," he worte of his patriarchal French comrade, Proudhon, "but the Peruns of home and family life are somehow 'waterproof,' they always bob up."[21] Herzen's insistence that revolutionaries pay more attention to patterns of domestic as well as political life resonates with considerable power in the context of an autobiography that dwells, with remarkable frankness, on the failure of his own marriage. Probably the most influential of all Russian utopias, N. G. Chernyshevsky's *What Is to Be Done?*, is concerned primarily with the reconstruction of the family and only secondarily with communism; and we may sense the centrality of this "question" in Russian utopianism when we discover that even Dostoevsky's *Diary of a Writer*, which emphatically rejects equality of nationalities or religions, advocates the equality of the sexes. The Russian identification of their utopian tradition with radical feminism is, in fact, a target of Joseph Conrad's historically insightful anti-utopia, *Under Western Eyes*. Conrad's chief revolutionary, Peter Ivanovich, foresees a victory for the Russian revolution because, he explains, Russian radicals rely not on their workers but on their women. "In Russia it is different," he repeats a *topos* common to both Slavophiles and revolutionary populists. "In Russia we have no classes to combat each other. . . . We have only an unclean bureaucracy in the face of a people as great and as incorruptible as the ocean. No, we have no classes. But we have the Russian woman. The admirable Russian woman! I receive most remarkable letters signed by women."[22]

An Inter-generic Dialogue: The Nature and Proper Function of Literature

Utopias are in general agreement about the proper social function of literature—and about the failure of all existing literature, as the corrupt product of a corrupt world, to fulfill it. When citizens of utopias read nineteenth-century novels, they tend to find them puerile and self-indulgent, if not positively dangerous. "I say flatly that in spite of all their cleverness and vigour, and capacity for story-telling, there is something loathesome about them," Clara tells the "praiser of past times" in *News from Nowhere*. In the world to come, utopias tend to argue, art will either have no place at all or will be as radically transformed as society itself. Specifically, art will no longer serve the function of presenting alternative worlds, inasmuch as perfection needs no necessarily imperfect alternatives. "As for your books," Clara tells the eccentric reactionary, "they were well enough for times when intelligent people had but little else in which they could take pleasure, and when they must needs supplement the sordid miseries of their own lives with the imaginations of the lives of other people" (169). In Clara's world, however, life itself, which has realized the dreams of the past, fulfills the imaginative and speculative functions of art better than art ever could (168-169):

> "Books, books! always books, grandfather! When will you understand that after all it is the world we live in which interests us; the world of which we are a part, and which we can never love too much? Look!" she said, throwing open the casement wider and showing us the white light sparkling between the black shadows of the moonlit garden, through which ran a little shiver of the summer night-wind, "look! these are our books in these days! —and these," she said, stepping lightly up to the two lovers and laying a hand on each of their shoulders. . . . Yes, these are our books; and if we want more, can we not find work to do in the beautiful buildings that we raise up all over the country (and I know there was nothing like them in past times), wherein a man can put forth whatever is in him, and make his hands set forth his mind and his soul."

In *Nowhere*, Morris' delineator explains, there is no need for a separate aesthetic function or for works of art at all, because day-to-day life *is* now a work of art. "The production of what used to be called art . . . has no name amongst us now, because it has become a necessary part of the labour of every man who produces" (149).

Hostility to traditional art has been a motif of utopias since Socrates, in the *Republic*, banished or censored poets for "the worst of all faults—misrepresenting the nature of gods and heroes, like an artist whose picture is utterly unlike the object he sets out to draw" (69). Socrates' central argument, which he applies to representations of Republican guardians as well as of gods and heroes, is that poets must never show imperfections of any sort in those presumed to be perfect. In the Republic that he designs, the guiding principles of artists are consequently to be, first, that "heaven is not responsible for everything, but only for what is good" (72) and, second, that "things in the most perfect condition . . . [would] be the last thing to suffer transformation" (72-73), because, Socrates reasons, perfection could change only by becoming imperfect. It follows for Socrates that gods must never be described as vicious nor guardians as contentious. He argues that, by definition, there can be no conflict among perfect beings in a perfect society. "If by any means we can make them [the guardians] believe that no one has ever had a quarrel with a fellow citizen and it is a sin to have one, that is the sort of thing our old men and women should tell children from the first; and as they grow older, we must make the poets write for them in the same strain" (70). As this passage suggests, Socrates' description of Republican art is largely in the negative, in terms of what is to be deleted or avoided. "We shall ask Homer and the poets in general not to mind," he explains at the conclusion of the longest of such negative descriptions, "if we cross out all passages of this sort. . . . So we will have none of it; and we shall encourage writing in the opposite strain" (76-77). Specifically, Socrates would excise "the wailing and lamentations of the famous heroes" (77), since their sorrow might imply that the world is ruled by misfortune; nor, in his view, should heroes be shown to suffer fear, to experience self-division, or to "be overmuch given to laughter" (78), all of which might lead an audience to believe that values are essentially in conflict and that the wisest course of action is not necessarily apparent. For where there is unresolvable doubt or conflict, utopian authors from Plato to the present have understood, there can be no perfection.

One might ask, as critics of utopia frequently have, how narrative art is possible at all without conflict and change; for what, if not change, could be narrated? In a curious way, the question of theodicy—if God is all good, how can evil exist?—re-emerges as an aesthetic question for utopia: if heaven and the Republic are perfect, how can there be narratable events? "If everything in the universe were sensible, nothing would happen" (780), the devil in *Karamazov* observes. "And that, of course, would mean the end of every-thing, even of magazines and newspapers, for who would take them in?" (787-788). Perfection would seem to exclude plot, and utopias have had some difficulty in explaining what a plotless narrative would be. To be sure, the best *possible* state of a commonwealth can still contain some unavoidable conflicts, and so long as there are conflicts, there can be stories about them. The specification of the kinds of conflict that are and are not appropriate for narrative art in a post-revolutionary world has been an important and recur-rent question in the theory of utopia's heir, Socialist Realism, which has, by and large, allowed literature to represent social problems so long as the gods— in this case, the Party—are not responsible for them and the algorithm for solving them is clear. Some utopian authors (e.g., Skinner) have envisaged a similar answer; very few have been as brave as Morris, whose visitor to No-where becomes convinced that inasmuch as narrative art requires competition and misfortune, it is not worth the price. Most frequently, utopias have fol-lowed the example of much theodicy, and have left the problem of narrative art for the wiser citizens of the future to solve in a way that we cannot fore-see. Bellamy, for instance, describes not the sublime literary works of the future, but the rhapsodic experience of reading them. "I sat up in my room that night reading *Penthesilia* [the masterpiece of the future writer, Berrian] till it grew gray in the east, and did not lay it down till I had finished it," Bellamy's visitor, Julian West, recalls (121-122):

And yet let no admirer of the great romancer of the twentieth century resent my saying that at the first reading what most impressed me was not so much what was in the book as what was left out of it. The story writers of my day would have deemed the making of bricks without straw a light task compared with the construction of a romance from which should be excluded all effects drawn from the contrast of wealth and poverty, education and ignorance, coarseness and refinement, high and low, all motives drawn from social pride and ambition, the desire of being richer or the fear of being poorer, together with sordid anxieties of any sort for one's self or others; a romance in which there should, indeed, be love galore, but love unfretted by artificial barriers created by differences of station or possessions, owning no other law but that of the heart.

Because West's account is addressed to his new contemporaries, who have presumably all read *Penthesilia*, no further description of the work is presented. Nevertheless, Bellamy's delineator confidently pronounces the literature of his times an achievement "to which no previous age of the world offers anything comparable" (116).

Utopia, as a literary genre of the pre-utopian world, has usually conceived of itself as transitional to the sublime art of the future; so, in fact, it has been honored by Soviet Socialist Realism, which regards itself as that long-awaited art. Anachronistic in the contemporary world because of its anticipation of another, utopia tends to oppose itself to all literature yet written, to offer itself not just as another genre in the hierarchy of genres, but as a radically different *kind of genre* standing outside that hierarchy. We shall see in a later chapter that some of those traditional genres—especially the novel and anti-utopia—have parodied utopia's self-conception, and have measured the justice and humanity of alternative worlds by their very ability to respond to traditional art—to the literature, as the narrator of Eugene Zamyatin's *We* puts it, "of the antediluvian time of all those Shakespeares and Dostoevskys."[23]

Structure: Questions and Answers

Utopias may be regarded as a genre of "wisdom literature," a term sometimes used to describe narratives about how a sage (say a rabbi, Solomon—or Socrates) solves or tries to solve a difficult problem.[24] Like much wisdom literature, utopias are often divided into two sections: one, set in the world that readers and authors share, posing the problem of social injustice, the other, set in or describing the perfect alternative world, giving the "unexpected" but correct answer. It is especially interesting to compare utopia with another modern genre of problem solving, the detective story—a genre which emerged in the "golden age of utopia," the nineteenth century and which, like utopia, also reflects a faith in the adequacy of reason to solve all problems. Both genres are centrally concerned with crime and its hidden causes: as the detective solves the problem of *a* crime, the utopian delineator solves the problem of Crime itself. So the wise Socrates solves that larger question, as he has solved so many others, in utopia's exemplar, the *Republic*. Dostoevsky seems to have been well aware of the connections between popular and esoteric "wisdom" genres, which he wove together into complex philosophical thrillers—for example, about a murderer who kills to prove a theory and a metaphysical detective or priest who sees in each transgression the Cause and causes of all.

There is also, of course, an important difference between utopias and detective stories: whereas the latter are primarily concerned with the logical process of solving a problem, the former recommend not only that process but also—and especially—the specific answer. Utopias are, in short, politically programmatic, and for this reason their second section, which corresponds structurally to the concluding explanation of all mysteries in a detective story, becomes the principal part of the work, its importance marked by its formal separation from the "question" section. This formal division is already present in utopia's exemplars, *Utopia* and the *Republic*. In More's work, book 1 describes an inconclusive conversation about English social conflicts; in book 2, Hythloday explicates the Utopian prescription for their resolution. The transition between the two books, which is also a "passage" between two worlds, has its structural equivalent in almost all utopias. "I beg and beseech you," says "More" at the end of book 1 (109),

> "give us a description of that island. Do not be brief, but set forth in order the terrain, the rivers, the cities, the inhabitants, the traditions, the customs, the laws, and, in fact, everything which you think we should like to know. And you must think we wish to know everything of which we are ignorant."
>
> "There is nothing," he declared, "I shall be more pleased to do, for I have the facts ready to hand."

From this point on, dialogue yields to diatribe, an address to a silent interlocutor. Plato's transition occurs at the end of book 2, when, as Socrates recalls, "Glaucon and the others begged me to step into the breach and carry through our inquiry into the real nature of justice and injustice, and the truth about their respective advantages. So I told them what I thought" (55). During that telling, which occupies the remaining eight books of the *Republic*, Socrates' previously argumentative audience simply assents to everything he says, Glaucon's speech now consisting of the prescribed answers to Socrates' rhetorical questions and of formulaic expressions signifying complete agreement. If not diatribe, this part of the *Republic* is something like catechism.

In utopias written as narratives rather than dialogues, the transition usually describes not a change of *topic*, but a change of *place*. Instead of a turn in the conversation, there is *a sudden turn of events*. The questioner (who is usually a citizen of the reader's own society) finds himself, by a process recounted in the transition passage, in the ideal kingdom. He may, as in *Looking Backward*, *News from Nowhere*, and Granville Hicks' *The First to Awaken*, fall

asleep for a century and "wake up to" the truth; or he may sail across perilous seas and, the sole survivor of shipwreck, "arrive at" the answer to all his
questions. In the seventeenth-century utopia *Christianopolis*, the allegorical
nature of the journey is made explicit:

> While wandering as a stranger on the earth, suffering much in patience
> from tyranny, sophistry, and hypocrisy, seeking a man, and not finding
> what I so anxiously sought, I decided to launch out once more upon the
> Academic Sea though the latter had very often been hurtful to me. And so
> ascending the good ship, Phantasy, I left the port together with many
> others and exposed my life and person to a thousand dangers that go with
> desire for knowledge. . . . Very few escaped death, and I alone, without a
> single comrade, was at length driven to a very minute islet, a mere piece of
> turf, as it seemed.[25]

In most narrative utopias, the question section and the transition together
comprise a brief opening chapter, the title of which often describes its two
parts—for example, "Discussion and Bed" in *News from Nowhere*, "The
Reason for the Journey, and the Shipwreck" in *Christianopolis*. For the duration of the questioner's visit to utopia, the progress of the plot is suspended:
in utopia peripeteia is mere prologue, the introduction to a series of rhapsodic
invocations and static descriptions of a world in which history itself has been
overcome. In *News from Nowhere*, this formal division into narrative and
catechism is further marked by a shift from first to third person in the second
chapter.

Structure: Dream and Reality

The formal division of utopias represents their characteristic thematic opposition between the real world and the imagined world. A key point I would like
to make is that utopias insist on that familiar paradox: the "real" world is an
illusion and the imagined world is the higher Reality. In this respect, all utopias are Platonic, each, like the *Republic*, stressing the ontological primacy of
the timeless pattern—what Socrates calls "the realities themselves as they are
forever in the same unchanging state" (189)—over the everyday ephemeras
that seem so substantial. The delineator of *Looking Backward*, for instance,
describes his world as the realization of such a pattern, as nothing less than
the "codification of the law of nature—the edict of Eden . . . the logical outcome of the operation of human nature under rational conditions" (89). Nine-
teenth- and twentieth-century utopias frequently contain a chapter—"How
the Change Came" in *News from Nowhere*, "How It All Happened" in *The
First To Awaken*—that tells the story of the establishment of those "rational
conditions" and the creation of a society previously regarded as impossible
and "utopian."

Utopian society is, indeed, the no-place that will take place. It will exist
when the essentially Real is at last realized, and when society is consequently

in accord with the timeless pattern of justice. Or as the delineators of many utopias declare, it is the coincidence of historical reality with the vision of the poets. We may recall here that in *News from Nowhere* art is no longer necessary because the world itself *is* a work of art. In utopia, the boundary between fact and fiction is at last overcome: mimesis has been reversed and reality has imitated art.

Utopias characteristically set up a series of homologous oppositions— fact and fiction, possible and impossible, real and fantastic, wakefulness and dream, sane and insane, history and poetry, practical and visionary—that correspond to the two parts of its structure and the two worlds they represent. In ostentatious defiance of what it condescendingly characterizes as "common sense," the utopian work assigns primacy to the second term in each of these oppositions. An epistemological parable, it tells the story of how a questioner, who begins with untested assumptions about history, society, and human nature, comes to believe in what he had previously considered unbelievable. An encounter with a visitor from utopia, for instance, may oblige the questioner not only to confront the social institutions so far taken for granted, but also to reconsider the traditional justifications of those institutions. Thus, whenever the narrator of William Dean Howells' *A Traveler from Altruria* (1894) rationalizes an American injustice by saying, "that's human nature," the Altrurian asks mildly, "it is?" Howells' Americans are faced with an emissary from a society whose very existence refutes their complacent assumptions about what is possible. "I know something of the state of things in Altruria," the banker observes, "and, to be frank with you, I will say that it seems to me preposterous. I should say it was impossible, if it were not an accomplished fact."[26] In *Walden Two*, the philosopher, Castle, is also placed in the uncomfortable position of denying the possibility of an "accomplished fact," a phrase that, with a few variants, is recurrent in the genre. "'I'm still skeptical,' said Castle. 'Of course, I'm still at a disadvantage in arguing against an accomplished fact.' Frazier nodded his head violently" (122). As a rule, the questioner who, let us say, denies the possibility of communism or the eradicability of crime is answered not just theoretically, but also in the way Hythloday answers Giles and More (*Utopia*, 107):

> "I do not wonder," he rejoined, "that it looks this way to you, being a person who has no picture at all, or else a false one, of the situation I mean. But you should have been with me in Utopia, and personally seen their manners and customs as I did, for I lived there more than five years and would never have wished to leave except to make known that new world. In that case you unabashedly would admit that you had never seen a well-ordered people anywhere but there."

In those utopias where the questioner himself visits the ideal society, the utopian citizen, like Clara in *News from Nowhere*, can simply throw open the window and say, "Look!"

In some utopias, the questioner becomes aware of the perfect society in a dream or vision. Upon awakening, he concludes that the imagined world is realer than the real, and that his prophetic dream is truer than waking truth. He may, like the narrator of "The Dream of a Ridiculous Man" (*Diary of a Writer*, April, 77, II, 1), meditate at length on the nature of dreams and the kinds of knowledge they can impart. "They tease me now, telling me it was only a dream," he observes during one such meditation. "But is it not all the same whether it was a dream or not, if that dream announced the Truth to me? For once you have recognized the Truth and seen it, you know that it is the Truth, and that there is no other and there cannot be, whether you are asleep or awake" (end of ch. 2). The very distinction between dream and reality now seems problematic to him. "Let it be a dream, but all this could not *not* be," he begins the account of the end of his paradise. "You know, I will tell you a secret: perhaps it was not a dream at all! For then something happened so awful, so terribly true, that it could not have been imagined in a dream. . . . How could I have invented it or imagined it in my dream? Could my petty heart and capricious, trivial mind have risen to such a revelation of truth?" (end of ch. 4).

The implicit answer is, of course, that they could not. When utopias include dreams, visions, or myths to outline the perfect society or to reveal the principles on which that society depends, they tend sharply to separate such dreams from the rest of the text and so to mark their special, axiomatic status. The meditations on dreams as vessels of ultimate Truth serve this separating function in Dostoevsky's story, much as meditations on fiction as "higher Realism" separate the stories themselves from the rest of the *Diary*. One important source of the *Diary*'s alternation of political journalism with revelatory fictions is the *Republic*'s alternation of argument with embedded myths and allegories, such as the Myth of Er and the Allegory of the Cave. Unlike novels that embed dreams (including idyllic or "utopian" ones, as in *Oblomov*), utopias do *not* invite psychological interpretation of their embedded visions, because such interpretation would necessarily subject the visions to an "irony of origins" and so limit their absolute Truthfulness. No less than the Revelation to St. John, utopian revelations are designed to be *in*explicable wholly in terms of individual experience or personality. They are designed, in short, not to be convincing, but to convince.

The Masterplot

Now if a man believes in the existence of beautiful things, but not of Beauty itself, and cannot follow a guide who would lead him to a knowledge of it, is he not living in a dream? Consider: does not dreaming, whether one is awake or asleep, consist in mistaking a semblance for the reality it resembles?

I should certainly call that dreaming.

Contrast him with the man who holds that there is such a thing as Beauty itself and can discern that essence as well as the things that partake of its character, without ever confusing the one with the other—is he a

dreamer or living in a waking state?
He is very much awake. (*Republic*, 183–184)

An apparently foolish visionary, the only one awake, is usually the central
character of the narrative I take to embody the genre's masterplot: the Allegory of the Cave, in book 7 of the *Republic*. With remarkable consistency,
the works of this highly determined genre repeat that plot, either in part or
in its entirety. There is hardly an incident in Socrates' narrative or an observation in his interpretation that has not been developed at length in later
utopias. This epistemological "parable"—as Socrates calls it—tells of a journey
to light and knowledge and a return to darkness and ignorance. It begins in a
cave, where men chained from childhood see only the shadows passing in
front of them and so take those shadows for reality. "It is a strange picture,"
Glaucon observes, "and a strange sort of prisoners." "Like ourselves" (228),
Socrates replies, for all people tend to mistake skill in predicting the sequence
of phenomena, which are simply the shadows of reality, for true knowledge.
Socrates supposes one of these prisoners is set free and compelled to turn and
lift his eyes to the light. "What do you think he would say, if someone told
him that what he had formerly seen was meaningless illusion, but now, being
somewhat nearer to reality and turned towards more real objects, he was getting a truer view?" Socrates' answer, in most utopias enacted in a question
and answer section, is that the former prisoner would be "perplexed," would
doubt what he was told, and would have to be guided, step by step, out of
the subterranean darkness to the light of truth—and even then "he would
need . . . to grow accustomed before he could see things in that upper world"
(229). The third stage of the journey is his return to liberate the other prisoners, who, regarding him as "awkward and ridiculous" (231), refuse his help.
"They would laugh at him and say that he had gone up only to come back
with his sight ruined; it was worth no one's while even to attempt the ascent.
If they could lay hands on the man trying to set them free and lead them up,
they would kill him" (231), much as they were to kill Socrates himself. "Yes,
they would," Glaucon agrees in the concluding line of this parable, as he perhaps begins his own perilous journey to the light.

Most utopias describe a similar journey from darkness to light, followed by
a real or imagined return. Liberated against their will—another recurrent utopian paradox that can be traced to the Allegory of the Cave—shipwrecked or
resuscitated travelers are led by a Socratic "guide" to a knowledge of justice
and the society that embodies it. They then return, like Hythloday, "to make
known that new world," but are mocked and threatened. In utopias set in the
future, the return usually takes place in a dream or reverie. When the travelers
awaken a second time, they fully understand the superiority of the new world
to the old. They understand that those who mocked them in their dream
would in reality follow others preaching the same truths. Most modern utopias, in other words, add a happy ending to the story that Socrates leaves
portentously open.

Bellamy summarizes the plot of *Looking Backward* in the preface to its sequel, *Equality*. That summary, which is approximately the same length as Socrates' allegory, tells essentially the same story and repeats many of Socrates' metaphors. Julian West—utopias frequently name their traveler (or delineator) everyman—awakens in the perfect society after a century's sleep. Just as Socrates' prisoner is at first blinded by the unfamiliar light and tries "to escape and turn back to the things which he could see distinctly" (229), so West at first finds the new world alien and regrets his loss of the old. "His shock on learning what had befallen him," Bellamy summarizes, "was so great as to have endangered his sanity but for the medical skill of Dr. Leete, and the not less sympathetic ministrations of the other members of the household, the doctor's wife, and Edith the beautiful daughter."[27] Like the ascent of Socrates' prisoner, West's education—his "leading out"—is gradual. "Step by step, almost as to a child, his hosts explained to him, who had known no other way of living except the struggle for existence, what were the simple principles of national co-operation for the promotion of the general welfare on which the new civilization rested" (viii), principles that Bellamy summarizes in a series of sentences beginning, "He learned that . . . " (Needing to derive dramatic power from their inevitable lists, utopias make frequent use of anaphora.) When West's education is complete and his homesickness overcome, he is engaged to Edith and so becomes a full citizen of the future. This romantic addition to the Socratic plot was subsequently used often in American utopias—so often, indeed, that in *The First to Awaken* (1940) a woman familiar with the genre blushes allusively when she meets the traveler from the past. The brief third part of West's story, his return to 1887, takes place in a dream. "His cup of happiness now being full," the final paragraph of the sequel's preface begins (ix-x),

> he had an experience in which it seemed to be dashed from his lips. As he lay on his bed in Dr. Leete's house he was oppressed by a hideous nightmare. It seemed to him that he opened his eyes to find himself on his bed in the underground chamber where the mesmerizer had put him to sleep. . . . Then he knew that all this wonderful matter about the year 2000, its happy, care-free world of brothers and the fair girl he had met there were but fragments of a dream. His brain in a whirl, he went forth into the city. He saw everything with new eyes, contrasting it with what he had seen in the Boston of the year 2000. . . . He felt like a sane man shut up by accident in a mad-house. After a day of this wandering he found himself at nightfall in a company of his former companions, who rallied him on his distraught appearance. He told them of his dream and what it had taught him of the possibilities of a juster, nobler, wiser social system. He reasoned with them, showing how easy it would be, laying aside the suicidal folly of competition, by means of fraternal co-operation, to make the actual world as blessed as that he had dreamed of. At first they derided him, but, seeing his earnestness, grew angry, and denounced him as a pestilent fellow, an anarchist, an enemy of society, and drove him from them. Then it was that, in an agony of weeping, he awoke, this time awakening really, not

falsely, and found himself in his bed in Dr. Leete's house, with the morning sun of the twentieth century shining in his eyes.

Looking backward again, he knows for sure that the world in which he was born was no less a dream than his return to it.

Some utopias, especially those in which the truth is revealed in a dream or vision, double the masterplot by repeating it in the embedded dream as well as in the embedding narrative. That is, questioners may learn the truth in a dream (or vision) in which they or another questioner learn the truth in a second dream. When the "outer" questioners awake they imitate the convert of their dream and endeavor to convert others. In *What Is to Be Done?*, for example, the heroine, Vera Pavlovna, dreams that she is liberated from a cellar and cured of paralysis by the goddess Love of Mankind, who enables Vera to liberate and cure other young women. When she awakes, she liberates young women in reality by organizing sewing cooperatives, which are, moreover, emblems of the coming utopia Vera sees in other dreams with the same plot structure. The *Diary*'s fictions, which reveal the timeless patterns behind the everyday events reported in its journalism, are the structural analogues of these dreams. In a sequence that the work often repeats, the author first doubts, then is inspired with a prophetic fiction, and finally, like the ridiculous man, preaches utopia to his readers. These fictions, moreover, also repeat the masterplot, revelation taking the form of an unexpected reminiscence in "The Peasant Marey" and, of course, of a dream in "The Dream of a Ridiculous Man."

To put it somewhat differently, the opposition between dream and reality in "The Dream," like the analogous oppositions in other stories of the *Diary*, corresponds both thematically and structurally to the opposition between the stories themselves and the nonfictional sections of the *Diary* that introduce and comment on them. In structure as in rhetoric, utopias tend to repeat themselves and to multiply formal oppositions intended as homologous to the genre's many thematic pairs. This singular class of works, as H. G. Wells observed in the introduction to *A Modern Utopia* (1905), does not seem to be able to count beyond two.[28] In that introduction, Wells considered a few of the hybrid forms I have discussed, including certain kinds of "ancient dialogue," the juxtaposition of novelistic narrative and sociological discussion, and an "interplay between monologue and commentator" (xxxii); he described his own work as "a sort of shot-silk structure between philosophical discussion on the one hand and imaginative narrative on the other" (xxxii). *A Modern Utopia* also juxtaposes its fictional section as a whole with framing sections of nonfiction, one of which is, indeed, the introduction itself. In short, more than one kind of formal doubling frequently occurs in a single utopia, and it is especially common to double an already divided fiction by embedding it in nonfiction. Bellamy and Cabet (*Voyage en Icarie*) use the most common form of nonfictional frame, an afterword or conclusion that summarizes the utopian program and predicts its realization. Cabet's summary is quite lengthy. Entitled "Résumé de la Doctrine ou des Principes de la

Communauté," it is "divided" into one "chapitre unique," "Explications de l'Auteur.—Doctrine Communitaire," which is, like the preface, signed "Cabet." "Hail, Christian Reader," the nonfictional preface to *Christianopolis*, refutes the work's critics in advance; and in Mercier's *L'An 2440*, a series of footnotes applies the doctrine of the fiction to the reader's own world.[29] The exemplar for this kind of doubling is More's *Utopia*, which includes marginal glosses and is framed by letters that have frequently been taken as nonfictional and un-ironic endorsements of Hythloday's doctrine. When they are so taken, the two-part account of a meeting with Hythloday may itself constitute one part of a doubly divided work.

Utopia as Threshold Art

Utopias "by contraries/ Execute all things" (*The Tempest*, II, i). Like the second, encyclopedic kind of threshold literature described in chapter 2 of this study, they consist of sections usually considered antithetical or incompatible. As *War and Peace* is a novel that is "not a novel," so utopias are fictions that are not wholly fictions. The experience of reading them is likely to prove unsettling, and so it is meant to be. Designed to overcome epistemological complacency, utopias render habits of classification and interpretation problematic. Themselves given to categorical assertions, they systematically defamiliarize received categories—especially those that distinguish the credible from the incredible. "Dream? What is a dream?" asks the ridiculous man. "And isn't our life a dream?" (end of ch. 5). The diarist frequently echoes these questions with another that is no less a *topos* of the genre: isn't our reality a fiction? In most utopias, this question is self-referential, explicitly challenging a boundary implicitly blurred by the work's very structure. *I am suggesting, in other words, that utopias lie on the boundary between fiction and nonfiction because they are about that boundary, or, to be precise, about the analogous boundary between social "fact" and social "fictions."* As utopian ideology expects history to combine one set of opposites, so utopian literature conjoins the other. Utopia is a threshold genre that is about reality on the threshold. Its paradoxical structure answering to its oxymoronic title, utopia describes the place that is no place in fiction that is not fiction.

Utopias use a number of strategies to blur the distinction between fiction and nonfiction. In the nonfictional part of a utopia, for instance, the author may declare that the fictional part is "no fiction," but was only presented as one in order, as H. G. Wells describes this technique, to "pander to the vulgar appetite for stark stories" (*A Modern Utopia*, xxxii). The author alternately speaks "as if" and "as if as if," first asks us to suspend our disbelief, then to suspend our suspension of disbelief. In the form of a "romance," a "fantastic story," or a "novel," he or she presents an apparently incredible tale and then retracts those characterizations, telling the reader that the tale is incredible only to those who have not learned the hero's lessons about what is believable and possible. "You laugh, this seems incredible to you?" the diarist asks in "The Golden Age in the Pocket" (*Diary*, January, 76, I, 4). "I am glad I made you laugh, and yet all the things that I have just been exclaiming are not a paradox but the perfect truth ... Your whole trouble is that they are incredible to you" (ellipsis in original).

The author may also dismiss the work's literariness, as well as its fictionality, as something offered to readers so that they can learn not to need it.[30] Chernyshevsky's utopia, for instance, constantly reproaches its readers for being interested in its romantic plot; and Cabet distinguishes the first reading of his work from subsequent ones, in which the reader will have learned to be interested in the text as treatise rather than as novel. "Sous la forme d'un ROMAN, le *Voyage en Icarie* est un véritable TRAITÉ de morale, de philosophie, d'économie sociale et politique, fruit de longs travaux, d'immenses recherches et de constantes méditations," he writes in the genre's characteristically authoritative and didactic tone. "Pour le bien connaître, il ne suffit pas de le lire; il faut le relire, le relire souvent et l'étudier."[31] Existing on both sides of the boundary of literature as well as of fiction, utopia is doubly double encoded, twice a form of threshold art.

Utopias characteristically have it, or rather give it, both ways; they invite us to have our cake and eat it, too. The structure of their readers' experience thus corresponds to what Gregory Bateson has called a "double bind."[32] In a double bind situation, one is caught between a set of instructions about how a message is to be taken and a second set of instructions that countermands the first, but, itself nondefinitive, is also countermanded by the first. In the resulting "no-win" situation, message conflicts with meta-message, and meta-message with meta-meta-message. Repeated exposure to such situations, Bateson proposes, probably contributes to the development and "epidemiology" of schizophrenia. It is interesting that a number of Dostoevsky's characters are experts at setting double binds: so Smerdyakov drives Ivan Karamazov mad by repeated interpretations, and interpretations of previous interpretations, of a coded conversation,[33] and it is by setting double binds of labyrinthine proportions and complexity that Porfiry Petrovich drives Raskolnikov to confession and eventual repentance. Threshold genres in general, and utopia in particular, set a double bind for their readers, whose likely reaction is, if not schizophrenia, then hermeneutic perplexity—which, in turn, is designed to produce something not unlike confession and repentance.

In some cases, the double encoding of utopias as both fiction and nonfiction, literature and nonliterature, is given from the start—Andreae and Cabet forewarn their readers—but more often the second set of instructions, which characterizes the text as not a fiction or not "just literature," is delayed and the reader consequently led astray. It is not entirely surprising, then, that readers of utopias often feel exploited as well as perplexed. That feeling may be the result not so much of having been led to read a literary work that turned out to be bad as having been led to read one that turned out—or did it?—to be no literary work at all. Belatedly discovering that the literary and fictional contracts had hidden clauses, readers may feel themselves to be the victims of literary fraud. "It was not easy to make sure of such innocence as prompted this inquiry of my Altrurian friend," the narrator of Howells' utopia recalls. "For a moment I did not know but I had fallen victim to a walking-delegate on his vacation, who was employing his summer leisure in going about the country in the guise of a traveler from Altruria, and foisting himself upon people who would have had nothing to do with him in his real character" (29). The narrator's suspicion, which is untrue of the traveler from Altruria, is nevertheless an apt characterization of *A Traveler from Altruria*—and of literary utopias in general.

In the *Republic*, Socrates argues the necessity of "noble lies" in the education of Republicans. Intensely aware of the manifold forms of complacency and recalcitrance that keep society imperfect, he contends that the establishment and continuation of perfection will require deceit and compulsion. "The ignorant have no single mark before their eyes at which they must aim in all the conduct of their own lives and of affairs of state; and the others will not engage in action if they can help it," he tells Glaucon (233):

> It is for us, then, as founders of a commonwealth, to bring compulsion to bear on the noblest natures. They must be made to climb the ascent to the vision of Goodness, which we called the highest object of knowledge; and when they have looked upon it long enough, they must not be allowed, as they now are, to remain on the heights, refusing to come down again to the prisoners or to take part in their labours and rewards, however much or little these may be worth.

Short of compulsion, Socrates contends, "there may well be an art whose aim would be to effect this very thing, the conversion of the soul, in the readiest way; not to put the power of sight into the soul's eye, which already has it, but to ensure that, instead of looking in the wrong direction, it is turned the way it ought to be" (232). Utopian literature itself is intended by its authors to be just such an art of re-education "in the readiest way." Like other forms of didactic literature, it seeks to convert the experience of reading into the experience of conversion.

The Poetics of Didactic Literature and Fiction[34]

The author of a didactic work (of whatever genre) takes advantage of readers' willingness to think in unfamiliar or nonhabitual ways for the duration of their reading. The "entertainment" of points of view that one might otherwise dismiss as dangerous or frivolous is, indeed, one of the principal social functions of literature's "entertainment," as well as an important source of pleasure in reading. Because fiction is understood to be counterfactual and literature to be liberated from a specific context of communication demanding an immediate response, we are more likely to assume the role of the work's implied reader than we might when, let us say, reading a polemical article or listening to a sermon. Knowing it is "just literature" or "only a story," we suspend our beliefs—not just our disbelief—and allow our expectations to be shaped not primarily by what we know about the real world but by what the author gives us to know about the represented one. We trade metaphysics for genre, exchange principles for conventions. It follows that a would-be sermonizer might choose to write, as Cabet does, "in the form of a novel," and so to exploit an audience's more favorable disposition. The strategy would then be to make the readers' assumption of an unfamiliar way of thinking carry over into their other, everyday experience. Didactic writers therefore make orthodox, if disingenuous, use of the opening frame—this is only a story—but elude as much as possible the power of the closing frame. They must, so to speak, not allow the curtain to fall. In this sense, didactic works tend to remain open, and utopias in particular have developed a special set of closural—or, rather, anti-closural—devices. Systematic anti-closure is especially characteristic of *The Diary of a Writer*, where it is closely related to the work's periodical, therefore potentially endless, form.

The didactic poet exploits a kind of doubleness in the moment of reading. As a playground exists in the real world and a game's suspension of historical time is itself historically locatable, so the reading of a fiction takes place in real time and the experience of aesthetic detachment occurs under historically determinate conditions and at biographically locatable moments. Critics of art from Plato to Tolstoy have been aware of the potential abuse of this peculiar kind of simultaneity. Himself a didactic writer, Tolstoy was concerned with the ways in which art can affect its audience. His frequent descriptions of the experience of theatrical audiences were, I think, intended as metaphoric of all aesthetic experience. Tolstoy saw the theatre as casting a penumbra of theatricality over its audience and as mirroring the suspension of actors' personal responsibility for their represented speech and action with an analogous, and insidious, suspension of the audience's moral responsibility for actions impermissible outside the theater. It is then possible, as Pozdnyshev observes in *The Kreutzer Sonata*, for "the first immoral man who turns up"[35] to prolong this theatrical mood outside the theater and, by so doing, to use art as a means of seduction. So, in *War and Peace*, Natasha's seduction begins at the opera and continues at a dramatic reading. Pozdnyshev goes so far as to argue that it is *because* of such potential "abuse" that society values art. "Everybody knows that it is by means of those very pursuits, especially music, that the greater part of adulteries in our society occur" (406), he tells the narrator (410-411):

> What is music? What does it do? And why does it do what it does? They say music exalts the soul. Nonsense, it is not true! It has an effect, an awful effect . . . but not of an exalting kind. . . . Music makes me forget myself, my real position; it transports me to some other position not my own. Under the influence of music it seems to me that I feel what I do not really feel, that I understand what I do not understand, that I can do what I cannot do. I explain it by the fact that music acts like yawning, like laughter: I am not sleepy, but I yawn when I see someone yawning. . . . In

China music is a state affair. And that is how it should be. How can one allow anyone who pleases to hypnotize another, or many others, and do what he likes with them?

In the *Republic*, Socrates also speaks of the danger that actors and audiences may become "infected with the reality" (83) that the dramatic fiction represents, and so reverse mimesis. A central paradox of the utopian genre is that its works are designed to take advantage of an experience that the societies they advocate would restrict or disallow.

Reading as Journey

Utopia's aim is just such an "infection" of its audience with the "reality" of its fiction. In this particular sense, the genre is magical, seeking to make the representation of a nonexistent state of affairs the means for its realization.[36] Utopias therefore often repeat the masterplot in yet another way: they project it outward, into the real world, as well as inward, into a dream or vision. Either explicitly in the nonfictional afterword, or implicitly by a series of metafictional references to the very process of reading the narrative, utopias characteristically set up a metaphorical equation of the journey to the utopian world with the reading of the utopian work. That equation, in effect, places readers in the traveler's position, so that they can then be urged to repeat the traveler's conversion. The readers, too, receive "news from nowhere" —that is, from fiction—and are then invited to make nowhere their home. They discover belatedly that the narrative is an embedded one, and that they are the protagonists of the frame tale.

Most utopias, in other words, are constructed as allegories of the process of reading them. Once the identification of reading with traveling—and of tour with guidebook—has been made, readers can dismiss utopian doctrine only at the risk of a further identification with the scoffers who refuse liberation, in which case their condemnation of them would become self-condemnation. In some utopias, two or more characters may function as metaphoric readers and, taken together, define a typology of receptivity to the truth. *Walden Two*, for instance, contrasts its narrator, who eventually overcomes his skepticism and joins the commune, with his friend the philosopher, who raises sterile metaphysical objections and returns to his classroom. *A Modern Utopia* also describes the growing hostility between the narrator and his unregenerate fellow-traveler. As the title of its preface, "Hail, Christian Reader," suggests, *Christianopolis* explicitly predicts its own reception and the ways in which it is likely to be distorted. "I see two classes of men in the commonwealth" (133), begins the preface, which then equates those two classes with two groups of potential readers of *Christianopolis*: those who, approving it, prepare to embark on the same journey, and those who, rejecting it, "answer me with some sophism" (140). Writing in the second person—if you answer me, if you find our state at all attractive—Andreae insists that his readers make a self-defining choice.

In those utopias where the perfect society is described in Europe to a skeptical European audience, a typology of readers may be represented by a typology of listeners. Book 1 of the *Republic* and part 1 of *Utopia*, for instance, describe at length how people do—or do not—listen to what they do not wish to know. Themselves didactic, utopias are intensely aware that listening is an action which one must choose to perform and which, like any other action, can be performed skillfully or ineptly. As there is such a thing as false speaking (i.e., lying) there is also, utopias imply, such a thing as false listening[37]—that is, behavior in which one avoids following or seriously considering lines of reasoning that may lead to unwelcome conclusions. Faced with this possibility, false listeners misconstrue what is said or, indeed, even refuse their attention altogether. The *Republic* begins with a wry allusion to these forms of protective hypocrisy. In his address to his unspecified audience —the *Republic* being framed as a description of a previous conversation—Socrates recalls how Polemarchus persuaded him to remain a while longer after the festival (3):

> Socrates, said Polemarchus, I do believe you are starting back to town and leaving us.
> You have guessed right, I answered.
> Well, he said, you see what a large party we are?
> I do.
> Unless you are more than a match for us, then, you must stay here.
> Isn't there another alternative? said I; we might convince you that you must let us go.
> How will you convince us, if we refuse to listen?
> We cannot, said Glaucon.
> Well, we shall refuse; make up your minds to that.

So the prisoners in the cave refuse to listen to their enlightened companion, and so, it is implied, the Athenians will silence Socrates himself. It is possible, indeed, that the audience of Socrates' long recollection includes members of his future jury, and that Plato intended the unspecified audience of Socrates' address to correspond to his own unknown readers, whom Plato implicitly cautions against similar self-protection. In *A Traveler from Altruria*, the Americans also guard against the truth by interrupting the Altrurian whenever he begins to describe the society they would rather believe to be a fiction. In much the same way that Plato links his readers with Socrates' audience, Howells' use of a "well-known novelist" as narrator threatens to assimilate his readers into the Altrurian's listeners.

The Self-Implicating Question

As the traveler is shown the new world, he inquires about its institutions and social philosophy. Inasmuch as the questions are ones readers themselves are likely to be posing, another form of didactic frame-breaking becomes possible. In most utopias, the traveler's questions are self-implicating in that their presuppositions, which the utopian citizens do not share, are revealed as the ideology of immoral people or an immoral society. It is common for a delineator to answer what the reader might take to be an innocent and obvious question by interrogating the questioner. Pointing out the question's presuppositions, he reproaches the questioner and, by extension, the reader. Asked how crime and selfishness can possibly be avoided, for instance, the delineator may curtly observe that his visitor apparently accepts the long-discarded theory of original sin or inherent corruption—a theory that was simply a convenient excuse for exploitation. Like the narrator of *A Traveler from Altruria*, most questioners discover that their anthropology is their ethics. "Oh Stranger!" the Tahitian exclaims to the chaplain in one utopian section of Diderot's *Supplement to Bougainville's "Voyage"*, "That last question of yours finally reveals to me the last depths of your country's wretchedness."[38] In Morris' angry romance, the traveler is met with outrage when he asks about utopian prison conditions (47–48):

> As soon as the words were out of my mouth, I felt I had made a mistake, for Dick flushed red and frowned, and the old men looked surprised and pained; and presently Dick said angrily, yet as if restraining himself somewhat—
> "Man alive! how can you ask such a question?"

Faced with a number of responses of this sort, the narrator gradually learns to deduce his own answer from the known pattern—a process of self-education that is presumably recommended to the reader as well.

At times, indeed, the questioner has no other choice, since the utopians, who have lost the words for the vices he regards as natural, often answer him with mute incomprehension. As Orwell understood, a generic *topos* is that vocabulary is an index to character. "I am glad that it is of *me* that you ask that question," the delineator of *News from Nowhere* responds to an inquiry about Utopian politics (94):

> "I do believe that anybody else would make you explain yourself, or try to do so, till you were sickened of asking questions. Indeed, I believe I am the only man in England who would know what you mean; and since I know, I will answer your question briefly by saying that we are very well off as to politics,—because we have none. If ever you make a book out of this conversation, put this in a chapter by itself, after the model of old Horrebow's Snakes in Iceland."
> "I will," said I.

This passage is, in fact, a whole chapter of *News from Nowhere*, which thus engages in yet another form of self-reference.

What Is to Be Done? *and What Is to Be Inferred*

What Is to Be Done? is probably the utopia that makes the most extensive use of metaliterary techniques for implicating its readers. In much the same way that Tolstoy in his later years wrote literary works about the harmfulness of art and literature, Chernyshevsky framed his utopia as a novel about the harmfulness of novels. Constantly discussing, incorporating, and parodying the novel's traditional forms and plots, Chernyshevsky's anti-novel takes its target genre as the emblem and representative product of the world to be destroyed. Behind the novel's characteristic plots, Chernyshevsky finds mistaken philosophical presuppositions and immoral values; he sees its effect on the reader as an education in self-indulgent and "unhealthy" interests. Specifically, Chernyshevsky faults the novel for (1) its emphasis on personality, and on romantic love as the consummate expression of personality; (2) its implicit belief in the inevitable complexity of social relations and in the unchangeable corruption of "human nature"; and, above all, (3) its concern with, and acceptance of, the irrational vicissitudes of history, from which, Chernyshevsky and all other utopian writers insist, society can and must escape. Like so many Russian nihilists, Chernyshevsky saw the novel as a doomed Babylon's last flower, exquisite in its unnecessary luxury and fascinating in its distracting design. The duplicitous strategy of his work is to encourage the readers' fascination with novelistic plots and themes, and then to reproach them for that very fascination. The readers' novelistic expectations thereby become both the sign of their moral weakness and, it is hoped, the means for their regeneration. Genre corrupts, antithetical genre purifies.

What Is to Be Done? consists of a constant alternation of narrative and metanarrative. In Chernyshevsky's work, the outermost frame of most utopias —the section that explicitly refers to and implicates the experience of reading —repeatedly interrupts the story with inquisitions of the reader and essays about the harmfulness of the aesthetic. Generally written in the second person, these essays describe what "you" no doubt expect at this point in the novel, based on "your" knowledge of other novels; how "you" are probably responding to the frustration of those expectations; and, indeed, what "your" reaction to having words put in "your" mouth is likely to be. So common are these metanarrative intrusions that the work often resembles a sort of socialist Sterne, a didactic *Don Quixote*. "Baring" by exaggeration the devices it employs, Chernyshevsky's work can be taken as a textbook model of the utopian genre's techniques, particularly its techniques of didactic frame-breaking. I would therefore like to quote in full the work's first direct address to the reader, which, like analogous passages in Sterne and Pushkin, takes the form of a displaced preface. Following the opening description of the hero's mysterious apparent suicide, the preface interrupts the story to discuss the conventions of novelistic storytelling:

"The subject of this tale is love, the principal character is a woman— that is good, even if the tale itself should be bad," says the female reader.

"That's true," say I.

The male reader is not restricted to such easy conclusions—cognitive ability being naturally stronger and much more developed in man than in woman. He says—and the female reader probably also thinks so but considers it unnecessary to say it, and I therefore have no grounds to argue with her—the male reader says: "I know that this gentleman who has just shot himself did not really shoot himself." I seize upon the word "I know" and say: you do not know that, because you have not yet been told it, and you know only what you are told. You yourself know nothing, not even that the way I have begun my tale was designed to insult and mock you. So you didn't know it—right?—well, know it now.

Yes, the first pages of this story reveal that I think very badly of the public. I used the usual sly technique of novelists: I began the tale with "effective" scenes, extracted from its middle or end, and covered them in fog. You, public, are good, very good, and so you are both undemanding and slow-witted. You could not be expected to be able to discern from the first pages whether the content of a novel is worth the reading. You have very poor intuition, and need help, and this help is of two kinds: either the name of an author, or effectiveness of manner. I am narrating my very first tale to you, and you are not yet able to judge whether the author has artistic talent (after all, there are so many writers to whom you have ascribed artistic talent). My signature could not yet have seduced you, and so I must throw you a line baited with "effect." Don't blame me for it—you yourself are to blame: your simplehearted naiveté forced me to lower myself to this vulgar device. But now you have fallen into my hands, and I can continue the story in my own way, which is to say, without any ruses. There will be no further mystery, and you will always see the denouement of each situation twenty pages in advance. I'll take the first opportunity to tell you the denouement of the whole tale: it ends happily, with raised glasses and song; there will be neither "effect" nor embellishments. This author is not up to embellishments, because he constantly thinks about the muddle in your head and about the unnecessary, completely unnecessary suffering the wild confusion in your thinking causes for everyone. It is pitiful and ridiculous for me to look at you: you are so impotent and so wicked because of the extraordinary amount of nonsense in your head.

I am angry at you because you are so wicked to people, and the people are, after all, you: Why are you so wicked to yourself? That is why I am reviling you. But you are wicked from a certain mental impotence, and so while reviling you, I am obliged to help you. How can I begin to help— Well, perhaps I can begin with what you are thinking right now: what sort of writer is this who talks with me with such insolence? Well, I will tell you what sort of writer I am.

I don't have even a shadow of artistic talent. I even handle language itself badly. But it doesn't matter: all the same, read, my most precious public! You'll find some benefit in reading it through to the end. Truth is a good thing; it makes up for the defects of a writer who serves it. Therefore I will say to you that if I had not warned you, you might have expected that the story would be written artistically and that the author would have much poetic talent. But I have forewarned you, I have no talent. You know that the worth of my story is in its truthfulness alone.

And so, my most precious public, when chatting with you it is necessary to spell everything out; for you are seekers, not masters, of guessing what has been left unsaid. When I say that I don't have a shadow of artistic talent and that my tale is very weak in execution, don't take it into your head to conclude that I am admitting to you that I am worse than your other writers whom you consider great and that my novel is worse than their compositions. I am not saying that. I am saying that if it is compared with the works of men genuinely gifted with talent, then my story—make no mistake—is, though weak in execution, still as well or better executed than the works of your famous writers. There is still more artistic talent in it than in them, you may rest assured on that score.

Thank me then: since you are so fond of bowing to those who denigrate you, bow to me, too.

But there are among you, public, a number of people—by now already a significant number—whom I respect. With the vast majority of you, I am insolent—but only with them, and it is only with them that I have been speaking so far. With those other people whom I have just mentioned, I would speak modestly, even timidly. But with them it would not be necessary to explain myself. I value their opinions, but I know in advance that we will agree. Good and strong, honest and able, it was not long ago that you arose among us; and yet there are already more than a few of you, and your number is rapidly growing. If you were the public, I would not need to write; if you did not yet exist at all, it would not be possible for me to write. As it is, you are not the public and yet you exist among the public— and therefore it is still necessary and already possible for me to write.[39]

Like most utopian writers, Chernyshevsky divides his readers into two groups, a larger one whom he "reviles" and a smaller one whom he flatters. In Chernyshevsky's case, this division probably derives not only from earlier utopias, but also from apocalyptic writing—a tradition on which utopias frequently draw for both millenarian imagery and prophetic rhetoric.[40] In both utopias and apocalypses, the explicit division of the audience functions as a provocation to choose one side or the other. The logic of both traditions is that of the excluded middle: there can be no innocent bystanders at the apocalypse, no disinterested contemplators of the revolution. The chapter of many utopias that describes "how the change came" usually tells the story of how a polarized situation forced liberals and centrists to take sides; and utopias themselves seek to provoke their readers, by strategies of implication, to make that choice. The genre seems to say to its readers what John writes to the Laodiceans: "I know thy works, that thou art neither cold nor hot: I would thou wert cold or hot" (Revelation, 3:15).

Chernyshevsky's reference to "guessing what has been left unsaid" implicitly points to something *he* has left unsaid, but expects to be widely understood: namely, that this very work, which was written through a censor— in fact, more than one, since Chernyshevsky composed it in prison—contains meanings beyond its apparent meanings. Using "Aesopian language," the Russian phrase for this kind of hidden political allegory, Chernyshevsky's text invites an esoteric, as well as an exoteric, reading. *What is To Be Done?*, therefore, relies on yet another kind of double encoding, this one with the censor as dupe and the readers—or more accurately, some readers—as partners in deceit. In short, reading becomes a form of complicity, which is to say, a political act.

This kind of double (or multiple) communication has, of course, been quite common in Russia—a circumstance that has probably left its mark on Russian semiotics and hermeneutics. I strongly suspect that the constant presence of arbitrary and unpredictable censors, and the consequent development of strategies for concealing subversive messages behind apparently innocent prose, is an important reason that Russian literary theorists have been so aware of multiple encoding and of the dependence of meaning on variable interpretive procedures and conventions. Meaning, they must have reasoned, could not be "in the text," because any text can be *made* to mean so many contradictory things. In *The Diary of a Writer*, Dostoevsky argues that the very possibility of a hidden meaning in a text—and where there is a censor, this possibility always exists—inevitably encourages readers to find such a meaning even where none is intended by the author. As Shklovsky reasoned that the context of an obscene joke potentially renders every word a double entendre,[41] so Dostoevsky stressed the irony that censorship makes every message potentially subversive—even denials of subversive intent. That irony, I take it, is the point of the title of one of the *Diary*'s articles: "Thirst for Rumors and for What 'They Conceal'—The Words 'They Conceal' May Have a Future, and Therefore Measures Should Be Taken in Advance" (July–August, 1877, I, 2).

To be sure, it is commonplace to note, and a pastime to look for, political double meanings in Russian literature, just as it has become a ritual of Anglo-American literary criticism to lament (at times, in a preface to a careless translation) the distortions produced in great works by obtuse censors. The point I would like to make here is that in Russia (and probably elsewhere) the censorship has functioned not only as a literary distortion, but also as a "literary fact" itself. The censor became a *conventional* implied reader, in much the same way that the romantic young lady and the dissolute young gentleman were conventional implied readers. Pushkin, for instance, makes subtle use of all three. In "Tsar Nikita and His Forty Daughters"—a narrative poem that Prince Mirsky professed to find too pornographic for even a euphemistic plot summary[42]—a conventional narrator confides in conventional young rakes about how to titillate conventional young lady readers while still eluding the conventional prudish censor. The obvious impossibility of publication must have been an added source of irony to those few readers who, knowing the poem had never even been submitted to a censor, read it in manuscript. There are, it seems, works that open publication can actually spoil. Later Russian writers made a tradition of exploiting foreign, infrequent, or *samizdat* publication as literary facts, Tolstoy in his later years being particularly adept at strategies for communicating in "ex-communication."

In *What Is to Be Done?*, Aesopian language is not just a technique for speaking the unspeakable, it is also one of the work's principal themes. Indeed, the technique (or techniques) of double communication *is* one of the most important lessons the work is designed to teach, a lesson that the readers are encouraged to learn as thoroughly as the characters do. It is, I think, with this kind of surreptitious education in mind that Chernyshevsky includes so many scenes in which characters communicate, and instruct others in communicating, past an unsuspecting listener. These scenes, moreover, are frequently followed by a "conversation" with the "penetrating reader" about how to guess what has been "left unsaid." In part 1, for instance, Lopukhov explains utopian socialism and materialist psychology to Vera Pavlovna in such a way that her mother, who, as both are aware, is eavesdropping, takes him to be saying something quite different. Vera consequently learns, as the reader is implicitly asked to learn, revolutionary semiotics as well as revolutionary economics. She has no trouble, therefore, in deciphering the letter that Lopukhov later writes from abroad under a pseudonym and in code. In that letter, moveover, Lopukhov describes the strategies by which he has been deceiving the police, assuming false identities, and delivering unmentionable, but evidently political, messages. After this letter appears in the text, the following conversation with the reader takes place (321-322; ellipses in original):

> "And, for my part, I know ... "
> What's this?—a familiar voice ... I look around—and so it is! It's he, he himself, the penetrating reader, so recently expelled for the disgrace of not knowing the first thing about art. He's already back again, again with his former penetration, again knowing something already!
> "Ah! I know who wrote that ... "
> But I hurriedly grab the first thing at hand that suits my purpose—which happens to be a napkin, because, having just copied over the letter of the former student, I sat down to eat—and so, I grab the napkin and stuff up his mouth: "Well, know then; but why shout it out to the whole town?"

Chernyshevsky's narrator refers here to the chapter "A Conversation with the Penetrating Reader, and His Expulsion," in which the reader is asked to "guess" why the character Rakhmetov, who plays almost no role in the novel's plot, is described in such detail. "The penetrating reader has perhaps guessed that I know more about Rakhmetov than I say" (281), he observes enigmatically, but "decent people understand each other without entering into explanations" (303). The answer to the narrator's question is that Rakhmetov, who is evidently a revolutionary conspirator, is the hero of the work's *real* story, the one it cannot tell: the subtitle of Chernyshevsky's work is

"*From* Stories about New People" (italics mine). This answer was so obvious to Chernyshevsky's actual readers that a harder question is why the censor ever let it pass.[43]

The adversary relationship between censors and writers that Chernyshevsky describes is not the only one that can and does obtain. Again, his work makes use of a conventional censor, whose behavior may, but does not necessarily, correspond to that of actual censors. At times, writers and censors may and do develop a working relationship, in which the former do not so much try to deceive the latter as to *enable* them to pass a work without problems from their own overseers. The censors may duplicitously play the public role of adversaries, in order to deceive more formidable adversaries (whose own position may also involve similar ambiguities); and so the semiotics of censorship may be complex, indeed. Moreover, the censor may try to guide the writer through the labyrinth at minimal cost to the work: "Well, Dmitri, just change a few lines over here, and we won't have any trouble."

Periodical Apocalypse

The *Diary*'s periodical form made possible an especially interesting generic innovation in a utopia's outermost frame, that is, in the story of the readership's response to the text. In most utopias, the author must leave this story largely untold, even though it may be projected explicitly in an afterword or implicitly in the description of fictional characters' response to the same utopian doctrine. A narration of the work's actual reception is, of course, only possible when a second edition or a sequel allows for retrospection—and utopian writers have, indeed, taken advantage of these opportunities. For example, in the second edition of *Looking Backward*, which has become the standard text for most subsequent editions, Bellamy included an afterword that "looked backward" on responses to the first edition. "*To the Editor of the Boston Transcript*," Bellamy's afterword, entitled "The Rate of the World's Progress," begins. "The *Transcript* of March 30, 1888, contained a review of *Looking Backward*, in response to which I beg to be allowed a word" (220). Inasmuch as *Looking Backward* already contained a fictive preface from a twentieth-century editor of "West's" *Looking Backward*, Bellamy here adds frame to frame. It is interesting that subsequent editions of *Looking Backward* (and of other classic utopias) have sometimes included an additional preface or afterword tracing the expanding influence of the work, and so reassessing the "rate of the world's progress," since the author's death and the previous edition.[44] As we shall see, the multiple framing of some utopias— a practice for which the commendatory letters to More's *Utopia* were probably exemplary—has become a common target of anti-utopian parody.

In order to include the story of its own reception, a work must have a method of temporal layering. A periodical is, of course, a form that is necessarily composed at a series of times, and in the *Diary* Dostoevsky takes advantage of serial publication and intermittent reading in two principal ways.

First, in his role as *author*, he reports the fulfillment (or explains the apparent disconfirmation) of his earlier political predictions. The first chapter of the September, 1877, *Diary*, for instance, reviews former predictions as it embarks on new ones. "I have already written in the May-June issue of my *Diary*, long before the manifesto of the Marshall-President [MacMahon of France], about the legions, that is, about the new force coming to occupy its place in European civilization—and now everything has happened as I felt it would at that time," he writes in the chapter's second article. In the third, "Reference to What I Wrote Three Months Ago," he observes that even though "no one paid any attention" to his assertion in May-June that "the key to present and future events in all of Europe *lies in the Catholic conspiracy* and in the approaching, inevitable and enormous movement of Catholicism" that will surely take place when a new pope is elected, nevertheless that prediction, too, is being rapidly and unmistakably confirmed. By the time he is composing the chapter's last article, the tempo of events has so increased that predictions made in the first articles are already coming true: "When I began this chapter, those facts and reports which have now suddenly filled the whole European press were still absent, so that everything I wrote in this chapter as conjecture has now been confirmed almost precisely. My *Diary* is not to appear until next month, on the seventh of October; today is only the twenty-ninth of September, and the 'predictions,' so to speak, on which I ventured, taking risks—will, in part, turn out to be old and accomplished facts from which I copied my 'prophecies'" (September, 77, I, 5). With its publication slower than events, the *Diary* develops a method for temporal layering within a single issue.

Dostoevsky also makes use of his work's periodical form in his editorial, as well as authorial, role. Frequently receiving letters from subscribers, he prints and responds to some of those letters, and, in this way, makes the text an ongoing exchange. The editor selects those letters so as to define a typology of readers, a typology that implicitly corresponds to the typology of listeners in the *Diary*'s utopian fictions. Thus, as the ridiculous man regrets that he has "lost the words" with which to persuade others, Dostoevsky speculates on the effectiveness of his own rhetoric; and, admitting that he, like his fictional dreamer, may appear "ridiculous" (June, 76, II, 4) because of his utopian hopes, resolves to go on preaching all the same. For among his readers he also finds a number with whom he can "serve the good cause together. I write, *together*, because I directly consider my many correspondents to be my co-workers" (December, 77, II, 5). In one case, a "co-worker" comes in person to the editor's office while he is in the process of completing an issue; an account of their conversation becomes a second ending, and, consequently, another device for temporal layering. "I was about to finish my *Diary* and was already reading proof when a girl suddenly called on me," the diarist writes in June, 1876. The young woman, it seems, is preparing to become a nurse in the Eastern War, which this very issue has been urging as a messianic campaign to establish the Kingdom of God on earth. Inasmuch as this issue, which Dostoevsky has just written and we have presumably just read, also predicts that women will inspire and lead the utopian crusade, its second conclusion constitutes an almost immediate confirmation of that prediction.

The August, 1880, *Diary* is probably the best example of temporal layering within a single issue. The only issue published in that year, it replaces the succession of times usually achieved over several months by an explicit designation of separate times of composition for each of its three chapters. This tripartite temporal layering defines a narrative with beginning, middle and end—or, more accurately, with middle, beginning, and end, inasmuch as the order of the events (*fabula*) does not coincide with the order of their presentation (*sjužet*). Taken as a whole, the issue tells the story of Dostoevsky's Pushkin speech: how, having divined the prophetic significance of that poet, Dostoevsky proclaimed Russia's ability to "utter the final word of great, universal harmony, of the final brotherly concord of all tribes according to Christ's evangelical law!" (80, II); how, after the speech, " strangers embraced each other" (80, III, 4) and lifelong enemies made peace; and how, at last, skeptical Westernizers, not comprehending or perhaps even resenting the possibility of a Russian-dominated reign of "universal, worldwide brotherly unity" (80, III, 4), are now rejecting the opportunity for peace. But that rejection, according to Dostoevsky, need not be final, because it is in the power of his readers to respond to this very issue as enthusiastically as the original audience responded to his speech.

The issue begins *in medias res*. Written shortly after the speech, its first chapter breathlessly summarizes the author's utopian hopes and urges their immediate realization. The text of the speech itself, the second chapter of the issue, acquires new meaning from its contextualization in the *Diary*. Rather than the simple transcript of an oration, it becomes the first action in a narrative; and the readership is invited to consider *both* the content of the speech *and* the enthusiasm of its initial reception. They are, as Dostoevsky writes, asked to consider the "event," not just the content, of his address. One of the *Diary*'s "unplanned" second endings, the issue's third chapter describes the first published response to the speech. "I was about to conclude my *Diary*, confining it to my speech delivered in Moscow on June 8 and the preface to it," Dostoevsky begins with his characteristic reference to the chronology of composition. "But having read your criticism, Mr. Gradovsky, I delayed the publication of the *Diary* in order to supplement it with my reply" (80, III, 1). The remainder of the article is written primarily in the second person, a form of address that is designed to include vicariously the speech's third audience, the readers of this very issue. Although I know you will be incapable of understanding me, Dostoevsky addresses Gradovsky, I answer you "solely because I have others in mind who will judge between us, that is, my readers. It is for them that I am writing" (80, III, 1). As in most utopias, the reader is presented with exemplary converts and scoffers, and asked to take sides. The closing lines of the issue once again promise the resumption of regular publication to trace the progress of the prophecy.

4. Recontextualizations

PART 1: Theory of Parody

Parody and Intertextuality

The functions of parody as a literary phenomenon are illuminated by the fact that parody is not only a literary phenomenon. There are pictorial as well as verbal parodies, and various social or institutional aspects of the artistic "environment"[1] may also become parodic targets. The dadaists and the Russian Serapion Brothers, for instance, not only parodied artistic works but also artistic movements, their mock manifestos and self-conscious exhibitions focusing irony on both the pretension of artists and the conventional responses of audiences. Moreover, parody is not limited to the arts, but can be found—under the names of "mimicry," "mockery," "spoofing," "doing a takeoff," and so forth—in the most diverse forms and most various contexts of everyday life. Indeed, it appears that any symbolic act, whether artistic or nonartistic, verbal or nonverbal, can become the object of parody. The converse is also true: when we parody someone's behavior, we are attributing symbolic significance to it. Thus, an important social function of mimicry (which may be regarded as a form of nonverbal parody) is to reveal the covert semiotic value of apparently unmotivated actions. That is, in mimicry we make the usually subliminal and peripheral world of gestures and mannerisms the center of our attention, and so render a usually unacknowledged channel of communication available for scrutiny. Literary parody is, in short, a special form of a more general communicative possibility, and many aspects of its nature and function are revealed when we begin to ask certain questions suggested by its more general communicative status: Under what circumstances do we engage (or refrain from engaging) in parody, and when do we respond (or fail to respond) to others' parodies? What functions does parody serve for the parodist, and what relation is implicitly set up between the parodist and his or her audience? How does parody resemble and differ from other types of utterances directed at the utterance or utterances of another speaker?

The work of Bakhtin and his close associate V. N. Voloshinov on intertextuality (or, to use Bakhtin's term, metalinguistics) offers a good starting point for answering these questions.[2] I should therefore like to summarize their approach to intertextuality before (1) identifying the class of texts that I shall call parodies, and (2) describing those texts' essential methodology, by which I mean the ways in which a parody subverts its target and the relationship it establishes between the parodist and his or her audience.

Concerned with developing a sociology of language and literature, Bakhtin and Voloshinov considered the relation of utterances to their "extraverbal and verbal (i.e., made up of other utterances) milieu" and, especially, the *"active relation* of one message to another" (*Marxism*, 96, 116). Unlike some of their Formalist predecessors, they were interested not so much in how utterances are interpreted with reference to the transcontextual "system" of the language, but in how they function as components of the ongoing stream of communication. In their view, interpretation is not a matter of passive "decoding," but rather of an active and complicated process of orientation of a potential speaker to a previous speaker. That process involves selection, evaluation, the supplying of unstated premises, the invocation of social rules signaled by contextual cues, and, finally, the formulation, at least in inner speech, of a reply—a reply which is, in turn, constructed in anticipation of a similar process of active reception. For Voloshinov, the forms of reported speech (direct discourse, indirect discourse, and "quasi-direct discourse") and, for Bakhtin, parody and stylization, were, in effect, documents of that process of active reception, documents that could be used to formulate a typology of how utterances interact. Rather than viewing parody as a particular literary genre, or as a form of satire, or a special type of comedy, therefore, Bakhtin describes it in terms of the relation of any utterance, whether literary or nonliterary, to the context of its origin and reception.

For Bakhtin, parody and stylization are types of what he calls "double-voiced words," or utterances that are designed to be interpreted as the expression of two speakers. The author of a double-voiced word appropriates the utterance of another *as* the utterance of another and uses it "for his own purposes by inserting a new semantic orientation into a word which already has—and retains—its own orientation" (*PDP*, 156). The audience of a double-voiced word is therefore meant to hear both a version of the original utterance as the embodiment of its speaker's point of view (or "semantic position") *and* the second speaker's evaluation of that utterance from a different point of view. I find it helpful to picture a double-voiced word as a special sort of palimpsest in which the uppermost inscription is a commentary on the one beneath it, which the reader (or audience) can know only by reading through the commentary that obscures in the very process of evaluating. The distinction between double-voiced words, such as parody and stylization, and their closest single-voiced relatives, such as imitation (in the narrowest sense), is, according to Bakhtin, that in imitation the two voices are intended to merge completely so that only one is heard. Unfortunately, Bakhtin does not consider a range of intertextual utterances that his model would be well equipped to describe. For instance, imitation in the broader sense of a free adaptation of another text (e.g., Dr. Johnson's "Vanity of Human Wishes" as an imitation of the tenth satire of Juvenal) could be classed as a special type of double-voiced word, probably lying between parody and stylization.[3] Bakhtin's model might also be extended to utterances in which the audience is deliberately misled about the text's voicing. Plagiarism, for instance, denies the fact of an original speaker by attributing the utterance entirely to the

second speaker; forgery misrepresents a doubleness as a singularity by denying the second speaker and attributing the utterance falsely to the "first." A
consideration of plagiarism and forgery is helpful for stressing an important
point about all intertextual utterances: namely, that they are best described
not simply as an interaction of two speech acts, but as *an interaction designed
to be heard and interpreted by a third person* (or second "second person"),
whose own process of active reception is anticipated and directed. For this
reason, successful forgers do not imitate an original as *they* perceive it, but
rather the way such an original is likely to appear *to their intended victims*,
perhaps subtly exaggerating what the latter are likely to regard as the original's most characteristic features and hence as the marks of its authenticity.
Considered purely in terms of formal features, therefore, a forgery may sometimes resemble a parody, the difference lying in their anticipated reception or
intended effect. One man's forgery may be another man's parody (and vice
versa). Because both parody and forgery are constructed to foreground aspects of the original regarded as most characteristic, they may, indeed, serve
as valuable documents for a history of perception and interpretation. That is,
critics of one period may wonder how critics of another could have been deceived by an "obvious" forgery; and historians of art may take the earlier
critics' *de*ception as evidence for their *per*ception of the original. The success
of Ossian may be indicative of how Macpherson's contemporaries read Homer.

In Bakhtin's formulation, the difference between stylization and parody is
to be found in the different relation that obtains in each between the first utterance and the second. In parody, the two utterances are antithetical, in
stylization corroborative. "Stylization stylizes another style in the direction
of that style's own tasks" (*PDP*, 160), Bakhtin observes. "The body of devices of another person's speech is important to the stylizer precisely as the
expression of a particular point of view" (*PDP*, 157) with which the stylizer,
though maintaining independence from the predecessor, largely agrees. Nevertheless, the very fact that the original utterance is subject to evaluation at all
makes it inevitable that "a slight shadow of objectivization" (*PDP*, 157) is
cast over it. In becoming characteristic of someone's particular point of view,
it becomes conditional; instead of being simply asserted, it is defended and
hence implicitly in need of defense. It is perhaps for this reason that cultures
often protect their sacred texts from stylization—and from all other forms of
dialogue—by recording them in an alien script or a dead language: there are
some utterances with which we do not have the right to agree.

A parodic utterance is one of open disagreement. The second utterance represents the first in order to discredit it, and so introduces a "semantic direction" which subverts that of the original. In this way the parodied utterance
"becomes the arena of conflict between two voices. . . . the voices here are
not only detached and distanced, they are hostilely counterposed" (*PDP*,
160)—counterposed, moreover, with the second voice clearly representing a
higher "semantic authority" than the first. The audience of the conflict
knows for sure with whom it is expected to agree.

Criteria

We may now identify the class of texts to be called parodies. To be what I refer to as a parody, a text or utterance must satisfy *each* of the following three criteria: (1) It must evoke or indicate another utterance, which I will allude to henceforth as its "target," "object," or the "original utterance"; (2) it must be, in some respect, antithetical to its target; and (3) the fact that it is intended by its author to have higher semantic authority than the original must be clear.[4]

(1) If the first criterion is not satisfied (i.e., if the audience sees no indication of a second utterance), the text will be taken as "single-voiced" and hence not as a parody. Sometimes this means mistaking an intended parody for its object, a misidentification that is especially likely to occur when the audience is remote from, and so unaware of, the original utterance. The parodies of alien cultures are particularly likely to go unrecognized, or, when they are recognized by a few who are well acquainted with that culture, to be difficult to translate or present to a broader audience. It is possible, indeed, that some of our evidence of past or remote cultures consists of parodies of what we take it to be.

If the authors of parodies anticipate the passing of interest in, or knowledge of, their dialogue with their targets, they may design their texts to be of interest on other grounds as well. In this case, the identification of the text as single-voiced will not be a misidentification of the author's intentions, but simply a partial appreciation of them. For most Western readers, *Notes from Underground*, which was understood by its original readers as a parody of *What Is to Be Done?*, functions, as it was probably designed to function, apart from its unfamiliar target. It is also possible for a parodied text to survive and function primarily as the object of a parody that was itself designed or discovered to be meaningful in other ways: for example, *Amadis of Gaul*, the life of which has been prolonged by *Don Quixote*. When this happens, an ironic consequence may be that the parody helps in the revival of its object at a time when readers react against the parodist's point of view and identify the target as their forerunner: for example, the romantic revival of medieval literature, a process that often involved "amadisizing" the *Quixote* itself.

Furthermore, some texts that were originally designed to be single-voiced may later be "discovered" (or "re-authored") to be double-voiced—to be, in effect, parodies of themselves. This process is especially likely to occur with the inferior productions of great writers. Critics perplexed by what they regard as a platitudinous Shakespearean sonnet (say, 116) may re-interpret it as a parody of what it had previously appeared to be—and are likely to be faulted for doing so by others who either do not find it platitudinous or think the author should be allowed occasional platitudes. Conversely, a major work designated as a parody may not be taken as one when the culture of its origin "needs" to take it as a "serious" work: for example, nineteenth-century Russian readings of their first great novel, *Eugene Onegin*, as a romantic allegory of Russian cultural history or a mythic expression of national identity (as in Dostoevsky's Pushkin speech). Both kinds of re-interpretation may be regarded as part of the more general process that keeps a heritage vital through continual revision and reassessment of its canon.

(2) The parodist must be seen to be in some way disagreeing with or disapproving of the target. Because there are an indefinitely large number of grounds for disagreement with any utterance, the parodist must indicate the grounds in any of a number of ways (for example, by exaggerating key passages in the original).

(3) When the third criterion is not satisfied—that is, when readers do not know with which utterance they are expected to agree, or suspect that the second utterance may be no more authoritative than the first—then we do not have parody, but another dialogical relation, metaparody, which I shall discuss below.

The main thesis of this chapter can now be anticipated: there exist two classes of texts that enter into dialogical relation with utopias, namely *anti-utopias*, which parody utopias, and *meta-utopias*, in which utopia and anti-utopia themselves enter into an ultimately inconclusive dialogue.

It is instructive at this point to consider a number of criteria *not* included in this identification of parody. Parody is often described as a comic literary work that imitates another literary work by means of exaggeration.[5] By contrast, the class I have described requires neither the parody nor its target to be a literary work; nor does it require the target to be a single work. Some literary parodies, for instance, are designed to discredit a writer's total oeuvre, or a literary movement (e.g., romanticism) or a genre (e.g., romance, pastoral, epic, folktale, utopia—or, in principle, any other genre).

As I shall use the term, moreover, parody is not always comic. Parody re-contextualizes its object so as to make it serve tasks contrary to its original tasks; but this functional shift need not be in the direction of humor. As negation can be on an indefinitely large number of grounds, parody can, in principle, adopt an indefinitely large number of tones. The direction and tone of the parody will depend on the nature of the parodist's disagreement with or disapproval of the original and the point of view from which he disagrees or disapproves. As Tynyanov observed, "if a parody of a tragedy results in a comedy, a comedy parodied may turn out to be a tragedy" (*Poètika*, 226). For instance, in parodying romantic novels for their frivolity and lack of serious ideological commitment, *What Is to Be Done?* is positively solemn; and *Notes from Underground*, which parodies the naive optimism of *What Is to Be Done?*, retells key incidents from the original in a context of dark psychological complexity. One might also recall the Renaissance tradition of "sacred parody," in which the devices and language of love poetry were used, with critical intent, for religious purposes (e.g., Herbert's lyric "A Parodie"). "Poets by abusing their talent, and making the follies and faygnings of love the customarie subject of their base endeavours," wrote Southwell of the objects of his sacred parodies,

have so discredited this facultie, that a Poet, a Lover, and a Lyer, are by

> many reckoned but three words of one signification. . . . For in lieu of solemne and devout matter, to which in duety they owe their abilities, they now busie themselves in expressing such passions, as onely serve for testimonies to how unworthy affections they have wedded their wills. And because the best course to let them see the errour of their works, is to weave a new webbe in their own loome, I have heere laid a few course threds together, to invite some skillfuller wits to goe forward in the same, or begin some finer peece; wherein it may be seene how well, verse and vertue sute together.[6]

"To weave a new webbe in their own loome" and so to induce them, or others, to "see the errour of their works"—this, not comedy, is the essence of parody.

Exaggeration, moreover, is not essential to parody. Exaggeration is, rather, simply one of several techniques parodists use (1) to inform readers that the text is a parody, which is to say that it refers to another, antithetical, text, and (2) to indicate what is objectionable in the original. Both of these goals can, however, be achieved without exaggeration. Parodists may, for instance, use the opposite technique, understatement, to deflate exaggeration itself (e.g., in the *New Yorker*'s brief replies to advertisements and announcements in other publications); or they may exploit the double meaning of a pun to double-voice a text. An especially common technique is the introduction of an element—an incident in the plot, let us say, or an unexpected choice of words—that is incongruous with the tone or generic conventions of the original. In this case, readers are implicitly invited to discover the new point of view from which the incursion was made, and a new structure that would resolve the incongruity. If this new structure is designed and adapted to survive after the parodic reference to an earlier work is no longer of interest, then it could prove exemplary for works to come. For example, *Joseph Andrews*, which was designed not only as a parody of *Pamela* but also, according to its preface, as a "species of writing . . . hitherto unattempted in our language,"[7] was to prove exemplary for the realistic novel. By creating a new kind of structure that incorporates elements from an old structure (or structures), parody can thus serve as an important laboratory—or perhaps, as Tynyanov argues,[8] the most important laboratory—for emerging forms and new genres.

Indeed, it is possible to "weave a new webbe" without even changing the old web at all. That is, a parody can be *verbally identical* to its original if the parodist uses contextual, rather than textual, change to indicate the fact and grounds of double-voicing. He could, for instance, repeat the original in a significantly inappropriate social or literary setting. In everyday speech, inappropriate (and ironic) intonation are frequently used to discredit another's utterance, a technique that can be particularly effective precisely because the parody is "identical" to its target. Authors of literary parodies can exploit the implicit directive to read their text as a coherent whole in order to suggest a discrediting counterinterpretation of any "exact" citation or reproduced document. It is likely, for instance, that we would read any document that

Sterne should have chosen to include in *Tristram Shandy*—as we read a number of documents that he did include, such as the Latin decree on baptism of the unborn—as parodically double-voiced, because the alternative—that is, to interpret the novel so that the document was not the object of parody—would defy plausibility or strain ingenuity. Moreover, not even *that* alternative is available when the original is reproduced "straight" in an anthology of explicitly designated "parodic works," a strategy Dwight Macdonald used in his anthology to discredit one of Eisenhower's political speeches.[9] A brief introduction and an ironic footnote indicate the two things Macdonald finds most objectionable in the original, namely the president's faulty logic, as reflected in his chaotic syntax, and his claim to be speaking impartially when he praises his own party. "As a bipartisan," Macdonald's footnote mimics the speech, "I must point out that, although [in this sentence] the syntax seems to put the Republican Party on record against freedom and liberty, the speaker almost certainly intended to say the opposite" (450n.).

The Etiology of Utterance

The function and techniques of parody can now be described. Parody aims to discredit an act of speech by redirecting attention from its text to a compromising context. That is, while the parodist's ironic quotation marks frame the linguistic form of the original utterance, they also direct attention to the *occasion* (more accurately, the parodist's version of the occasion) *of its uttering*. The parodist thereby aims to reveal the otherwise covert aspects of that occasion, including the unstated motives and assumptions of both the speaker and the assumed and presumably sympathetic audience. Unlike that audience, the audience of the parody is asked to consider why someone might make, and someone else entertain, the original utterance. By pointing to the unexamined presuppositions and unstated interests that conditioned the original exchange, the parodist accomplishes what Fielding calls "the discovery of affectation" (preface to *Joseph Andrews*, 11)—the divergence between professed and unacknowledged intentions—or the discovery of naiveté, the difference between belief and disconfirming evidence. He or she does not, therefore, quote "out of context," as the targets often respond, but rather in "too much" context—in a context the targets would rather have overlooked. Parody is the etiology of utterance.

Parodies are usually described and identified as being of (or "after") a particular *author* or *work*, but the parodist's principal target may, in fact, be a particular *audience* or *class of readers*. The etiology of utterance includes the pathology of reception. For example, from *Don Quixote* to *Madame Bovary*, parodies have frequently been aimed at readers naive enough to mistake fiction and romanticism for realism. Parodies have also been aimed at the complacency and hypocrisy, as well as the naiveté, of audiences. Tolstoy's parodies of opera in *War and Peace* and *What Is Art?*, for instance, are primarily concerned with why "rich, idle people" should enjoy such immoral artifice.[10] After describing the behavior of spectators during the entr'acte, Tol-stoy concludes that their sanctimonious tributes to "great art" are an obvious cover for their cultivation of "refined and vicious feelings flowing from sex-love" (*What Is Art?*, 157). It may also be suggested that Fielding's *Shamela* was aimed primarily at the sanctimonious relationship that *Pamela* established with its readers, a relationship in which a moral lesson served as an excuse for titillation. Like many parodists, Fielding implies that readers must not be too ready to accept the invitations authors extend, and that reading is an action which, like any action, can be performed responsibly or irresponsibly.

This analysis suggests that the distinction drawn between "material" parodies and purely "formal" parodies, or, as it is sometimes put, between parodies of content and parodies of style, is oversimplified and in need of re-formulation.[11] For in addition to its reliance on vague or questionable assumptions regarding the relation of form to content, this distinction also contributes to the misunderstanding of parody's basic nature and function. We cannot parody words, syntax, or any other element, whether "formal" or "material," out of which utterances are made, but only utterances themselves —that is, speech acts as discourse in a context. To the parodist, form and style are of interest because they betray, or can be shown to betray, the values, motives, and assumptions of those who would use or respond to that style on that occasion. The parodist recognizes language as dialect or idiolect, as *characteristic* of some group or speaker. Taking speech as an index of its speaker or listener, he or she selects and draws attention to whatever most clearly uncovers their affectation or folly.

The distinction of formal from material parodies is probably made in order to take account of comic imitations that neither discredit very much nor seem especially hostile to the original. In approaching such texts, we might note, first, that not all comic imitations are parodies (there are, for example, comic imitations of comedies) and, second, that parodies can be, as Bakhtin observes, "shallow" as well as "deep" (*PDP*, 160), which is to say, directed at superficial as well as fundamental faults of the original. As well as being more accurate, the distinction between shallow and deep, rather than formal and material, parodies is also more helpful in understanding the complex ways in which parodies are used. For instance, shallow parody is sometimes used to pay an author an indirect compliment. The opposite of damning with faint praise, this parody with faint criticism may be designed to show that no more fundamental criticism *could* be made. We have here an instance of a semiotic universal which I have often had occasion to describe in this study: every convention that can be used can be abused, any set of rules carries the possibility of its strategic violation. Those texts might best be called false parodies; for, under *cover* of parody, they do not function as parodies at all.

Even a true parody cannot help paying one compliment to its original, namely that the original is important enough to be worth discrediting. One only discredits what others might credit, one only reveals as counterfeit what others might take for true coin. Parody implies currency. For this reason, works of remote times and cultures are rarely parodied; because parody lo-

cates a text in its compromising context, we tend not to engage in parody
when that context is either unfamiliar or uninteresting. We speak ill of the
dead, and parody their works, only to the extent they remain vital and present to *someone*; we discredit foreigners only when they are, or are becoming,
influential among "us." To be precise, then, on those occasions when a work
of a remote culture is parodied, the target is usually its circulators or readers
in *our* culture. The parody may, for instance, be directed at inadequate translations, as in A. E. Housman's "Fragment of a Greek Tragedy," or at an enthusiastic group of imitators, as in many Russian verse parodies of the early
nineteenth century. These "readdressed parodies," as Tynyanov calls them
(*Poètika*, 288), are particularly common in works that belong to an anti-
genre, like anti-utopia or mock-epic. Mock-epic allusions to Homer and Virgil
are usually allusions to contemporary epic allusions to Homer and Virgil; not
More and Plato but their latter-day imitators and followers are the targets of
anti-utopian references to the *Utopia* and the *Republic*.

PART 2: Anti-utopia as a Parodic Genre

"Fortunately, the antediluvian time of those Shakespeares and Dostoevskys (or what were their names?) is past," I said in a voice deliberately
loud.—*We* (41)

Anti-genres

Anti-utopia is an anti-genre. Before turning to an examination of anti-utopia,
we may consider briefly the nature of anti-genres in general. As a special type
of literary genre, an anti-genre (or, as we shall sometimes call it, a parodic
genre) may be identified, as are all other genres in this study, by (1) the membership of its works in a tradition of similar works, and (2) the existence (or
readers' assumption of the existence) of a set of conventions governing the interpretation of those works. The distinctiveness of anti-genres lies in the fact
that those conventions establish a *parodic* relation between the anti-generic
work and the works and traditions of another genre, the target genre.[1]

(1) As I shall identify the class, anti-generic works are written in the tradition of previous works of the anti-genre. Like other genres, anti-genres have
their classic texts and exemplars (e.g., for mock-epic, *The Dunciad* and the
Homeric *Battle of the Frogs and Mice*, respectively). Anti-genres do not, however, necessarily have exemplars—that is, acknowledged originating works—
because the broader tradition of literary parody may provide models. An anti-
genre may therefore develop a tradition of allusion to a parodic text that does
not belong to that anti-genre. *Don Quixote* has been, in this sense, exemplary
for anti-utopia.

If the anti-genre has more than one type, its subgenres will have their own
classic texts and may also have an exemplar or exemplars. Thus, Zamyatin's
We has been made by its successors into an exemplar of the modern "dys-

topia," a type of anti-utopia that discredits utopias by portraying the likely effects of their realization, in contrast to other anti-utopias which discredit the possibility of their realization or expose the folly and inadequacy of their proponents' assumptions or logic. As in other genres, the tradition of an anti-genre creates the possibility of networks of allusions and references among its works. As *1984* and *A Clockwork Orange* develop motifs that occurred in *We*, *We* itself develops those of *Notes from Underground* and the legend of the Grand Inquisitor; and *Notes* and the legend allude, in turn, to *Candide*. Tradition may thus make, and frequently remakes, early works interesting as the source of motifs in later ones. Anti-generic motifs may also be drawn from a body of nonliterary texts, a knowledge of which is part of the competence the anti-genre presumes and encourages in its readers. Thus, just as utopias may require and reward familiarity with a tradition of nonliterary utopian ideology, anti-utopias often allude to a tradition of counterideology.

(2) An anti-generic work must parody a target genre. That is, it must discredit not a single work in the target genre, but the genre as a whole. When a particular work is singled out for discreditation, it must be discredited, so to speak, synecdochically—that is, as representative of the genre. So *Notes from Underground* parodies *What Is to Be Done?* as a contemporary, and especially dangerous, example of a kind of literature and thinking extending back to the *Republic*. I shall not class a work as a member of an anti-genre when broader parody of the tradition is not intended (or presumed to be intended). For example, the class I identify as anti-utopias does not include a number of works that parody the specific utopian program inferable from *Looking Backward* (or any other utopia) without taking exception to utopianism *per se*. Rival utopias are not anti-utopias.

Because they allude to another generic tradition, works of an anti-genre may have two kinds of exemplars, namely the positive models of its own tradition *and* the negative models of the target genre. The *Republic* and *Utopia* served not only as positive models for utopia, but also as negative models for anti-utopia. Grounded in two traditions, a passage in an anti-genre is often designed to be understood in terms of both the motifs of the target genre and the countermotifs of the anti-genre. In *1984*, for instance, the essay on Newspeak alludes both to utopian plans for a universal, unambiguous language and to anti-utopian parodies of utopian languages, such as the projectors' replacement of words by sacks of things ("an universal language to be understood in all civilized nations")[2] in *Gulliver's Travels* and by mathematical symbols in *We*. When Winston Smith discovers Shakespeare, and the hero of *Fahrenheit 451* discovers the Bible, readers may discover not only positive allusions to *Brave New World* and *We* but also negative ones to Plato's suspicion of poetry and Morris' rejection of novels.

It will be recalled that my concern in this study is *not* to regulate or account for the use of *terms*, but rather to identify and characterize classes of texts. We may note in this regard that not all works which have been *called* anti-utopias or mock-epics necessarily belong to the classes to which those terms will be applied in the present study. For example, some works which have been called mock-epics use the divergence between epic virtues and contemporary vices not to parody epic but to satirize those vices; and *insofar as* those works do not discredit epic (or its contemporary readers or imitators), they will not be classed as mock-epics, nor as members of an anti-genre, *as those terms are used in the present study*—though, to be sure, they might so be classed in another generic system. A similar point could be made with regard to certain "mock encomia" which, rather than discrediting encomia, reveal the inadequacies of the person "praised"; and with regard to some "anti-utopias" which are aimed not at utopias, but at contemporary social evils (e.g., *Erewhon*). Of course, it is difficult to avoid some generic parody even when it is not the primary point of the work, and it is common for authors to have, and for readers to take them as having, both targets in mind. That is, such a work may be offered and taken as both social satire and generic parody.

Anti-utopian, mock-epic, and other anti-generic works are, in fact, frequently offered or taken as members of two generic traditions—that is, as related not only to the works of the anti-genre, but also to works of another genre or anti-genre. For example, *The Praise of Folly* may be regarded as both a parodic sermon and a mock encomium, and *Joseph Andrews* as both a mock-epic and a novel. The novel has been especially hospitable to anti-utopia (cf. *Notes from Underground*, *The Possessed*, *Under Western Eyes*, and some of Turgenev's works), probably because the novel's presuppositions are antithetical to those of utopia and because utopias have characteristically disapproved of traditional novels. For both reasons, an important theme of some anti-utopian novels is their own "novelness":[3] implicitly answering utopian criticisms of the genre of the novel, a particular work may self-consciously affirm what other novels simply assume, specifically, the existence of personality, the complexity of psychology, and the value of aesthetic experience. Responding to Chernyshevsky's attacks on these novelistic assumptions in *What Is to Be Done?*, *Notes from Underground* is just such a self-conscious novel— which is to say, it is, as an anti-utopia, an *anti*-anti-novel. More recently, many anti-utopias, such as Sinyavsky's *Lyubimov*, Bradbury's *Fahrenheit 451*, and Bulgakov's *Heart of a Dog*, have easily combined with and appropriated some of the conventions of science fiction, which, like anti-utopia, functions as a genre of fictional "thought experiments" examining present social trends, technological possibilities, or philosophical beliefs, by taking them to an extreme.

Although an anti-generic work may be related to the tradition of a second genre, it need not, for that reason, constitute an example of what I have called threshold literature. For instance, in the cases just cited, the hermeneutic principles of the combined genres are not in principle incompatible or discontinuous. It is quite possible to read *Notes from Underground* as both a novel and an anti-utopia, *Joseph Andrews* as both a novel and a mock-epic, *Fahrenheit 451* as both science fiction and anti-utopia, *The Dunciad* as both social satire and mock-epic, and *The Praise of Folly* as both parodic sermon and mock encomium without confronting mutually exclusive interpretive directives. In other words, while such generic doubling does not necessarily lead to what I have called "hermeneutic perplexity," it may permit and encourage different readers, or the same reader at different times, to emphasize different aspects of the work. Depending on the tradition in which the reader chooses to locate the work, different allusions or generic *topoi* will become visible or predominant.

Parody and History

I have suggested that parody works by etiology. The parodist uncovers for each target an "irony of origins," which is to say, he or she reveals the relation of the text to the compromising and conditionalizing context of its utterance. A text or genre will be vulnerable to parody, therefore, to the extent that it ignores or claims to transcend its own originating context: parody is most readily invited by an utterance that claims transhistorical authority or implies that its source does not lie in any interests or circumstances of its speaker. The parodist typically reveals the historical or personal circumstances that led someone to make or entertain a claim of transhistoricity. Parody historicizes: and in so doing, it exposes the conditions that engendered claims of unconditionality.

In his study of *Gargantua and Pantagruel* as a composition of parodic genres, Bakhtin described medieval parodies of liturgies, prayers, wills, epitaphs, and grammars as expressions, in the face of official claims to eternal truth and unchangeable social norms, of a sense of the "gay relativity" of all things and the historical character of all rules.[4] We may add that the conventional semantic positions of these forms, in which truths and rules are handed down from an anonymous or impersonal source, must have invited parodic identification of the social or personal interests these forms often served. Modern dictionaries, grammars, and encyclopedias are also easy targets: the parodist returns the codification to the codifier, dates each attempt to arrest history. The well-known definitions in which Dr. Johnson expressed his personal opinion regarding what a word denotes (e.g., Whig, the name of a faction) or characterized the circumstances in which it is often used (patriotism, the last refuge of a scoundrel) were probably intended as what we might call preemptive self-parody—preemptive, that is, of such works as Ambrose Bierce's *Devil's Dictionary*. Like Bierce, who defined a lexicographer as "a pestilential fellow who, under the pretense of recording some particular stage in the development of a language, does what he can to arrest its growth" and who claimed for a chronicle the authority of a statute,[5] Dr. Johnson saw his own efforts and hopes as yet another example of the vanity of human wishes. He had begun his dictionary, its preface states, with the hope that it would check the history—he said decay—of English, which had been "suffered to spread, under the direction of chance, into wild exuberance; resigned to the tyranny of time and fashion; and exposed to the corruptions of ignorance, and caprices of the imagination." He had wished, he wrote, "that the instrument of language might be less apt to decay, and that signs might be permanent, like the things which they denote."[6] He knew, however, that such a wish was utopian; and in other places the preface anticipates those wry definitions that point away from words and toward their codifier. "To enchain syllables, and to lash the wind, are equally the undertakings of pride," Johnson wrote of lexicographers and academies (*Rasselas* . . . , 233–234):

> Those who have been persuaded to think well of my design, will require that it should fix our language, and put a stop to those alterations which time and chance have hitherto been suffered to make in it without opposition. With this consequence I will confess that I flattered myself for a while; but now begin to fear that I have indulged expectation which neither reason nor experience can justify. When we see men grow old and die at a certain time one after another, from century to century, we laugh at the elixir that promises to prolong life to a thousand years; and with equal justice may the lexicographer be derided, who being able to produce no example of a nation that has preserved their words and phrases from mutability, shall imagine that his dictionary can embalm his language, and secure it from corruption and decay, that it is in his power to change sublunary nature, and clear the world at once from folly, vanity, and affectation.

In short, *denial of history is invitation to parody*. More particularly, parodies are often directed at narrative genres in which the action unfolds in a time radically different from everyday time or discontinuous with the time of reading (for example, epic, romance, and pastoral). Parodies of these genres typically re-narrate their characteristic incidents in everyday time, and so use double narration as a means of double-voicing. Thus, the *Quixote*, which parodies all three genres, answers each of its hero's generically orthodox descriptions of his adventures with a counterdescription by Sancho or the narrator. As he tells of giants and they of windmills, the text becomes a dialogue of simultaneous times. So do *Candide* and *Ruslan and Lyudmila*, both of which call attention to the kind of time in which the action of the romance unfolds. As Bakhtin has observed, time in romance bears no relation to biological chronology.

> At the novel's outset the heroes meet each other at a marriageable age, and at the same marriageable age, no less fresh and handsome, they consummate the marriage at the novel's end. Such a form of time, in which they experience a most improbable number of adventures, is not measured off in the novel and does not add up; it is simply days, nights, hours, moments clocked in a technical sense within the limits of each separate adventure. This time—adventure-time, highly intensified, but undifferentiated—is not registered in the slightest way in the age of the heros.[7]

But that time *is* counted in Voltaire's and Pushkin's parodies. *Candide* marries Cunegonde and Pushkin's wizard finally wins the love of his proud maiden when they are already hags. Has it been long since I left you, the wizard asks.

"Rovno sorok let/ Byl devy rokovoj otvet" (Exactly forty years/ Was the maiden's fateful answer).[8] Here the wizard encounters not only time, but also his genre, and the reader is returned to the world of mutability in which he or she reads—and lives. In *Ruslan and Lyudmila*, and in his numerous other generic parodies (e.g., *Gabrieliad*, *Tsar Nikita*, *Count Nulin*, and that encyclopedia of parodies, *Eugene Onegin*), Pushkin also resembles his favorite models, Cervantes, Voltaire, and Sterne, in taking the stylized *language* of his target genres as an emblem of their distance from biographical time and historical flux. Juxtaposing their language of "remote allusions and obscure opinions" (to quote Dr. Johnson's well-known description of pastoral [*Rasselas* . . . , 450]) to a language that is clearly marked as characteristic of a particular group at a particular time, these parodists answer implicit claims to permanence and historical transcendence with the passing speech of a passing world.

Certainties and Skepticisms

> . . . all truths are mistaken; the dialectical process is precisely that today's truths become tomorrow's errors; there is no last number.
> —Eugene Zamyatin[9]

These observations suggest two reasons why utopia is especially vulnerable to parody. First, utopia frequently incorporates other genres that are themselves vulnerable: for example, romance, pastoral, catechism, and sermon (all of which are present in *News from Nowhere or An Epoch of Rest, Being Some Chapters from a Utopian Romance*—that work's full title). Second, and more important, utopia's basic presuppositions and explicit ideologies are radically anti-historical—which is, indeed, one reason that it does draw on other genres that are distant from history. Designed in accordance with what they represent as the unchanging essence of human nature, utopias claim to be, like their ideal of justice itself, timeless. We may recall that Socrates argues in the *Republic* that "things in the most perfect condition" enjoy an "immunity to change" (72-73) from the outside; neither, he adds, would something perfect allow change from within, inasmuch as change from perfection is necessarily deterioration. In utopias of the Christian era, it has been common to cite the promise of the millennium in support of the conceivability and possibility of a fundamentally different kind of temporality—of an age when "the former things are passed away" (Revelation, 21:4) and indeed of a time when "there should be time no longer" (Revelation, 10:6). Utopia is uchronia.

To be sure, there is disagreement among utopias as to whether history will, at a predestined time and by its own laws, transcend itself, or whether escape from history could be accomplished at any point that certain plans are put into effect (e.g., in *Walden Two*—where Rogers asks, "Why don't we just start all over again the right way?"—9). In either case, however, utopias do generally agree that the future will be qualitatively different from, and no mere extension of, the present and past. When Julian West wakes to a world that is, he understands, "the 'new heavens and the new earth . . . ' which the prophet [of the Apocalypse] foretold" (141), he is now able to evaluate his "former contemporaries"—a paradox that is probably designed to stress the change *in* time as well as the passage *of* time—as they could not have evaluated previous societies. "Looking Backward, 2000–1887" is utterly unlike looking backward from 1887 to any earlier time—much as the Last Judgment is unlike any merely historical judgment, and the vision of Plato's escaped prisoner is unlike that of his former comrades in the cave. For the escaped prisoner perceives Reality, not just appearances, has Knowledge, not just opinions; and his many utopian counterparts have escaped an epoch of dreams, for a "time to awaken." News from nowhere differs from all other news in that it will never be outdated. Thus, when the citizens of Morris' pastoral paradise condemn nineteenth-century urban architecture, they are not simply expressing the opinion of one period and civilization about another. They are, rather, voicing a final determination of aesthetic value, one which, unlike any of our evaluations, will never become but one chapter in the history of taste. Utopia anachronizes anachronism.

Anti-utopia tends to regard this kind of revelation—or nonhistorical knowledge—as in principle unobtainable. Its generic presuppositions are radically historical, in the sense that it imagines all futures as other presents, admits no radical discontinuities of temporality, and sees all judgments as limited by the circumstances that occasioned them. As the spirit of utopia is Platonic, that of anti-utopia is, we might say, Heraclitian: for this parodic genre, "everything is in flux" and "all truths are mistaken," by which Zamyatin meant tentative. For anti-utopia, there can be no knowledge in the Platonic sense of certain understanding of Reality, nor can there be any way of achieving Bacon's projected determination of "the Causes, and secret motions of things; and the enlarging of the bounds of Human Empire, to the effecting of all things possible."[10] For anti-utopia, there is, at best, the possibility of continual progress of hypotheses and new hypotheses, with no final determination—no "last number." In short, utopia claims to know, anti-utopia asks why we think we know. Like the novel, it "speculates in categories of ignorance"[11] of both causes and values. When it affirms the existence of universals of human nature, those universals are, characteristically, humanity's unchanging need for growth, creativity, and change itself. To be sure, anti-utopias, at their most complex, may extend considerable sympathy to quixotic seekers after an impossible kind of knowledge or, like Don Quixote himself, after a restored golden age (to which he dedicates himself in bk. 1, ch. 11). Nevertheless, in emphasizing the strength of the need for such a belief, anti-utopias point to the insubstantiality of the grounds; they call attention to the ways in which desire rather than reason has shaped a set of ideas that is as dangerous as it is foolish.

Counterplot #1: Systems and Labyrinths

Memento. For the rest of my life. Write the Russian *Candide*.—
Dostoevsky's notebooks[12]

Like utopia, therefore, anti-utopia is a form of "wisdom literature" or philosophical parable. But instead of telling the story of how the representative of a society faced with apparently unsolvable problems learns the answer to them, it tells one of a number of counterstories about the unavailability of such an answer: it parodies the masterplot with counterplots. One such parody of the Allegory of the Cave is what might be called the allegory of the labyrinth—a labyrinth from which, like those of Borges, there is no escape. Unlike Plato's prisoner and the heroes of most utopias, the heroes of this allegory believe at first in the possibility of definitive answers and timeless truths; but they achieve at last a wise epistemological modesty, a recognition of the inadequacy of all human explanatory systems to account for the complexities of nature and human nature. In short, they begin where their utopian counterparts end, and end where the latter begin—with an understanding that there can be no way out of what Tolstoy's utopian dreamer, Pierre Bezukhov, calls time's "labyrinth of lies."

Rasselas is a good example of this allegory. Believing that happiness "must be something solid and permanent, without fear and without uncertainty" (543; ch. 17), and that he can find the formula for "a perfect government" (597; ch. 44), Rasselas questions the reputedly wise and interviews the apparently good, but discovers at last that the truly wise are those who, like Imlac, understand the limitations of human understanding itself. "Thus it is," Rasselas' sister paraphrases Imlac's thought, "that philosophers are deceived. There are a thousand familiar disputes which reason never can decide; questions that elude investigation, and make logick ridiculous; cases where something must be done, and where little can be said" (556; ch. 29). In order to establish personal and general happiness on unshakable foundations, Rasselas enquires into the cause of good and evil; but he learns that "the causes of good and evil . . . are so various and uncertain, so often entangled with each other, so diversified by various relations, and so much subject to accidents which cannot be foreseen, that he who would fix his condition upon incontestable reasons of preference must live and die inquiring and deliberating" (542; ch. 16). Rasselas comes to a realization still more subversive of his utopian hopes: that goods may exclude each other—"that nature sets her gifts on the right hand and on the left" and that "there are goods so opposed that we cannot seize both, but, by too much prudence, may pass between them at too great a distance to reach either" (567; ch. 29). Rasselas at last becomes convinced of the vanity of looking for goods that are "solid and permanent" when we are fluid and changing. As Imlac has told him, "our minds, like our bodies, are in continuous flux; something is hourly lost, and something acquired" (579; ch. 35). Rasselas' lessons seem to be reflected in *Rasselas*' structure, which closes with "The Conclusion, in Which Nothing Is Concluded." It ends, that is, with a designed non-ending which is emblematic of both the impossibility of final determinations and the artifice of all human constructs—including the construct of narrative art itself.

The most striking example of anti-utopian anti-closure is to be found in *Notes from Underground*. The narrator of that work, it will be recalled, promises, but fails, to end his potentially endless series of self-referential para-doxes; and so the "editor" arbitrarily ends the text, substituting an ellipsis for the "missing" section. "The 'notes' of this paradoxicalist do not end here, however," the editor explains. "He could not resist and continued them. But it also seems to me that we may stop here" (115). The underground man's paradoxes of self-reference and infinite regress are closely related to one of his two key arguments against all-embracing explanatory systems: namely, that their starting points must be chosen arbitrarily and are consequently like-ly to appear, to someone not already committed to the system, as just what is most in need of justification. One system's axioms, he suggests, are another's theorems (and vice versa): there are no axioms *per se*. "Where are the primary causes on which I am to build?" he asks. "Where are my bases? Where am I to get them from? I exercise myself in the process of thinking, and consequently with me every primary cause at once draws after itself another still more pri-mary, and so on to infinity" (16). *Notes from Underground* itself is, indeed, the dramatization of this process, the logic of which is reflected not only in its non-ending, but also in its characteristic sequences of speech, speech about speech, and speech about speech about speech: "You will say that it is vulgar and base to drag all this into public after all the tears and raptures I have my-self admitted. But why is it base? . . . And yet you are right—it really is vulgar and base. And what is most base of all is that I have now started to justify myself to you. And even more base than that is my making this remark now. But that's enough, or, after all, there will be no end to it; each step will be more base than the last" (51).

The underground man's second argument against all-embracing explana-tory systems is that they fail to account for the complex facts of history and human behavior—facts which are, he suggests, essentially unamenable to sys-tematization. "Try it, and cast a look upon the history of mankind. . . . one may say anything about the history of the world—anything that might enter the most disordered imagination. The only thing one cannot say is that it is rational. The very word sticks in one's throat" (26–27). Describing history as a succession of the contingent, irrational, and hence anomalous, he concludes that "all these fine systems—all these theories for explaining to mankind its real normal interests, so that inevitably striving to obtain these interests, it may at once become good and noble—are, in my opinion, so far, mere logical exercises! Yes, logical exercises. . . . But man is so fond of systems and ab-stract deductions that he is ready to distort the truth intentionally, he is ready to deny what he can see and hear just to justify his logic" (20–21).

The first part of *Notes from Underground* could, indeed, be described as a series of encounters of system with anomaly. In chapter after chapter, the underground man (a) paraphrases a utopian explanatory system, (b) presents contrary cases from history or everyday behavior (e.g., the story of the educa-ted man of the nineteenth century with a toothache), and (c) supplies the evidently inadequate answers that his opponents would probably give to ex-plain away anomaly and so to "justify their logic." In chapter 7, in which the underground man's characterization of utopian explanatory systems as "logical exercises" occurs, this pattern is repeated a few times. "Oh tell me," he begins (18),

> who first declared, who first proclaimed, that man only does nasty things because he does not know his own real interests; and that if he were enlightened, if his eyes were opened to his real normal interests, man would at once become good and noble because, being enlightened and understanding his real advantage, he would see his own advantage in the good and nothing else, and we all know that not a single man can knowingly act to his own disadvantage. . . . Oh, the babe! Oh, the pure, innocent child!

The one who "first proclaimed" this theory, or a version of it, was, of course, Socrates; and the underground man here seems to be answering both the *Republic* and a contemporary utopian target, *What Is to Be Done?*, which outlines a similar theory. Dostoevsky's "paradoxicalist" responds with his characteristic examples of quite different kinds of behavior; then supplies the "gentlemen's" likely defense of their system; and, returning to his starting point, both describes and engages in still more examples of the sort of paradoxical behavior which, he says, "breaks down all our classifications, and continually shatters all the systems evolved by lovers of mankind" (20). The psychology of the underground thus refutes the Allegory of the Cave. In a number of chapters, the underground man concludes that "what is to be done"—he repeats the phrase a number of times—is not to escape from the "cellar" (as Chernyshevsky's heroine dreams) but to remain where the "sole vocation of every intelligent man is babble, that is, the intentional pouring of water through a sieve" (17).

System, anomaly, re-affirmation of system—this is also the pattern, repeated many times, of an earlier anti-utopia to which *Notes* alludes: *Candide, or Optimism*. From the Lisbon earthquake and the Grand Inquisitor's auto-da-fé to the tribe of Indians "in the pure state of nature"[13] who have monkeys for lovers, Candide constantly wonders how Pangloss could possibly reconcile each catastrophe or discovery with his optimistic theory. "Candide, terrified, dumbfounded, bewildered, covered with blood, quivering from head to foot, said to himself: 'If this is the best of all possible worlds, what are the others?'" (243). By the end of the narrative, Candide has learned that although the philosopher could find "sufficient reason" for anything, the greater wisdom would be to avoid philosophy altogether—to "work without theorizing" and "cultivate our gardens" (327-328).

Counterplot #2: The Madman

> "I experience through myself the great ideas that space and time are but a fiction. I dwell in all ages."
> " . . . But surely you will agree with me that you and I are both in this room, and that it is now"—the doctor consulted his watch—"half past ten on May the sixth . . . ?"—Vsevolod Garshin, "The Scarlet Flower"[14]

Taken to its extreme, blindness to disconfirmation is madness; and another common parody of utopian plots is, indeed, the story of the man who *thinks* he has found the Truth but who is, for that very reason, evidently insane. Here again, the *Quixote* has often been exemplary, as it probably was, for instance, for Garshin's remarkable allegory on Russian utopianism, "The Scarlet Flower." Set in a madhouse, Garshin's narrative concerns a man who has "discovered" that all the evil in the universe issues from three poppies growing in the asylum yard and describes his attempt to pick those poppies. Swift's Gulliver, who returns to England with hopes of making human society as rational as equine society, is also probably a descendant of Don Quixote as well as of Hythloday. Offering the fourth book of his *Travels* as a plan to "correct every vice and folly to which *Yahoos* are subject" (206), he ends the narrative with a description of what he takes to be his lonely knowledge of the Truth, but what we are likely to recognize as unmistakable signs of madness. As its English title implies, Dostoevsky's *Possessed* (more literally, *The Devils*) is an encyclopedia of such plans and a portrait gallery of such madmen: Shigalev believes that "there can be no solution to the social problem but mine" (409); Shatov places his faith in the messianic mission of the "God-bearing" Russian people; Kirillov has stopped his clock at the moment when he discovered that for him, and by his example for all people, "there should be time no longer." "When all mankind attains happiness then there will be no more time," he explains to Stavrogin, for time "will be extinguished in the mind." "That'll scarcely be possible in our time" (239), Stavrogin replies.

There is considerable irony in the fact that *The Possessed* is itself a *history* of attempts to escape history, a *chronology* of plots to arrest time. Or to put the point differently, Dostoevsky used the very fact that his work was a narrative, which is to say, an explanation of actions and events in terms of causal and temporal sequence, to question the logic of those attempts. As we observe Kirillov's brains splattered on the floor *the moment after* he has shot himself to escape from time and transcend the laws of nature, we may reflect on the impossibility of such an escape and on the inexorability of those laws. We may reflect as well on the biographical causes of such beliefs and on the connections between personality and professed ideology. That is, insofar as we read this narrative as a novel, we look for an "irony of origins" that conditionalizes each claim to unconditionality. It is, indeed, characteristic of political novels in general, as well as anti-utopian novels in particular, to subject ideologies to such unwelcome scrutiny. The kind of assertion that in a utopia (or some other genres) marks the hero's realization of the Truth becomes instead the sign of his madness or folly.

Questions and Inquisitors

Many modern anti-utopias, especially dystopias, are concerned not only with the untenability of claims to certainty, but also with the strength of the epistemological yearning that leads to such claims. The imaginary societies they describe are frequently based on the satisfaction of that yearning. That is, whereas most utopias have based a plan for perfection on a claim to certainty, their modern parodies have often represented the primary attraction of utopianism to be that claim itself. So the narrator of Borges' philosophical parable "Tlön, Uqbar, Orbis Tertius" explains how a conspiracy of idealist philosophers was able to replace our uncertain material world with what he calls a "brave new world"[15] without doubt—a world where people regard not materialism, but idealism as common sense. Having discovered that reason is ultimately inadequate to the real world and that every "system is nothing more than the [arbitrary and tentative] subordination of all aspects of the universe to any one such aspect" (10), people chose, he explains, to accept a fantastic world to which reason *is* adequate. So deep was the desire for such a world, he explains toward the end of his history (17-18), that:

> Almost immediately, reality yielded on more than one account. The truth is that it longed to yield. Ten years ago any symmetry with a semblance of order—dialectical materialism, anti-Semitism, Nazism—was sufficient to entrance the minds of men. How could one do other than submit to Tlön, to the minute and vast evidence of an orderly planet? It is useless to answer that reality is also orderly. Perhaps it is, but in accordance with divine laws—I translate: inhuman laws—which we never quite grasp. Tlön is surely a labyrinth, but it is a labyrinth devised by men, a labyrinth destined to be deciphered by men.

Believing that people cannot be happy so long as they doubt, the founders and rulers of some modern dystopias (e.g., *We* and *Brave New World*) knowingly preside over the falsehood that there are no more unanswered questions. In the context of the utopian literary tradition, that falsehood can be understood as an ironic allusion to the "noble lies" on which Socrates would found his Republic. A closely related dystopian motif, the scene in which the ruler acknowledges the falsehood to a rebel who has detected it, can, moreover, be taken as a parody of those numerous utopian exchanges in which the delineator reveals the truth. The climax of these dystopias, in other words, is the Revelation of the Lie—which is simultaneously the initiation into the Mystery. Having realized that there are indeed unanswered questions, the rebel—who is at odds with society through the very fact of asking such questions—at last confronts the ruler. "Let us talk as adults do after the children have gone to bed; let us talk to the logical end," the ruler of *We* responds to D-503 (200; ellipsis in original):

> I ask: what was it that man from his diaper age dreamed of, tormented himself for, prayed for? He longed for that day when someone would tell him what happiness is, and then would chain him to it. What else are we doing now? The ancient dream about paradise . . . Remember: there in paradise they know no desires any more, no pity, no love; there they are all—blessed.

Or to use D-503's own vocabulary, the new Eden is blessed with a "mathematically faultless happiness" (3) that has solved all equations and determined all unknowns. In *Brave New World*, Mustapha Mond advances a similar argument to the Savage.

Both of these dystopian arguments, as has often been pointed out, are indebted to Dostoevsky's Grand Inquisitor legend, which is, in turn, a development of anti-utopian sketches in *The Diary of a Writer* (e.g., "The Extraordinary Shrewdness of Devils . . . "–January, 76, III, 2). The "legend" is so well known that it is, I think, unnecessary to paraphrase it at length here; but it would be useful to recall that the Inquisitor bases his plan for "the universal happiness of mankind" (*Karamazov*, 305) not on "bread" (like the naive utopists he criticizes) but on saving people from the terror of "all that is exceptional, vague and enigmatic" (302). Indeed, one of his most daring paradoxes is that people have desired bread so strongly not only because it is something to eat, but also because it is something—perhaps the only thing— they can all agree to worship. For the Inquisitor, the attraction of materialism itself is nonmaterial, is mystical: people seek "so incessantly and so painfully . . . to worship what is established beyond dispute . . . and nothing is more certain than bread" (301-302). But even bread, he reasons, will never be enough to make people happy so long as "freedom, free thought and science . . . bring them face to face with . . . marvels and insoluble mysteries" (306), with "conflicting choices and unanswerable problems" (303). For the fact is, he argues, that the most important problems are essentially unanswerable; the truth is that there is no truth; and if life has any meaning at all, it is that God "must have meant to mock" (304) people by creating them to probe the void and put questions to the darkness.

It follows for the Inquisitor that the kingdom must be founded on "deception," on "mystery" (301, 305); or, as the "paradoxicalist" of the *Diary* contends, because there is no paradise we must delude ourselves with the "mirage" of paradise (July–August, 76, IV, 1). The Inquisitor's lie is that the rulers possess a secret Truth; his "firm foundation for setting the conscience of man at rest for ever" (*Karamazov*, 302) is that their secret enables them to resolve all moral problems. "The most painful secrets of their conscience, all, all they will bring to us, and we shall have an answer for all. And they will be glad to believe our answer, for it will save them from the great anxiety and terrible agony they endure at present in making a free decision for themselves" (308).

"And all will be happy, all the millions of creatures except the hundred thousand who rule over them," the Inquisitor concludes. "For only we, we who guard the mystery, shall be unhappy. There will be thousands of millions of happy babes, and a hundred thousand sufferers who have taken upon themselves the curse of the knowledge of good and evil" (308). We shall have more to say later about the extraordinary complexities of this last paradox, but we may observe here that, in a much simpler version, the theme of the suffering, self-sacrificing ruler over a "mirage of paradise" has also been borrowed by modern dystopias. Zamyatin's Benefactor, for instance, claims a similar heroism when he compares himself to those who took on the burden of crucifying Christ. "Does it not occur to you that the part which those above [who nailed Him to the cross] must play is the more difficult, the more important part? If it were not for them, how could that magnificent tragedy ever have been staged? True, they were hissed by the dark crowd, but for that the author of the tragedy, God, should have remunerated them the more liberally, should He not?" (199). In *Brave New World*, too, Mustapha Mond explains sadly that "happiness is a hard master—particularly other people's happiness. A much harder master, if one isn't conditioned to accept it unquestioningly, than truth."[16] Himself a former scientist, a reader of Shakespeare, and, indeed, a believer in God, he seems to echo the Inquisitor's paradoxes when he tells the Savage that in their world God "manifests himself as an absence" (159).

In an important respect, dystopian rulers go one step beyond the Inquisitor. Having a ready-made answer for all questions, they imply, may not be enough to secure the kingdom forever against rebellion. For that it would be necessary to make sure the questions were not asked in the first place. Hypnopedia (in *Brave New World*), hypnosis (in *Lyubimov*), brainwashing (in *1984*), and lobotomy (in *We*) are techniques for this preventive epistemology. Or to put it differently, they are ways of putting into practice the key dystopian insight that the mind, though perhaps incapable of fully understanding nature, is still capable of mind control. I find it interesting to regard that sinister insight as a collective and technological re-interpretation of Stoic doctrine: the gods, Epictetus held, did not give us dominion over the external world, but they did "put in our hands the one blessing that is best of all and master of all, that and nothing else, the power to deal rightly with our impressions."[17]

Counterplot #3: Escape to the Cave

When rebellion against utopia is still possible, anti-utopias may make use of another inversion of the utopian masterplot. This counterplot, which figures as a single incident in a number of anti-utopias written before the twentieth century, and which is usually the main story of modern dystopias, tells, in effect, of an attempt to return to the Cave. Or, to use the imagery of *We*, it tells of a conspiracy to bring about a second Fall, a Fall that would be fortunate not because it would be part of a larger drama that included a greater Return, but because Eden is itself unfortunate. In short, whereas utopias describe an escape *from* history, these anti-utopias describe an escape, or attempted escape, *to* history, which is to say, to the world of contingency, conflict, and uncertainty. Refusing perfection, the anti-utopian hero tries to convince the ruler and his fellow citizens of his paradoxical truths (which are, like their opposites in utopian works, regarded by most as absurd): truths such as the unhappiness of happiness, the desirability of desire, and the advantage of disadvantage. "I'm claiming the right to be unhappy," the Savage says to Mustapha Mond. "Not to mention," the ruler replies (63), "the right to grow old and ugly and impotent; the right to have syphillis and cancer; the right to have too little to eat; the right to be lousy; the right to live in constant apprehension of what may happen tomorrow; the right to catch typhoid; the right to be tortured by unspeakable pains of every kind." There was a long silence.

"I claim them all," said the Savage at last.

Mustapha Mond shrugged his shoulders. "You're welcome," he said.

Anti-utopias generally use this plot to examine and criticize utopian assumptions about the relation of history to human nature. For these anti-utopias, people are not, as utopias imply, beings somehow trapped, against their will and contrary to their nature, in the historical process. On the contrary, it is suggested, people are essentially historical in the sense that for them life can have meaning and action value only if they involve striving, on the basis of imperfect knowledge and in an uncertain world, for elusive goals —goals which are, indeed, valued in part for the difficulty of attaining them. It follows, according to these antiutopias, that to place people in a world where all "the blessings of nature were collected, and its evils extracted and excluded" and where "every desire was immediately granted" (*Rasselas*, 506; ch. 1) would be to inflict a great cruelty on them. So Rasselas, whose story begins in the "happy valley" where the stories of most utopian heroes end, comes to long for unhappiness itself. Sated with perfection, which admits no vicissitudes but "the soft vicissitudes of pleasure and repose" (508), Rasselas begins to desire something to lack so that he might have "something to pursue" (511; ch. 3). He discovers, in short, "The Wants of Him That Wants Nothing" (the title of the third chapter, which presages "The Conclusion, in Which Nothing is Concluded") and questions Imlac as to whether this displeasure with pleasure is unique. "Great Prince, said Imlac, I shall speak the truth: I know not one of all your attendants who does not lament the hour when he entered this retreat. . . . Those whose minds have no impressions but of the present moment, are either corroded by malignant passions, or sit stupid in the gloom of perpetual vacancy" (533–534; ch. 12). Still worse, he says, "the invitations, by which they allure others to a state which they feel to be wretched, proceed from the natural malignity of hopeless misery. . . . They envy the liberty which their folly has forfeited, and would gladly see all mankind imprisoned like themselves" (534; ch. 12). After their escape, Rasselas, who still wishes to establish a perfect kingdom, learns at last that he wishes for a contradiction. In the well-known passage where they survey the pyramids and speculate on the reason for such unnecessary labor, Imlac suggests that the pharaohs, like Rasselas in the happy valley, may have suffered from "that hunger of imagination which preys incessantly on life, and must be always appeased by some employment. Those who have already all that they can enjoy, must enlarge their desires. He that has built for use, till use is supplied, must begin to build for vanity, and extend his plan to the utmost power of human performance, that he may not be soon reduced to form another wish" (573; ch. 32).

Boredom, vacancy, and satiety leading to malignancy, vanity, and cruelty—

that is also the logic of Dostoevsky's use of this counterplot. In the first sketch on spiritualism in the January, 1876, *Diary*, for instance, Dostoevsky imagines the likely consequences of the immediate granting—say, by devils—of all human wishes. Though people would, at first, be rapturous and would exclaim that only now will humanity, liberated from the necessity of work, begin to reveal its potential, it is unlikely, Dostoevsky asserts, that this rapture would last even for a single generation (January, 76, III, 2; italics in original):

> People would understand that there can be no happiness in inaction, that thought dies without work, that one cannot love one's neighbor without sacrificing one's labor to him . . . and that *happiness is not in happiness but in the attaining of happiness.* Boredom and ennui would set in: everything is accomplished, there is nothing left to do; everything is known, there is nothing more to find out. Mass suicides—not just separate ones as we see today—would take place; people would gather in crowds, taking each other by the hand and exterminating themselves at once, by the thousands, by means of some new method revealed to them along with the other discoveries.

And then, Dostoevsky concludes his projected history, people would rebel against this "paradise" and reject the devils and their kingdom forever. No doubt, he observes wryly, the devils have foreseen this outcome, and that is why they have not tried to establish their rule in this way.

A similar argument and projected history are advanced in *Notes from Underground*, which is probably the most important single source of the modern dystopia. In a much cited passage, the underground man defends the familiar paradox that people strive for goals they would be unhappy—and instinctively know they would be unhappy—to reach. Humanity, he writes, "likes the process of attaining, but does not quite like to have attained, and that, of course, is terribly funny. In short, man is made comically; there is evidently a sort of pun in it all" (30). To extend Camus' reading of this passage, *only* Sisyphus can be happy. This paradox, the underground man reasons, is closely related to what he calls man's puzzling, "passionate love for destruction and chaos" (29): he destroys the edifice in order to avoid completing it. It follows for the underground man that certain happiness is certain unhappiness. Taking the utopian image of a world beyond history to an extreme, the underground man describes (22) a time when

> all human actions will . . . be tabulated . . . like tables of logarithms up to 108,000, and entered in a table; or better still, there would be published certain edifying works like the present encyclopedic lexicons, in which everything will be so clearly calculated and designated that there will be no more incidents or adventures in the world.
>
> Then . . . new economic relations will be established, all ready-made and computed with mathematical exactitude, so that every possible ques-

tion will vanish in a twinkling, simply because every possible answer to it will be provided. Then the crystal palace will be built.

And some time later, the underground man continues, it would be smashed. For boredom would ensue; masochism and sadism would follow; and at last, for no reason at all, "it would not surprise me in the least, if . . . a gentleman with an ignoble, or rather with a reactionary and ironical, countenance were to arise and, putting his arms akimbo, say to us all: 'What do you think, gentlemen, hadn't we better kick over all that rationalism at one blow, scatter it to the winds, just to send these logarithms to the devil, and to let us live once more according to our own foolish will!'" (23). Moreover, the underground man writes, the ironical gentleman would be sure to find followers who would also reject perfection and choose choice. "One's own free unfettered choice, one's own fancy, worked up at times to frenzy—why that is that very 'most advantageous advantage' which we have overlooked, which comes under no classification and through which all systems and theories are continually being sent to the devil" (23).

Zamyatin's *We* is the story of just such a revolt—in the name of foolishness, caprice, and unpredictability—against a world where there is "no place for contingencies" and where "nothing unexpected can happen" (129). Indeed, as D-503 explains in Record 6 of his manuscript, "the ideal (it's clear) is to be found where nothing happens" (24). Developing a complex network of allusions to *Notes*, *We* makes particularly extensive use of the underground man's mathematical metaphors for a world beyond history, especially the one he uses most frequently: "twice two makes four." As the underground man uses it, the logic of this metaphor would seem to be that an ideal world would exclude unforeseen events as surely as mathematics rules out unforeseen results from the multiplication of two numbers: like mathematical equations, utopia is, in other words, beyond the reach of personality, idiosyncrasies, or the particularities of experience that shape the lives of people in history. For this reason, the underground man finds the equation and its social analogue to be "insulting" and "simply a piece of insolence." "Two times two makes four," he declares, "is a fop standing with arms akimbo barring your path and spitting. I admit that two times two makes four is an excellent thing, but if we are to praise everything, two times two makes five is sometimes also a very charming little thing" (30). *We* probably alludes to this well-known passage when D-503 observes that "there are no more fortunate and happy people than those who live according to the correct, eternal laws of the multiplication table. No hesitation! No errors! There is but one truth, and there is but one path to it; and that truth is: four, and that path is: two times two. Would it not seem absurd for these happily multiplied twos suddenly to begin thinking of some foolish kind of freedom?—i.e. (is it not clear?), of a mistake?" (64). It is, of course, just such an "absurd" turn of events that the unruly "numbers" (so people are called in the world of *We*) conspire to produce. They want to shatter the "ideal," and to create a world where events are unforeseen, where choices can and must be made, and where actions consequently have value. To be sure, their rebellion ultimately fails; but insofar as they do create a brief period of uncertainty, the very fact of a rebellion already constitutes its partial, if ephemeral, success. As I-330 observes at the moment of greatest uncertainty, it is exhilarating to live in a day without a sure tomorrow. "Nobody knows what tomorrow will be," she exclaims to D-503. "Neither I nor anyone else knows; it is unknown! Do you realize that all that was certain has come to an end? Now things will be new, improbable, unforeseen!" (136-137).

The rebels of We seek to re-establish the possibility of possibility: the goal of their rebellion is, in this sense, rebellion itself. Choosing the name "Mephi," they hope to reconstitute that "indispensable minus," which, as Ivan Karamazov's devil observes, makes the world historical rather than "an endless church service" (781). The passages about the ideology of the Mephis may be designed to recall not only Dostoevsky's novel and numerous romantic images of a heroic Satan, but also the Russian anarchist critique of Marxism—a critique which, like the Mephis' rejection of perfection, involved a paradoxical celebration of negation and rebellion per se. Bakunin, for instance, argued, contra Marx, that negation and rebellion are not only means for changing the world, but are also the highest human faculty—the faculty which, in Bakunin's view, distinguishes man from other animals and makes him human. It followed for Bakunin that a world without rebellion would be a world to rebel against; and that Satan, in liberating man from such a world, enabled him to "constitute himself a man" and to begin "his distinctively human history."[18] In We, I-330 develops a similar mystique of negation and revolution, which are, she tells D-503, as infinite as numbers and, so long as people remain human, as sure to continue. Contrasting the "energy" of demonic rebellion with the "entropy" of angelic torpor, she seems to echo Bakunin's famous aphorism: "The will to destroy is a creative will" (58). Inasmuch as We closes with the final destruction (by lobotomy) of this power to destroy, its end, like that of many later dystopias, would seem to coincide with the end of humanity itself. In this self-conscious use of literary closure as an emblem of apocalyptic closure, We seems to allude to another kind of metaliterary play on endings in some earlier anti-utopias. As Notes from Underground and Rasselas each end with an ostentatious non-ending that marks the impossibility of final determinations, We ends with a conclusion in which everything is concluded.

The brief and final rebirth of contingency and alternative possibilities in D-503's world implies a re-emergence of personality as well—which is to say, of unique selves describable in terms of a particular history of choices and accidents in unforeseen and unrepeatable circumstances. The rebirth of history, in other words, entails the rebirth of biography. At the beginning of his manuscript, D-503 explains that the greatest achievement of his society is to have eliminated both personality and individual biography. Each "I," he observes, is now fully explicable in terms of a precise vocabulary available to all; "numbers" have become as transparent as the glass walls of their dwellings; "I" has ceased to be anything but a division of "We," a division, moreover, with no remainder. The irony of these confident declarations is, of course, that they are made in a manuscript that records D-503's discovery of such a remainder in himself. He develops "an incurable soul" (81) that is, as he puts it, opaque to the light of reason and irreducible to a mathematical formula.

Frightened by this disease of self, D-503 repeatedly attempts an impossible reduction of personality and idiosyncrasy to generalized mathematical formulae. Those attempts become a source of considerable wit in Zamyatin's work, as the narrator is led to more and more daring mathematical metaphors for a realm of experience that we are used to regarding as essentially unamenable to this kind of description. The effect is something like that of English metaphysical poetry, and the wit derives from the unexpectedness and unconventionality of the comparisons. For example, D-503 compares the soul to an irrational, imaginary root—"the square root of minus one"—the resemblance being that both are "strange, foreign, terrible" (37). Like the soul, "this irrational root . . . tortured me [because] it could not be thought out. It could not be defeated because it was beyond reason" (37). At another point, D-503 compares his discoveries to non-Euclidian geometry. Like Ivan Karamazov, to whose metaphorical use of Lobachevskian mathematics Zamyatin's work probably alludes, D-503 takes this counterintuitive and apparently absurd mathematical system as an emblem of a universe beyond the reach of any "Euclidian, earthly mind" (*Karamazov*, (279).

Stretching language and logic to their limits, D-503 begins to realize that, in self and in nature, there are worlds beyond words and realms unreachable by reason. Surveying the unfamiliar world beyond the Green Wall, he reflects on "the debris of logic" (95) and the failure of ordering systems. Appropriately enough, the chapter in which he makes this admission surrenders the headings that other chapters have used to describe and order their contents. "No Headings—It Is Impossible!" is the anti-heading of Record 27. The self-referential headings of some other chapters also record the breakdown of linguistic and logical control.

We *and the Rebirth of the Novel*

As D-503 changes, so does his manuscript. Like its author, the manuscript acquires a history, a history which D-503 narrates in some detail and which he describes as a change in the work's genre. His work begins as a sample of the literature of his world, but step by step, before his amazed eyes, it is transformed into a sample of the literature of ours. Answering the summons of the Benefactor to write "treatises, poems, manifestoes, odes, and other compositions on the greatness and beauty of the United State" (3)—didactic works to aid in convincing other planets to submit to utopian rule—D-503 decides to record "the things I see, the things I think, or, to be more exact, the things *we* think. Yes, 'we'; that is exactly what I mean, and *We*, therefore, will be the title of my records" (4). Because all lives are the same, he reasons, a description of his experiences will be "a derivative of our life, of our mathematical, perfect life in the United State" (4). But as he acquires an "I," his *We* becomes our *We*. Describing unexpected events, his "poem" or treatise becomes a narrative; and as a narrative about the emergence and development of personality, it becomes a novel. "With great sorrow," D-503 writes of his failure to compose the sort of work he intended, "I notice that instead of a correct and strictly mathematical poem in honor of the United State, I am writing a fantastic adventure novel" (97)—"an ancient, strange novel" (167) about mysterious dreams, social conflict, and self-division. Speculating on the simultaneous re-emergence of personal history and the ancient novel, he comes to agree with I-330, who draws an interesting connection between the two: "Man is like a novel," she observes. "Up to the last page one does not know what the end will be. It would not be worth reading otherwise" (151).

A novel about the birth of the novel, literature about literature's rediscovery, *We* is rich in self-reference. Beginning with its title, which names both D-503's "poem" and Zamyatin's novel, *We* tells the story of *We*. That is, the text frequently describes its own history, not only as a re-emerging literary genre, but also, after the manner of Sterne and Shklovsky, as a physical manuscript. Record 4, for instance, tells how a tear blotted Record 4; and in Record 19, D-503 uses the open pages of *We* to cover an incriminating pink check (106; ellipses in second paragraph in original):

> I quickly opened this manuscript, *We*, and with its pages I covered the check. . . .
>
> "See here, I am still busy writing. Already 170 pages . . . Something quite unexpected comes out in this writing . . . "

D-503 eventually realizes that he can no longer use his poem in honor of the United State as a "cover" for his conspiratorial activities because *We* itself has become the most incriminating evidence of all. "Quick! To my desk!" he writes in Record 28. "I opened this manuscript and took up my pen so that they [the Guardians] should find me at this work, which is for the benefit of the United State. Suddenly I felt every hair on my head living, separated, moving. 'What if they should read even one page of those most recently written?'" (154). Zamyatin also seems to glance at his Formalist contemporaries when his narrator knocks the manuscript onto the floor, scattering the pages. Perhaps, D-503 remarks wryly, they are now an apt emblem of the world they describe. "Even if I put them back in the right order there will be no real order," he observes. "There will still be thresholds, gaps, x's" (125).

As D-503 grows more and more distant from his world, he even begins to suspect its fictionality. "Oh, if only this were a novel, and not my actual life" (97–98), he wishes upon first discovering the resemblance of his records to the ancient genre—a wish that is, from the reader's point of view, a wish-come-true. So he himself seems on the verge of realizing when, three records later, he imagines telling his fellow characters that they do not exist outside the pages of *We*. "Perhaps all of you are only my shadows," he thinks during one encounter with the woman from the Ancient House (113),

Did I not populate these pages, which only recently were white quadrangular deserts, with you? Without me could they whom I shall guide over the narrow paths of my lines, could they ever see you?

Of course I did not say all this to the old woman. From experience I know that the most torturing thing is to inoculate someone with a doubt as to the fact that he or she is a three-dimensional reality, and not some other reality.

Exempting himself from this ontological threat, D-503—for whom events are "as distant . . . as though written in a book" (70)—seems to think of himself as between two worlds. From this liminal position, he enjoys a unique relationship with his readers. "I believe you will understand that it is harder for me to write than it ever was for any other author throughout human history. Some of them wrote for contemporaries, some for future generations, but none of them ever wrote for their ancestors" (23). Although ostensibly addressed to his interplanetary readers, who are like D-503's ancestors in being primitive, this passage can also be taken to refer to his real readers—his "ancestors" from "the antediluvian time of all those Shakespeares and Dostoevskys."

Anti-utopian Metafiction

As I have been suggesting throughout this chapter, this kind of self-referential play on the fictional frame is not uncommon in anti-utopias. Anti-utopias are often rich in such play not only because, like the works of all anti-genres, they recontextualize the works of another genre, but also because their target —utopia—is itself a genre of threshold literature. Themselves fictional, anti-utopias characteristically parody—bare the devices of and the motives for—utopian classificatory ambivalence.

The many envoys to the reader in *We* probably allude to similar passages in *Notes*: the underground man, it will be recalled, tells his readers that they are only "an empty form—I shall never have readers" (35), a declaration to which one of his readers, the "editor," seems to respond when he describes the author of the *Notes*, and the *Notes* themselves, as "of course imaginary" (3). In *Lyubimov* (English title: *The Makepeace Experiment*), this peculiar dialogue of text with footnote becomes an open and ongoing argument between the narrator and a voice "from under the ground,"[19] which is to say, with a footnoter who interrupts the text with his distracting numbers, provokes the narrator with his unwelcome qualifications, and, at last, invades the text itself, briefly displacing the narrator to the footnotes. "We are writing the book jointly, in layers" (58), he explains, in the text, to the narrator with whom he shares authority. We may also observe metaliterary "layering" in Shklovsky's brief anti-utopian narrative, "Bundle."[20] The inner of two frames to *The Knight's Move*, "Bundle" embeds its lecture against communist epistemology and aesthetics in a story within a story within a story within a story. No less self-conscious, Borges' "Tlön, Uqbar, Orbis Tertius" leads its readers through a labyrinth of frames and contradictory textual self-characterizations. By the end of the story a few readers may recognize that it is itself the hypothetical work the narrator and his friend plan in the opening paragraph. "We became lengthily engaged in a vast polemic," the narrator recalls, "concerning the composition of a novel in the first person, whose narrator would omit or disfigure the facts and indulge in various contradictions which would permit a few readers—very few readers—to perceive an atrocious and banal reality. From the remote depths of the corridor, the mirror spied upon us" (3). Perhaps *Rasselas* is also reflected in its own mirror when the prince, who has discovered the inefficacy of all remedies or consolations for human misery, discovers as well "the inefficacy of polished periods and studied sentences" (547; ch. 18).

To be sure, the metafictional aspects of Borges', Shklovsky's, and Zamyatin's anti-utopias probably reflect not only certain traditions of this antigenre, but also their respective authors' interest both in the theory of literature and in the more general self-consciousness of literary modernism. It is likely, indeed, that the attraction of anti-utopia for some twentieth-century authors and audiences can be partially attributed to its traditional combination of literary self-consciousness and epistemological skepticism—much as, for that matter, the attraction of utopia for other authors and audiences (e.g., in the Soviet Union) can be attributed to its traditional combination of didacticism and epistemological certainty. In general, a number of factors interact to make or keep a genre vital, interesting, and current for writers and readers. Changes in the relative importance of those factors are likely to make different aspects of a generic tradition prominent and, consequently, to affect the genre's evolution; in particular, literary modernism seems to have "foregrounded" anti-utopia's traditional concern with its own language and literariness. It would be useful to stress, however, that self-conscious play on the boundaries of fiction is by no means limited to *modernist* anti-utopias. It appears, as we have noted, in *Rasselas* and *Notes from Underground* as well, and may be found as early as *Gulliver's Travels*. As early or earlier, it is also particularly common in the meta-utopias to be discussed below (e.g., in More's *Utopia* and Diderot's *Supplement to Bougainville's 'Voyage'*). In his framing letter, Gulliver complains that some readers "are so bold as to think my book of travels a mere fiction out of my own brain; and have gone so far as to drop hints that the Houyhnhnms and Yahoos have no more existence than the inhabitants of Utopia" (207). Swift here refers to the framing letters to More's work, letters which vouched for the veracity of Hythloday's account and of More's report of it. Swift probably also alludes to the debates since the Renaissance (and before) on the relation of fiction to both lies and history and to those many "extraordinary voyages" that tried to deceive credulous readers with descriptions of improbable adventures and unreal societies.[21] As Swift was no doubt aware, parodies of such claims of veracity, and of readers who could be taken in by them, occur in the *Quixote*—which in this respect, too, has been exemplary for anti-utopia—and in some ancient menippean satires such as Seneca's *Pumpkinization* and Lucian's *True History*.

Of course, most utopias have not claimed to describe an *existing* ideal society. But they have often advanced an analogous claim which, from the anti-utopian point of view, is likely to appear all the more dangerous for being less obviously incredible and not evidently falsifiable. As we observed in the second section of this study, utopias from Plato on have tended to contrast the ephemeral world before our eyes with the timeless ideal of the perfect society, which, because of either its conformity with the essential nature of things or its inevitable realization in the future, is the higher Truth. In some utopias, such as "The Dream of a Ridiculous Man" and *What Is to Be Done?*, the questioner sees that society in a dream or vision and awakens to an understanding that what he or she has seen is "not a dream," but Reality. In others, such as *News from Nowhere*, the questioner learns that what has always been regarded as the idle fiction of poets is no fiction, but future fact. Utopia, I pointed out earlier, is often presented as the place where "fiction" and "reality" merge, where mimesis has been reversed and reality has imitated art. I suggested as well that utopian literary works blur a distinction analogous to that between vision and reality, namely that between fiction and nonfiction. They often do so, for example, by embedding the utopian fiction in a non-fictional frame that claims to be less, not more, real than the embedded fiction; the framing section may also claim that "all the things I have just been exclaiming are not a paradox, but the perfect truth . . . Your whole trouble is that they are incredible to you" ("The Golden Age in the Pocket," *Diary*, January, 76, I, 4).

Asserting and then denying its own fictionality, utopia is a threshold genre about reality on the threshold. In parodic contrast, anti-utopia insists on the danger of confusing fiction with nonfiction—or social "fiction" with social fact—and both locates the causes and examines the consequences of that confusion. Thus, in "The Dangerous Prevalence of Imagination," the chapter in *Rasselas* that deals with the mad astronomer who has come to believe he controls the heavens, Imlac discusses the ease with which dreamers succumb to madness (596):

> "To indulge the power of fiction, and send imagination out upon the wing, is often the sport of those who delight too much in silent speculation. . . . In time some particular train of ideas fixes the attention, all other intellectual gratifications are rejected, the mind, in weariness or leisure, recurs constantly to the favourite conception, and feasts on the luscious falsehood whenever she is offended with the bitterness of truth. By degrees the reign of fancy is confirmed; she grows first imperious, and in time despotick. Then fictions begin to operate as realities, false opinions fasten upon the mind, and life passes in dreams of rapture or of anguish."

The princess herself then confesses that she has so succumbed to dreams of a pastoral paradise that she can sometimes hear the sheep bleat; and Rasselas admits that he has given in to "an indulgence of fantastick delight more dangerous than yours. I have frequently endeavoured to image the possibility of a perfect government, by which all wrong should be restrained, all vice reformed, and all the subjects preserved in tranquility and innocence.... and I start, when I think with how little anguish I once supposed the death of my father and my brothers." Their teacher then draws a key anti-utopian lesson: "Such, says Imlac, are the effect of visionary schemes: when we first form them we know them to be absurd, but familiarise them by degrees, and in time lose sight of their folly" (597; ch. 44).

To defamiliarize this familiarization is an important goal of anti-utopian writers. Whereas utopias frequently obscure the boundary between the fantastic and the real, and the analogous boundary between fiction and nonfiction, anti-utopias tend to emphasize those boundaries. We have seen that one way in which they do so is to tell the story of someone who crosses, or leads others to cross, those boundaries unawares. Another is to use metafictional devices, which—by that "logic of anomalies" which the Formalists discussed so well—may call attention to the distinction between fiction and nonfiction through a systematic and ostentatious failure to observe it. *It is, in other words, in order to parody the ways in which utopias function as a genre on the boundaries of fiction that anti-utopias play so frequently on their own fictionality and literariness.* Themselves unambiguously fictional and literary, anti-utopias *represent* threshold works that exploit a double status. Implicitly responding to numerous utopian frames that assert a fiction to be "no fiction," for instance, anti-utopias sometimes include unmistakably fictional frames that deny even their own fictionality. Or they may parody utopias' characteristic embedding of dreams and visions by leading their readers through an extensive labyrinth of frames, and frames within frames. It would seem to be the hope of anti-utopian writers that the experience of negotiating such a literary labyrinth, and of having to distinguish levels of fictionality, will alert its readers to the more sinister labyrinths constructed by those who would obscure the distinctions between political reality and political "fictions," myths—and lies.

Utopia, Anti-utopia, and Their Readers

Itself a didactic genre, anti-utopia bares the devices of another didactic genre in order to deprive those devices of their effectiveness. Its counterlessons, in other words, concern not only the danger and folly of utopian lessons, but also the duplicitous strategies by which those lessons are taught. To recall one such strategy toward which anti-utopias have frequently directed attention, utopias often set up a metaphorical equation between the journey to the utopian world and the reading of the utopian work—an equation which, in placing readers in the traveler's position, may be helpful in persuading them to repeat the traveler's conversion. Utopias that use this strategy may also mirror the typology of listeners *in* the work with a typology of readers *of* the work: as the listeners choose to be either converts or scoffers, the readers are asked to make the same choice. As H. G. Wells observes in the afterword to *A*

Modern Utopia, utopias characteristically end with the "formation of committees, and even the commencement of subscriptions" (371) from readers newly dedicated to realizing the fiction. Wells might have added that authors of utopias also tend to anticipate, as Andreae and Dostoevsky do, a hostile reaction from readers who are likely to "answer me with some sophism" (*Christianopolis*, 140) or to "laugh at all these 'dreams' about Russian destiny" (*Diary*, June, 76, II, 4). Prefaces or afterwords that project such histories of the work's reception have been a frequent target of anti-utopian parody. Gulliver's introductory letter to his *Travels*, for instance, exemplifies both the pride and paranoia that exaggerated expectations of either approval or condemnation imply. Writing to his cousin Sympson about his disappointed hopes for making people as rational as horses, Gulliver complains (205-206) that

> instead of seeing a full stop to all abuses and corruptions, at least in this little island, as I had reason to expect: behold, after above six months warning, I cannot learn that my book hath produced one single effect according to my intentions: I desired you would let me know by a letter, when party and faction were extinguished; judges learned and upright; pleaders honest and modest, with some tincture of common sense; and Smithfield blazing with pyramids of lawbooks; the young nobility's education entirely changed; the physicians banished; the female *Yahoos* abounding in virtue, honor, truth and good sense; courts and levees of great ministers thoroughly weeded and swept; wit, merit and learning rewarded; all disgracers of the press in prose and verse, condemned to eat nothing but their own cotton, and quench their thirst with their own ink. These, and a thousand other reformations, I firmly counted upon by your encouragement; as indeed they were plainly deducible from the precepts delivered in my book. And, it must be owned, that seven months were a sufficient time to correct every vice and folly to which *Yahoos* are subject . . .

The extraordinary arrogance of Gulliver to his readers—like that of utopians from Plato to Skinner toward the benighted citizens they would instruct—reaches a paroxysm of vanity in Gulliver's concluding lines. "I must freely confess," writes this ancestor of Shigalev (208),

> that since my last return, some corruptions of my *Yahoo* nature have revived in me by conversing with a few of your species . . . else I should never have attempted so absurd a project as that of reforming the *Yahoo* race in this kingdom; but I have now done with all such visionary schemes for ever.

Purportedly written six months after the rest of his *Travels*, Gulliver's letter seems to look forward to—or, in Shklovsky's phrase, to "parody in advance"—the frames of later utopias. It will be recalled that some utopias have developed techniques of temporal layering in order to tell, and, so far as possible, to control, the story of their own reception—techniques which have in-

cluded prefaces, afterwords, letters from readers, and, in the case of the
Diary, a periodical form. The second book of the *Quixote*, in which Cervantes' heroes encounter readers of the first book, has probably been an important exemplar for numerous anti-utopian parodies of such layering. Thus,
"Tlön, Uqbar, Orbis Tertius," which was actually written in 1940, represents
a work consisting of an article published in 1940 and a postscript dated 1947.
"I reproduce the preceding article just as it appeared in the *Anthology of
Fantastic Literature* (1940), with no omission other than that of a few metaphors and a kind of sarcastic summary which now seem frivolous" (14), the
postscript begins its account of how, since the publication of the article, the
world has in effect *become* an "anthology of fantastic literature." Tracing the
secret history of the Encyclopedia of Tlön ("the vastest undertaking ever carried out by man"—15) from its beginnings in the time of "George Berkeley
. . . and the curious book by Andrea" (15) to the present "intrusion of this
fantastic world into the world of reality" (16), the author of the postscript
looks forward with deep sadness to the time when, in a world with only a
"fictitious past" and, indeed, with no concept that "the spatial persists in
time" (9), there will be no "place" for chronicles like his own. "Then English
and French and mere Spanish will disappear from the globe," he concludes a
narrative that will evidently have no readers. "I pay no attention to all this
and go on revising, in the still days at the Androgué hotel, an uncertain Que-
vedian translation (which I do not intend to publish) of Browne's *Urn Burial*"
(18).

Sinyavsky's parody of these utopian techniques is still more labyrinthine.
Like *We*, *Lyubimov* also tells two stories—one concerning the utopian community, the other concerning the composition and expected reception of the
manuscript itself—and for each Sinyavsky uses temporal layering. (The "co-
author," it will be recalled, describes the book as written "in layers.") In the
first story, footnotes confirm predictions made in the text (e.g., one footnote
proclaims that "History has since proved me right!"—41); in the second, a
preface and an afterword about the work's authorship parody the self-referential frames of many utopias. In an interesting inversion of utopian endings
(the "formation of committees" and the "commencement of subscriptions"),
the chronicler of this utopia, writing after its fall to the Soviet government,
concludes with regrets that he ever began the incriminating manuscript and
with hopes that it will have no readers at all. His closing words are an appeal
to his mysterious co-author to conceal the document from the secret police.
"Strictly between ourselves—but you really mustn't breathe a word, Profes-
sor—I told you a lie when I said that things were not as bad as they might
be," he says, retracting an earlier statement planted for a possible investigation (192):

> The fact is, they couldn't be worse. . . . Any moment there will be a new
> wave of arrests. If they search the house and find this manuscript under
> the floorboards, they'll pick up every single one of us. Listen to me, Pro-
> fessor. After all, you are my co-author. Will you hide this wretched book

away for the time being? Keep it in your inaccessible safe for the present?
. . . Look after it for a bit. You do recognise it as your property, don't
you?

Inasmuch as Sinyavsky himself published his work in the West under a
protective pseudonym (his own "co-author"), this concluding reference to
the perils of authorship evidently applies to him as well. As we have observed,
frame-breaking of this sort is not unusual in Russian literature, where it
has been a commonplace at least since Pushkin that one of the implied readers of literary works, especially dissident works, is the secret police. The fictional author of *Lyubimov* is, indeed, quite aware of this unwelcome potential audience as he begins his work with a description of a characteristically
Soviet form of writer's block. "I swear I'm not directly responsible," he defends his yet unwritten work (24-25; ellipses in original):

> . . . if I'm caught, I'll deny everything. If I have to stand my trial, hands
> and feet bound, face to face with a terrible judge, I'll recant, I'll say there's
> not a word of truth in it.—"Citizen Judge," I'll say, "I've been slandered
> and confused and tripped up. You can shoot me if you like but I'm an in-
> nocent man."
>
> Now I come to think of it, this may be the very reason why it's taking
> me such a time to begin. . . . It's simply that I want to stay alive! Well,
> who wouldn't? It's nice . . . Nice to have a drink and cigarette . . . Nice to
> read a book in peace and quiet (reading isn't like writing).

As Sinyavsky's readers were no doubt aware, however, reading can be almost as dangerous as writing when what one reads is *Lyubimov*. Sinyavsky,
in other words, alludes to the reading, as well as the writing, of his book. That
allusion becomes particularly interesting when one is aware, first, that the
Soviet Union, like the nightmarish societies of dystopian literature, claims to
be the realization of the utopian ideal; and, second, that a central action of
most dystopias (*Brave New World*, *1984*, *Fahrenheit 451*) is the reading of a
forbidden work of literature. In *Lyubimov*, that forbidden work is *Lyubimov*
itself, and its central characters, who read a novel in a post-novelistic world,
are its own endangered audience.

We have seen that for many utopias (including *What Is to Be Done?*, *News
from Nowhere*, *Looking Backward*—and, for that matter, the *Republic*) traditional literature is something to be overcome. For dystopias, it is something
to be regained: which is why the hero's discovery of personality and history
often takes the form of his rediscovery of pre-utopian authors. Quite frequently, a dystopia's measure of the inhumanity of a realized utopia is that
no one would appreciate the values or understand the presuppositions of traditional literature—including the dystopia itself. In a brave new world, no one
would comprehend *Brave New World*; *Fahrenheit 451* would be burned; and
the chronicle of Tlön, written in a dead language—our language—and addressed to an extinct readership, would be unread. Whereas utopias invite
their readers to contemplate a world in which they would at last be at home,

dystopias invite their readers to contemplate one in which they would have "no place" at all. Nowhere is to be populated by Nobody—or by nobody like us. Perhaps the most terrifying record of *We* is the last, which describes the death of literature (and of all that an understanding of literature requires) forever. Looking over his manuscript, the lobotomized narrator (his imagination has been removed) can no longer recognize his own work, nor make sense of his rediscovery of the world and literature of his "ancestors"—which is to say, of us. "Is it possible that I, D-503, really wrote these two hundred and twenty pages?" he asks. "Is it possible that I ever felt, or imagined I felt, all this?" (217). The end of *We* is the end of us. Zamyatin invites his readers to consider a world without them, a world in which, as Zamyatin once predicted, literature's only future will be its past.[22]

PART 3: Meta-utopia

> Some readers will probably want to know what I think of Pechorin's character. My reply may be found in the title of this book. "But that is a bitter irony!" they will say. I do not know.—Mikhail Lermontov, *A Hero of Our Time*[1]

Metaparody

The books written by Borges' inhabitants of Tlön "invariably include both the thesis and the antithesis, the rigorous pro and con of a doctrine. A book which does not contain its counterbook is considered incomplete" (*Labyrinths*, 13). We reserved the term "parody" for those double-voiced texts or utterances that clearly indicate which of their conflicting voices is to be regarded as authoritative. The audience of a parody—that is, the readers who identify a text as a parody—knows for sure with which voice they are expected to agree. We may now consider a class of texts that are designed so that readers do *not* know. In texts of this type, each voice may be taken to be parodic of the other; readers are invited to entertain each of the resulting contradictory interpretations in potentially endless succession. In this sense, such texts remain fundamentally open, and if readers should choose either interpretation as definitive, they are likely to discover that this choice has been anticipated and is itself the target of parody. Caught between contradictory hermeneutic directives—between "this is a parody" and "this is a parody of a parody"—readers may witness the alternation of statement and counterstatement, interpretation and antithetical interpretation, up to a conclusion which fails, often ostentatiously, to resolve their hermeneutic perplexity. We shall refer to texts that are designed to exploit this dialogue between parody and counterparody (or, as we shall see, between genre and anti-genre) as *metaparodies*. Inasmuch as they create resonance between contradictory hermeneutic directives, metaparodies constitute a special type of threshold art. Readers of a metaparody are expected to comprehend the work not as the compromise between book and counterbook, but as their ultimately inconclusive dialectic.

Metaparodies frequently work by first parodying an original, then parodying the parody of the original. Readers of the *Quixote*, for instance, may be reasonably sure that the first book is a parody directed at naive readers of romances and tales of knight-errantry. But they may be less sure about the second book, which seems to be directed at readers of the first book as well—readers who, we recall, appear as characters in the second book and are portrayed as growing increasingly trivial in their complacent and sterile mockery. If Don Quixote is foolish, then so are they who think him foolish—a paradox that corresponds to the essentially ambiguous vision of the work. Generally speaking, metaparodies anticipate readers of varying degrees of sophistication and appreciation of ambiguity, and are constructed to sort out, and so to define implicitly a typology of, their own readers. Ambiguities similar to those of the *Quixote* are also developed in Pushkin's metaparodic "novel in verse," *Eugene Onegin*, which has been interpreted both as a romantic novel and (as Shklovsky argued in his essay on "Pushkin and Sterne")[2] as a parody directed at readers of romantic novels. (Its prefatory verses, which describe the work as "a collection of motley chapters/ Half-humorous and half-sad," seem to invite both readings.) We may add that *Onegin* is also a parody directed at readers of parodies, and the readings it seems to anticipate and "parody in advance" include Formalist ones. Not simply a work in the tradition of Sterne and Byron, *Onegin* is also a parody of that tradition. *Onegin*, in effect, includes its own parody, and its essentially open dialogue is designed to exemplify a deep suspicion of all "statements" about the world—including its own. This openness of vision may be taken by the reader as the point of its nonending, which seems to be poised between the elegiac and yet another parody of the elegiac—an uncertainty that the poet deliberately leaves unresolved. "Blessed is he," he writes in his self-referential closing lines, "who left life's feast early,/ Not having drunk to the dregs/ Its beaker full of wine;/ Who did not read its novel to the end,/ And knew how to part with it suddenly,/ As I part with my Onegin."

Ambiguity of this sort may be a characteristic of a *genre* as well as of particular works. As there are genres and parodic genres, there are also metaparodic genres—that is, genres of works that are designed to be interpreted as a dialogue of parody and counterparody. When readers identify a work as belonging to a genre of this type, they will, in appreciating the conventions of the generic tradition, expect the work to exhibit this kind of hermeneutic resonance. One such genre is the rhetorical paradox, the praise of something regarded as essentially unpraisable.[3] Beginning in antiquity and including encomia to flies and fleas, to gnats and nuts, to baldness and incontinence, and to bastardy and the codpiece, this genre reaches a peak of complexity in Erasmus' *Praise of Folly*—which may also be taken as a metaparodic sermon (i.e., as both a parodic sermon and a parody of a parodic sermon). As many have noted, one cannot adequately comprehend the complexity of Erasmus' work by simply negating each of Folly's statements—or even by negating each of these negations. For as Folly herself points out, wisdom cannot be the unambiguous opposite of folly, because folly is necessary for wisdom—or, we may ask, is that simply Folly's foolish self-justification? Does she err when she argues that error leads to truth? Erasmus' work sharpens the paradoxes of self-reference and infinite regress traditional in praises of the unpraisable by allowing Folly herself to be the author of a rhetorical paradox in praise of Folly (she cites several generic precedents). It is, she argues, appropriate (and a wise choice) to have Folly praise folly—and praise self-praise as well. Repeatedly making statements which she subsequently calls foolish, she leaves no statement exempt from contradictory meta-statement, no meta-statement exempt from a potential meta-meta-statement. Everything she says implies (folds in upon) itself and includes (closes in upon) its opposite.

Folly's essentially unfinalizable dialogue of opposites ends (in much the same way that *Onegin* ends) with her refusal to resolve her contradictions with a summary—a refusal that is itself, paradoxically, an appropriate summary. No less appropriate and self-implicative is the work's prefactory dedication to Thomas More, in which Erasmus—whom Folly includes in her list of fools—treats his readers in much the same way that Folly treats her audience. "A satirist who spares none of mankind (himself included)," Erasmus writes, "is obviously concerned with human failings in general. . . . It follows that if anyone feels aggrieved by this book, he is discovering his guilt, or at least is afraid of having to do so."[4] Erasmus discovers his own folly when he observes, "Nothing can be a worse waste of time than a serious subject trifled with, nothing better worth while than nonsense turned to good account. It is for others to judge: still, unless the nymph *Self-Love* beguiles me, though I praise folly, I do not do so altogether foolishly" (5).

The rhetorical paradox will concern us again below when we consider More's *Utopia* and the arguments of the "paradoxicalist" in *The Diary of a Writer*, but we may observe here that a number of Dostoevsky's characters are masters of its self-cancelling strategies. In *The Brothers Karamazov*, for instance, when Smerdyakov praises apostasy, he uses the Biblical citations and jesuitical precision traditional for this mock-scholarly genre.[5] And in that novel's best-known chapter, "The Grand Inquisitor," Ivan praises the devil and an antichrist (if not *the* antichrist)—praises them, moreover, for their Christianity. Ivan is the devil's advocate in the literal sense of the phrase—but also in the idiomatic sense, which is to say, he plays the role of the devil's advocate, rigorously defending a position so that it can be triumphantly refuted. His paradoxes are sharpened still more when his double, the paradoxically petty Satan, himself *plays* the devil's advocate. In the novel, only Father Zossima understands the equivocation in Ivan's professions of atheism: "you don't believe your own arguments, and with an aching heart mock at them inwardly," the elder observes. "That question you have not answered, and it is your great grief, for it clamors for an answer" (79). Ivan's perplexed listener, Alyosha, seems almost to arrive at a similar understanding of his brother's contradictions when he declares that the legend is "in praise of Jesus, not in blame of Him—as you meant it to be" (309). Zossima would have understood that it is both. Ivan is, in fact, first introduced as the author of other paradoxes, such as the article on a controversial subject received favorably by both sides until "finally some sagacious persons opined that the article was nothing but an impudent satirical burlesque" (14)—or, more accurately, a rhetorical paradox. And Zossima's interpretation of Ivan's contradictory meanings occurs right after Miusov reports that once, "in a gathering principally of ladies," Ivan defended the assertion that crime, even to cannibalism, is the only "honorable" course of action for an atheist. "From this paradox, gentlemen, you can judge of the rest of our eccentric and paradoxical friend Ivan Fyodorovitch's theories" (79).[6]

The first part of *Notes from Underground* is an excellent example of the genre. The underground man—called a "paradoxicalist" by the editor of his notes—argues the self-interest of self-spite, the unhappiness of happiness, and the advantage of disadvantage—to the point where it is not clear what the words "advantage" and "disadvantage" mean. A descendant of that Cretan who swore that all Cretans are liars, he exhibits as well the genre's characteristic logical paradoxes of self-reference, especially through variations on the sentence "This sentence is false." "I was lying," he explains, "when I said just now that I was a spiteful official. I was lying out of spite" (4). The passage in which he declares (to whom?) that he will have no readers exemplifies a closely related type of self-contradiction, the sentence "You are not reading this sentence." And like Folly, the underground man leaves no statement exempt from a contrary meta-statement and presents no position as his final position. His self-cancelling self-cancellations reach a dizzying apogee at the beginning of the last chapter of part 1 (33–34):

> The long and short of it is, gentlemen, that it is better to do nothing! Better conscious inertia! And so hurrah for underground!
>
> Though I have said that I envy the normal man to the point of exasperation, yet I would not care to be in his place as he is now (though I will not stop envying him. No, no; anyway, the underground life is more advantageous!) There, at any rate, one can—Bah! But after all, even now I am lying! I am lying because I know myself as surely as two times two makes four, that it is not at all underground that is better, but something different, quite different, for which I long but which I cannot find! Damn underground!
>
> I will tell you another thing that would be better, and that is, if I myself believed even an iota of what I have just written. I swear to you, gentlemen, that I do not really believe one thing, not even one word, of what I have just written. That is, I believe it, perhaps, but at the same time, without knowing why, I feel and suspect that I am lying myself blue in the face.
>
> "Then why have you written all this?" you will say to me.... "You long for life and try to settle the problems of life by a logical tangle.... You talk nonsense and are pleased with it; you say impudent things and are constantly afraid of them and apologizing for them.... Lies, lies, lies!"

Of course I myself have made up just now all the things you say. That, too, is from underground.

Beginning on a paradox that he has examined before ("to do nothing"—as opposed to not doing anything) and proceeding through a maze of negations and negations of negations, this passage anticipates the *Notes'* own paradoxically appropriate non-ending.

Like the rhetorical paradox, *meta-utopia*—the subject of this chapter—is a metaparodic genre. A type of threshold literature, meta-utopias are designed to be interpreted as dialogues between utopia and the parody of utopia. One side of the dialogue—usually utopia—may seem to predominate, but that predominance is inconclusive and never free from the possibility of reversal. In some works, large sections may exhibit the *topoi* of utopian literature so well that, when considered separately or excerpted for anthologies, they appear to be utopian without qualification. Read in the context of the complete work, however, these sections are framed by others that do qualify them and may even make them seem to tend toward self-parody. Meta-utopias are perhaps best comprehended as examinations, rather than either endorsements or rejections, of the presuppositions of utopian thinking and literature—or, to cite the self-description of Wells' *A Modern Utopia*, as the dramatization of "the adventure of his [narrator's] soul among Utopian inquiries" (2). The author of a meta-utopia allows himself to entertain utopian or anti-utopian arguments, but does not ultimately commit himself to them. However uncompromising in tone or scornful of indecision, his pronouncements are both compromised and indecisive. Poised between statements and performance, they are tentative and "neither cold nor hot."

"Each Commenting on the Other": Wells' A Modern Utopia

A threshold genre that represents a dialogue between another threshold genre and its parody, meta-utopia tends toward great formal, as well as hermeneutic, complexity. H. G. Wells' *A Modern Utopia*, for instance, anticipates the accusations of inconsistency, carelessness, and incoherence sometimes leveled at meta-utopias, and, because of its explicit justification of its form, is worth considering first in some detail. To begin with, we may note that the work contains most of the formal complexities characteristic of *utopias*. "A sort of shot-silk texture between philosophical discussion on the one hand and imaginative narrative on the other" (xxxii), as Wells describes the work in its preface, *A Modern Utopia* not only combines essay and story in its fictional section but also juxtaposes the fiction as a whole to sections of nonfiction. As in numerous utopias, for example, the work's nonfictional footnotes (as well as the preface signed "H. G. Wells") refer the reader to specific passages in Cabet, Morris, and Bellamy; other notes cite lines from More; others criticize or recommend economic and sociological treatises (e.g., a footnote in the chapter on "Utopian Economics": "But see Gidding's *Principles of Sociology*, a modern and richly suggestive American work, imperfectly appreciated by the British student. See also Walter Bagehot's *Economic Studies.*"–92).

Wells' work also resembles a number of *anti-utopias* in embedding its narrative and essays in a series of ironic metaliterary frames (and frames within frames), which contain discussions of the presuppositions and conventions of utopian literature. In order to protect his work from misreading—for "it is certainly the fate of all Utopias," he observes in one note, "to be more or less misread" (99)—Wells forewarns his audience that what may seem like formlessness is in fact careful design, a well-considered "method." "That method," he writes, "assumes an air of haphazard, but it is not so careless as it seems. I believe it to be—even now that I am through with the book—the best way to a sort of lucid vagueness which has always been my intention in this matter. . . . I explain all this in order to make it clear to the reader that, *however queer this book appears at the first examination, it is the outcome of trial and deliberation, it is intended to be as it is*" (xxi–xxxii; italics mine).

Wells stresses that, unlike many utopias, his work is not offered as an unambiguous recommendation of a plan for social perfection. This work, he writes, is not likely to please the sort of reader who expects such a plan and who "likes everything in hard, heavy lines, black and white, yes and no. . . . Mentally he seems to be built upon an invincible assumption that the Spirit of Creation cannot count beyond two, he deals only in alternatives." Such a reader, Wells observes, is especially impatient "whenever there is any effect of obliquity, of incommensurables, whenever there is any levity or humour or difficulty of multiplex presentation" (xxxi).

Like other meta-utopias, Wells' work is above all one of "incommensurables" and of "multiplex presentation." To be sure, its predominant mode and longest sections are utopian, and a number of readers have, despite Wells' warning against simplistic and humorless interpretations, taken it as unambiguously utopian. "One day, in the distant future," writes Mark Hillegas in his introduction to a recent edition of Wells' work, "the citizens of a peaceful, just, and benevolent World State will look back at the evolving concept of the new order and honor *A Modern Utopia.* Along with such other key documents as Edward Bellamy's *Looking Backward*, William Morris's *News from Nowhere*, Lenin's *State and Revolution*, Freud's *Civilization and Its Discontents*, B. F. Skinner's *Walden Two*, and Herbert Marcuse's *Eros and Civilization*, it is central to what George Kateb calls 'modern utopianism.'"[7] It is possible that Hillegas and some of the other readers he mentions classed Wells' work as an unambiguous utopia on the strength of its plot (which describes a characteristically utopian journey to an ideal society and a return to a society of complacent skeptics), its extensive discussions of economic and social problems, and the general shape of the book as adumbrated in its table of contents (e.g., "Chapter the First—Topographical," "Chapter the Second—Concerning Freedoms," "Chapter the Third—Utopian Economics," "Chapter the Sixth—Women in a Modern Utopia"). They may also have recognized as a generic *topos* the narrator's assertion that his dream was reality and his compatriots' reality a dream: "'You may accept *this* as the world of reality . . .

not I. . . . You think this is real because you can't wake out of it,' I say. 'It's all a dream, and there are people—I'm just one of the first of a multitude—between sleeping and waking—who will presently be rubbing it out of their eyes'" (363-364). And once having taken *A Modern Utopia* as a work of the same semiotic type as *Looking Backward* and *News from Nowhere*, these readers would also have been likely to take as authoritative the narrator's recommendation that we unite to build this better world "where men and women are happy and laws are wise, and where all that is tangled and confused in human affairs has been unravelled and made right" (30)—an unraveling which, the narrator declares, "it would be easy to bring about . . . within a few decades, was there but the will for it among men!" (350).

But this sunny reading would have to overlook a number of deep shadows that Wells casts over his utopian passages. For example, he includes, as the work's appendix, the text of an anti-utopian speech that he delivered on another occasion. Reproduced here in a revised form and cross-referenced to specific passages in the narrative (where footnotes also refer the reader to the appendix), this speech, entitled "Scepticism of the Instrument," raises a number of traditional anti-utopian arguments against the adequacy of reason (the "instrument" of which Wells is skeptical) to know the world and solve its problems. Having studied evolution and natural science, Wells begins, I recognized man "incurably for what he was, finite and not final, a being of compromises and adaptations" (376-377)—a characterization that Wells applies to human knowledge, and even to human logic, as well. "Now to come to logic over the branching uplands of comparative anatomy," Wells traces the evolution of his own thinking (377-378),

> is to come to logic with a lot of very natural presuppositions blown clean out of one's mind. It is, I submit, a way of taking logic in the flank. When you have realised to the marrow, that all the physical organs of man and all his physical structure are what they are through a series of adaptations and approximations . . . and that this is true also of his brain and of his instincts and of many of his mental predispositions, you are not going to take his thinking apparatus as being in any way mysteriously different and better. . . . And as a consequence I found a sort of intellectual hardihood about the assumptions of logic, that at first confused me and then roused all the latent scepticism in my mind.

Wells observes that logic, as a method of reasoning about the relation of classes of phenomena, presupposes what he doubts, namely "*the objective reality of classification.* . . . I have it in my mind that classification is a necessary condition of the working of the mental implement but that it is a departure from the objective truth of things . . . " (379). For Wells, classification is not a description of how things are arranged in nature, but of how the mind arranges its perception of things; and syllogisms do not reveal the hidden connections between phenomena, but rather make explicit how the mind connects propositions. "I submit to you," Wells concludes, "that all hard logical reasoning tends to imply and is apt to imply a confidence in the objective reality of classification. Consequently in denying that I deny the absolute validity of logic. . . . *The forceps of our minds are clumsy forceps, and crush the truth a little in taking hold of it*" (382). A consideration of evolution, in short, leads Wells to conclusions about systematic thinking similar to the conclusions to which a consideration of history leads some other anti-utopian thinkers. It suggests an epistemological humility and skepticism that are at considerable variance with, if not the direct opposite of, the epistemological "confidence" and "hardihood" characteristic of utopias.

Wells' principal narrator (whom he calls the "Owner of the Voice") advances such skeptical arguments at a number of points in the fiction as well. For example, the narrator criticizes the traditional utopian ideal of an unchanging and unambiguous language for much the same reasons that it has been criticized by a number of anti-utopian thinkers. "You may make your ideal clear, a scientific language you demand, without ambiguity, as precise as mathematical formulae, and with every term in relations of exact logical consistency with every other," he addresses whatever believers in the Crystal Palace his audience may include (19-20):

> That, at any rate, is the sort of thing one hears demanded, and if only because the demand rests on implications that reach far beyond the region of language, it is worth considering here. It implies, indeed, almost everything that we are endeavouring to repudiate in this particular work. It implies that the whole intellectual basis of mankind is established, that the rules of logic, the systems of counting and measurement, the general categories and schemes of resemblance and difference, are established for the human mind for ever. . . .

It implies, in short, that humans and their knowledge can be nonhistorical—an assumption that this narrator, like Dostoevsky's underground man, emphatically rejects. "Nothing endures, nothing is precise and certain (except the mind of a pedant)," he declares. "Perfection is the mere repudiation of that ineluctable marginal inexactitude which is the mysterious inmost quality of Being. Being, indeed!—there is no being, but a universal becoming of individualities, and Plato turned his back on truth when he turned towards his museum of specific ideals. Heraclitus, that lost and misinterpreted giant, may perhaps be coming to his own . . . " (20-21, ellipsis in original). Like the world it may describe and the social world in which it functions, language, the narrator declares, is eternally in flux; it "serves only as it undergoes metabolism, and becomes thought and lives, and in its very living passes away" (21). At a later point in the fiction, the narrator extends his sense of epistemological and historical relativism to embrace axiological relativism as well. Again citing Heraclitus in preference to Plato, he denies the possibility of defining, for everyone and forever, what justice is. "So long as we ignore difference, so long as we ignore individuality, and that I hold has been the common sin of all Utopias hitherto," he writes, "we can make absolute statements, prescribe communisms or individualisms, and all sorts of hard theoretic arrangements. But in the world of reality, which—to modernise Heraclitus and Empedocles—is nothing more nor less than the world of individuality, there are no absolute rights and wrongs, there are no qualitative questions at all, but only quantitative adjustments" (37).

Wells and the Owner of the Voice also reflect on the "very definite artistic limitations" (9) of utopian literature. Agreeing that there is always "a certain effect of hardness and thinness" about utopian works, and that "their common fault is to be comprehensively jejune" (9), Wells and the Voice continually alternate utopian formulae with ironic discussions of those formulae, discussions that generally have the effect of parody. Repeatedly baring devices just before or just after using them, the Voice often accounts for sudden turns in the plot or unexplained leaps in his logic simply by invoking his prerogatives as an author of literature or by appealing to the conventions of the genre in which he is writing. That is, whereas utopias tend to obscure the boundary between fiction and nonfiction, Wells, like many anti-utopian writers, tends to emphasize that boundary by techniques of ostentatious frame-breaking. For example, the Owner of the Voice explains how he was able to speak with any citizen he met immediately upon his arrival in Utopia by observing, first, that it is "quite elementarily Utopian" (17) that there will only be one universal language to learn, and, second, that "by the conventions established in the beginning of this book, we are given the freedom of their tongue" (52). He counters objections that governments might abuse the great power with which he entrusts them by pointing out that in works of this genre "one *assumes* the best possible government" (142; italics mine): the reader who might object that there could never be so many well-educated citizens as his plan demands is asked to "take into consideration the general assumption [of improbabilities] one is permitted to make in all Utopian speculations" (151). And when his fellow-traveler to Utopia, the botanist, answers that he would make different assumptions and so create a different image of perfection, the Owner of the Voice, addressing the reader directly, observes peremptorily that "this is my book, and . . . the ultimate decision rests with me. It is open to him to write his own Utopia . . . " (67).

By authorial fiat, the Owner of the Voice also omits explaining how he and the botanist came to Utopia: without shipwreck or a century's sleep, they are brought immediately by the conventions of the genre. Because of this extraordinary means of transportation, the travelers have considerable difficulty in explaining their presence and their lack of identifying documents. "We are here by an act of the imagination," the Owner of the Voice tells the botanist in anticipation of a difficult official interview, "and that is just one of those metaphysical operations that are so difficult to made credible. . . . We have nothing to produce to explain our presence here, no bit of a flying machine or a space travelling sphere or any of the apparatus customary on these occasions" (133). When the expected interview does take place, the Utopian official understandably refuses to believe the travelers' "cock-and-bull story of an instantaneous transfer from some planet unknown to Utopian astronomy. That he and all his world exists only upon a hypothesis that would explain every one of these difficulties, is scarcely likely to occur to his obviously unphilosophic mind" (236). Only the anti-utopian botanist seems to understand his own fictionality and the remarkable kind of power his companion, who is also the author, has over him and the world in which they are both visitors. When the botanist sees the Utopian double of his earthly lady with another man, for example, he knows at once who is responsible for her "infidelity." "This is *your* doing," he says wrathfully to the Owner of the Voice. "You have done this to mock me" (356), an accusation that his companion acknowledges to be justified. On another occasion, the Owner of the Voice considers using his power to mock the botanist's conservative racial views. "It is my Utopia," he confides in the reader, "and for a moment I could almost find it in my heart to spite the botanist by creating a modern Desdemona and her lover sooty black to the lips, there before our eyes. But I am not so sure of my case as that . . . " (341).

Perhaps the most interesting examples of frame-breaking occur when yet another narrator, the editor (who calls himself the "intrusive chairman") and the Owner of the Voice reveal to their skeptical readers that by generic convention the skeptical botanist is the readers' fictional counterpart. In his introduction, the chairman predicts that the narrative will proceed only after "a preliminary complication [of the botanist] with the reader" (3), a prediction that is fulfilled when the Owner of the Voice remarks in his first chapter on how strange it is that "this figure of the botanist will not keep in place. It sprang up between us, dear reader, as a passing illustrative invention. I do not know what put him into my head, and for the moment, it fell in with my humour for a space to foist this man's personality upon you as yours and call you scientific—that most abusive word. But here he is, indisputably, with me in Utopia. . . . " (25). One genre of threshold art parodies another.

"Inspired by the Muse of Parody" (28), Wells leads his readers through a series of frames, and frames within frames. The work begins with "A Note to the Reader," signed "H. G. Wells," in which the author warns that his work is *not* directed to readers who may be impatient with experimental and idiosyncratic forms or unwilling to entertain unresolved contradictions in tone and point of view. After the table of contents, the work's first fictive speaker, the "intrusive chairman," tells us in italicized sentences that the major portion of the work will be spoken by another Voice, and that "*all that is not, as these words are, in Italics, is in* [*this*] *one Voice*" (1). Twice removed from Wells' "Note," "*this Voice . . . is not to be taken as the Voice of the ostensible author who fathers these pages*" (1) or even as the authoritative spokesman that those familiar with earlier utopian works might take him to be: "*You have to clear your minds of any preconceptions in that respect*" (1). Perhaps to emphasize his distance from authoritative utopian delineators, the Owner of the Voice is described as somewhat unattractive and as decidely unheroic. "*His front is convex. He droops at times like most of us, but for the greater part he bears himself as valiantly as a sparrow. Occasionally his hand flies out with a fluttering gesture of illustration. And his Voice (which is our medium henceforth) is an unattractive tenor that becomes at times aggressive*" (1-2).

What follows is his, not the author's or chairman's, utopia. And inasmuch as this utopia follows many of its predecessors in combining fictional and nonfictional sections, yet another frame is added to Wells' complex work. We might begin, the chairman tells us, by imagining the Owner of the Voice *"sitting at a table reading a manuscript about Utopias, a manuscript that he holds in two hands that are just a little fat at the wrist. The curtain rises upon him so. But afterwards, if the devices of this declining art of literature prevail, you will go with him through curious and interesting experiences"* (2) in his fictional utopian world. These devices prevail only briefly and tentatively, however; then they are repeatedly bared, and (2):

> *ever and again you will find him back at that little table, the manuscript in his hand, and the expansion of his ratiocinations about Utopia conscientiously resumed. The entertainment before you is neither the set drama of the work of fiction you are accustomed to read, nor the set lecturing of the essay you are accustomed to evade, but a hybrid of these two.*

It is, in short, threshold art.

In a probable (and ironic) allusion to Plato's Cave allegory, the chairman suggests that we may be better prepared for these shifts from fiction to nonfiction—or, more accurately, from thrice-embedded fiction to twice-embedded fiction (2-4; end of chairman's preface)—if we:

> *figure a sheet behind our friend on which moving pictures intermittently appear. . . . The image of a cinematograph entertainment is the one to grasp. There will be an effect of these two people [i.e., the botanist and the Owner of the Voice] going to and fro in front of the circle of a rather defective lantern, which sometimes jams and sometimes gets out of focus, but which does occasionally succeed in displaying on the screen a momentary moving picture of Utopian conditions. Occasionally the picture goes out altogether, the Voice argues and argues, and the footlights return, and then you find yourself listening again to the rather too plump little man at his table laboriously enunciating propositions, upon whom the curtain rises now.*

But even this curtain falls and rises again and again throughout the work, as the intrusive chairman interrupts the Voice's nonfictive exposition, in much the same way that the exposition interrupts the utopian fiction. There is more than one "defective lantern" that calls attention to itself as well as to the pictures it shows. Always unmistakable because of his italics, the chairman may, for instance, wryly describe the gestures that accompany the Voice's sententious pronouncements: for example, " (*You figure the heroic sweep of the arm that belongs to the Voice*)" (58).

As the opening of Wells' work describes a rapid descent to its deepest fiction, its conclusion (in the chapter "The Bubble Bursts") describes a rapid ascent. At the beginning of that chapter, the Voice observes that inasmuch as his utopia (unlike most others) is intended as "a thing of the imagination" rather than a blueprint for immediate political action, it "becomes more and more fragile with every added circumstance . . . [and] like a soap bubble it is most brilliantly coloured at the very instant of its dissolution. . . . Utopian individuals pass me by, fine buildings tower on either hand; it does not occur to me that I may look too closely" (352). Quite literally, this utopia will not bear scrutiny. The bubble bursts, and the frame breaks, for good when the botanist, who is annoyed at being a character in another's fiction, challenges his companion's authority. Suddenly, "there is no jerk, no sound, no hint of material shock. We are in London" (358), which overwhelms the "Utopist's feeling of ambitious unreality" (367) with its incessant, "re-echoing actualities" (368). Waiting in the confusion of traffic for a policeman to let him pass, the Owner of the Voice considers whether, as he would like to believe, his utopian plan seems unrealizable only because a few details are imperfect. "There will be many Utopias," he concludes with more hope than assurance. "Until at last from dreams Utopias will have come to be working drawings, and the whole world will be shaping the final World State, the fair and great and fruitful World State, that will only not be a Utopia because it will be this world. So surely it must be——" (370).

These are the Voice's last words. *"The policeman drops his hand"* (370), the curtain falls, and the intrusive chairman poses a number of questions his readers may be asking about the work's formal and thematic contradictions. You may wish to know, he asks, what you are expected to think of *"this irascible little man of the Voice, this impatient dreamer, this scolding optimist, who has argued so rudely and dogmatically,"* but who nevertheless may be *"dreaming dreams . . . that with all the inevitable ironies of difference, may be realities when you and I are dreams"* (371). Indeed, *"why was he intruded [at all] ? you ask"* (371), why have so many frames and levels of fictionality? *"It has confused the book, you say, made the argument hard to follow, and thrown a quality of insincerity over the whole. Are we but mocking at Utopias, you demand, using all these noble and generalised hopes as the backcloth against which two bickering personalities jar and squabble? Do I mean we are never to view the promised land again except through a foreground of fellow travellers?"* (371). You may also object, the chairman observes in a key characterization of his work, that despite its title, this book is in a number of important respects unlike other utopias (371–372):

> There is a common notion that the reading of a Utopia should end with a swelling heart and clear resolves, with lists of names, formation of committees, and even the commencement of subscriptions. But this Utopia began upon a philosophy of fragmentation and ends, confusedly, in dust and doubt, with, at the best, one individual's aspiration. Utopias were once in good faith, projects for a fresh creation of the world and of a most unworldly completeness; this so-called Modern Utopia is a mere story of personal adventures among Utopian philosophies.

It is a description that fits meta-utopia as a genre. Like other meta-utopias, *A Modern Utopia* is an account of an imagination in dialogue with itself, the "story" of an inconclusive consideration of utopian and anti-utopian philosophies. The chairman describes his work as a representation of a mind's constant alternation between a vision of a "comprehensive scheme" for universal happiness and a contrary vision of the forces that make the first vision absurd. This ambiguous utopia, he says, dramatizes *"the interplay of my vanities and wishes"* with an unwelcome wisdom that leaves *"the soul's desire turned to presumption and hypocrisy upon the lips. One grasps at the Universe and attains—Bathos"* (372-373). And yet, he continues, unless one is, like the botanist, a man of "spiritual anaemia, dull respectability, . . . [and] a cultivated pettiness of heart" (365), one grasps again and again, knowing one will fail but despising the complacency that sketpticism may justify or rationalize.

The chairman may also be taken as speaking for meta-utopia as a genre when he describes the work's complex form as a way of representing its complex dialectic of utopian and anti-utopian visions. *"The two visions,"* he writes, *"are not seen consistently together, at least not by me, and I do not surely know that they exist consistently together. . . . Nevertheless, I cannot separate these two aspects of human life, each commenting on the other. In that incongruity . . . inheres the incompatibility I could not resolve and which, therefore, I have had to present in this conflicting form"* (372-373).

Wells also offers his work's ambivalent vision as an explanation for its frequent juxtaposition of apparently incompatible tones—that is, for its sudden shifts from the dogmatic seriousness of the "scolding Optimist's" utopian lectures to the playful humor of the Voice's and chairman's self-conscious frame-breaking and "bubble-bursting." Discussing his work's complex seriocomic tone in the appendix, Wells observes that humor is, by its nature, inconsistent with utopia as a genre and contrary to the expectations of its readers. We recall that in the work's opening "Note to the Reader," Wells characterizes the implied, sympathetic readers of traditional utopias as impatient with ambiguity, "multiplex presentation," and all "levity and humour." The reason for their distrust, Wells now suggests, is that humor—especially self-referential and self-parodying humor—tacitly acknowledges an anti-utopian "Scepticism of the Instrument": that is, when our minds recognize their own inadequacy, we laugh. And we laugh hardest, Wells implies, at those—including ourselves—who may entertain the hope that moral and social problems have a final answer and that the universe's complexities admit resolution by a single explanatory system. A challenge to all philosophical monism and political totalism, laughter, in Wells' view, offers "hope of intellectual salvation from the original sin of our intellectual instrument" (392), that is, from our belief in the adequacy of human reason to justify any sort of certain and "universal claim" (391). "The repudiation of [certain] demonstration in any but immediate and verifiable cases that this Scepticism of the Instrument amounts to the abandonment of any universal validity for moral and religious propositions," Wells concludes (392),

> brings ethical, social and religious teaching into the province of poetry. . . .
> All these things are [but] self-expression. Such an opinion sets a new and

greater value on that penetrating and illuminating quality of mind we call insight, insight which when it faces inwards the contradictions that arise out of the imperfections of the mental instrument is called humour.

The spirit of laughter *is*, for Wells, the spirit of skepticism. Born of a Heraclitian sense of the relativity of all things, laughter tends to imply that "all truths are mistaken," all values in flux, and all explanatory systems themselves in need of explanation. According to Wells, utopias usually exclude laughter because laughter is implicitly anti-utopian. Far from being unique in this view, Wells here echoes a *topos* of utopian and anti-utopian literature, both of which have often characterized utopias as being, like Plato's Guardians, "not . . . overmuch given to laughter" (*Republic*, 78). In *We*, for instance, D-503's rebellion begins with an act of laughter, which, he observes, contains "a strange irritating x" for which he is unable "to find an arithmetical expression. . . . Somehow I was confused; with a somewhat hazy mind, I tried logically to explain my laughter."[8] A number of other works have attributed a similar anti-utopian significance to irony, which, like laughter, may challenge convictions of certainty by suggesting the possibility of alternative explanations and values. As the reluctant conspirator of *Under Western Eyes* learns, irony is incipient relativism: "Remember, Razumov," Sophia Antonovna tells him, "that women, children, and revolutionists hate irony, which is the negation of all saving instincts, of all faith, of all devotion, of all action" (235). Meta-utopias characteristically combine affirmations of "saving instincts" and faith with suggestions of humor and irony. By combining utopian ideology with its implicit negation, and utopian literature with a traditionally incompatible tone, meta-utopias create a dialogue of alternative visions and of antithetical genres, "each commenting on the other."[9]

Dialogue: The Tempest *and* From the Other Shore

A number of meta-utopias take the form, in whole or in part, of dialogues between a utopian dreamer—the sort of character who might be the delineator of a utopia—and a skeptical critic (or critics) of his or her views. In contrast to the catechism of utopias, these dialogues are balanced and open: neither speaker is in possession of the unqualified truth. Their contradictory arguments may be equally strong; or if one speaker is clearly superior in argument, the other is likely to be superior in character. It is, in fact, a commonplace of these works that skeptics and anti-utopians, despite their deeper appreciation of historical and political forces, tend toward a cynicism that may be more dangerous than utopian naiveté. We may consider, for instance, the exchange on utopianism in *The Tempest*, which dramatizes in the space of a brief passage the ambiguities and balanced contraries that meta-utopias develop on the scale of an entire work:

Gonzalo. Had I plantation of this isle, my lord—
Antonio. He'd sow't with nettle seed.

> *Sebastian.* Or docks, or mallows.
> *Gonzalo.* And were the king on't, what would I do?
> *Sebastian.* Scape being drunk for want of wine.
> *Gonzalo.* I' th' commonwealth I would by contraries
>   Execute all things. For no kind of traffic
>   Would I admit; no name of magistrate;
>   Letters should not be known; riches, poverty,
>   And use of service, none; contract, succession,
>   Bourn, bound of land, tilth, vineyard, none;
>   No use of metal, corn, or wine, or oil;
>   No occupation; all men idle, all;
>   And women too, but innocent and pure;
>   No sovereignty.
> *Sebastian.* Yet he would be king on't.
> *Antonio.* The latter end of his commonwealth forgets the beginning.
> *Gonzalo.* All things in common nature should produce
>   Without sweat or endeavor. Treason, felony,
>   Sword, pike, knife, gun, or need of any engine
>   Would I not have; but nature should bring forth,
>   Of its own kind, all foison, all abundance,
>   To feed my innocent people.
> *Sebastian.* No marrying 'mong his subjects?
> *Antonio.* None, man, all idle—whores and knaves.
> *Gonzalo.* I would with such perfection govern, sir,
>   T' excel the Golden Age.
> *Sebastian.* Save his Majesty!
> *Antonio.* Long live Gonzalo![10]

Neither side has the clear advantage in this exchange. To be sure, some of Antonio's and Sebastian's comments do not rise above trivial and cynical carping. But their responses to Gonzalo's promise that there will be "no sovereignty" on his isle allude to, and seem to anticipate the development of, one of the recurrent arguments against utopianism: namely, the contradiction between the image of perfection and the means that must be employed to realize it. Sebastian's reply—"Yet he would be king on't"—points to the political power that is required to abolish the rule of power and the historical action by people with historically compromised motives that is needed to escape from history. It is a contradiction which, later works will suggest, is likely to turn the promise of the millennium into the reality of hell, and the dream of innocence into the vacuity of a *Brave New World*. Modern readers—especially modern Russian readers—of Antonio's line ("The latter end of his commonwealth forgets the beginning") may, in particular, think of Shigalev's admission that "I am perplexed by my own data and my conclusion is a direct contradiction of the original idea with which I start. Starting from unlimited freedom, I arrive at unlimited despotism" (*The Possessed*, 409).

Nevertheless, even if we recognize Gonzalo's naiveté, we may still prefer him to his critics. For whereas their political shrewdness is soon to be implicated in a regicidal conspiracy, Gonzalo's foolish speech is designed to distract the king from his son's presumed death. This passage, in short, seems to offer a choice between honesty and intelligence, trustworthiness and truth; and it is by no means clear that the skeptics' truth is to be chosen. Indeed, we may reflect on whether truth is always what *should* be spoken, and on whether the occasion and motives for uttering a truth may compromise it. So Gonzalo seems to imply when, immediately before the utopian exchange, he reproaches Antonio and Sebastian for reminding the king of his responsibility for his son's loss. "My lord Sebastian," says Gonzalo, "The truth you speak doth lack some gentleness, / And time to speak it in. You rub the sore / When you should bring the plaster" (II, i, 141-144).

* * *

Herzen's meta-utopia, *From the Other Shore*, contains three inconclusive dialogues between a believer and a skeptic or, as the interlocutors themselves sometimes describe their exchange, between faith and truth. Placed among a number of articles which, despite disappointment and disconfirmation, continue to predict the imminent collapse of the old order and the creation of a utopian new one, these dialogues cast a deep shadow of doubt over the articles' already highly qualified statements of hope. In each dialogue a middle-aged skeptic and a young idealist (a man in two of the dialogues, a woman in the third) criticize each other's positions in a way that suggests considerable uncertainty as to the validity of their own and discuss, with a knowledge evidently born of experience, the ways in which each position may appeal to one's vanity or offer an unwarranted consolation. What the interlocutors share, and what the dialogues as a whole exemplify, is the familiar view that truth is to be found in the constant and unflinching *pursuit* of truth rather than in definitive statements. Or to put it differently, the dialogues implicitly place the highest value on the dialectical process itself, a potentially endless process in which admittedly tentative positions are tested and modified by encountering unexamined counterexamples and unconsidered alternatives.

"Self-reflection—the ability to make an object of one's deepest feeling, to set it before oneself, to bow down to it, and, perhaps immediately after, to ridicule it—was developed in him to the highest degree," Dostoevsky wrote of Herzen in the second article of *The Diary of a Writer* ("Old People," 1873). That ability is also highly developed in each of the interlocutors of *From the Other Shore*, which was probably the most important model for the *Diary* itself. At the close of the *Diary*'s first article ("Introduction," 1873), which wryly and inconclusively introduces the form and political orientation of his new work, Dostoevsky recalls that once

> while talking with the late Herzen, I praised one of his works, *From the Other Shore*, very highly. . . . This book is written in the form of a conversation between Herzen and his opponent.

"And what I especially like," I remarked in passing, "is that your opponent is also very intelligent. You will agree that he has you pinned to the wall several times."

"But that's the whole trick," Herzen began to laugh. "I will tell you an anecdote. Once, when I was in Petersburg, Belinsky dragged me to his place and sat me down to listen to his article, 'A Conversation between Mr. A. and Mr. B.,' which is passionately written. . . . In this article, Mr. A., evidently Belinsky himself, is portrayed as very intelligent, and Mr. B., his opponent, as inferior. When he had finished reading, he asked me with feverish expectancy:

"'Well, what do you think?'

"'Oh, it's very good, and it's obvious you are very intelligent, but why did you want to waste your time with such a fool?'

"Belinsky threw himself on the couch, buried his face in the pillow, and began to shout, while laughing with all his might,

"'You're killing me! You're killing me!'"

In this reminiscence, Dostoevsky seems to refer in particular to the first dialogue of Herzen's work. Entitled "Before the Storm" and set immediately prior to the 1848 revolutions, this dialogue between a "middle-aged man" and a "young man"—their only identification in this allegorical work—concerns the young man's hopes for a utopian transformation of society. Having recognized that no such transformation is imminent, the young man still believes—or tries to believe—that his ideal will surely be realized in times to come:

"Of all the hopes, of all the life that has slipped through our fingers (and how it has!) if there's anything left, it is faith in the future; sometime, long after our death, the house for which we have cleared the site will be built and it will be comfortable and pleasant—for others."

"Though of course [the middle-aged man replies] there is no reason to believe that the new world will be built according to our plans . . . "

. . . The young man gave a disconcerted toss of the head . . . "You are doing to me," he said, after a silence, "what robbers do to travellers; having stripped me completely, you are still not satisfied; you are after the last tatters which keep the cold from me . . . "[11]

The skeptic's reply in this passage anticipates an argument that he and the skeptical doctor of the later dialogue with the young lady develop at length: namely, that although change is inevitable, it is impossible to predict its nature and direction. For in the first place, the middle-aged man observes, we are ourselves products of a particular historical period and in principle cannot attain the perspective and objectivity needed to understand the historical process as a whole; and in the second place, there probably *are* no historical laws to guarantee socialism or any other political system. "There is no *libretto*. . . . In history, all is improvisation, all is will, all is *ex tempore*; there are no frontiers, no itineraries" (39), he tells the young man. "You want a book of rules, while I think that when one has reached a certain age one ought to be ashamed of having to use one" (28). The interaction of countless wills and un-identified forces, history, according to the middle-aged man, is unlikely to confirm the predictions or realize the plans of the theorist. "Life has its own embryo-genesis which does not coincide with the dialectic of pure reason," he observes, alluding to the great nineteenth-century historical models that have inspired his young companion. "Instead of realizing the Republic of Plato or the Politics of Aristotle, it created the Roman Republic and the politics of their conquerors; instead of the utopias of Cicero and Seneca, the fiefs of the Lombards and German Law" (31–32). You are misled, he concludes, "by categories not fitted to catch the flow of life" (35).

In a passage that may have influenced and certainly anticipates both *Notes from Underground* and *The Possessed*, the middle-aged man further observes that utopian models of history not only contradict experience, but also de-feat the humanitarian purposes they supposedly serve. For if our lives and ef-forts are meaningful only or primarily with respect to a goal we will never see, then all those who have ever lived have been mere "puppets" (35) in an ab-surd performance and everyone who will live before utopia is achieved be-comes, for the revolutionary, expendable material: it is, he suggests, a small step from *telos* to terrorism. Then "is it possible that in all this you do not see a goal?" the young man asks. "Quite the opposite," the older revolution-ary replies (36–37),

I see here only a consequence. If progress is the end, for whom are we working? Who is this Moloch who, as the toilers approach him, instead of rewarding them, only recedes, and as a consolation to the exhausted, doomed multitudes crying "morituri te salutant," can give back only the mocking answer that after their death all will be beautiful on earth. Do you truly wish to condemn all human beings alive to-day to the sad role ... of wretched galley slaves, up to their knees in mud, dragging a barge filled with some mysterious treasure and with the humble words "progress in the future" inscribed on its bows? Those who are exhausted fall in their tracks; others, with fresh forces, take up the ropes; but there remains, as you said yourself, as much ahead as there was at the beginning, because progress is infinite. This alone should serve as a warning to people: an end that is infinitely remote is not an end, but, if you like, a trap; an end must be nearer—it ought to be, at the very least, the labourer's wage, or pleasure in the work done.

In his allusion to the endlessness of history, the middle-aged man addresses a key point at issue between utopia and anti-utopia: namely, whether there can be a nonhistorical future, a world that neither retains unwanted aspects of the past nor develops in directions people cannot control. The middle-aged man contends that the tyranny of the "causal and provisional" (90) cannot be escaped and that even if socialism were realized, it would no more resem-ble our image of it than Christianity fulfilled the Gospels. "The fulfillment of socialism," he observes, "involves the same unexpected combination of ab-

stract doctrine and existing fact. . . . The new element born of the conflict between Utopias and conservatism enters life, not as the one or the other side
expected it—it enters transformed, different, composed of memories and
hopes, of existing things and things to be, of traditions and pledges, of beliefs
and science, of Romans who have lived too long, and Germans who have not
lived at all, united by one church, alien to both" (89-90). Once triumphant,
in short, nonhistorical ideologies are themselves historicized. To expect otherwise, the doctor tells the young lady, is to be false to science, which revolutionaries profess to accept; it is, indeed, to embrace a new religion. "Could
you please explain to me," he asks, "why belief in God is ridiculous and belief in humanity is not; why belief in the kingdom of heaven is silly, but belief in utopias on earth is clever?" (120).

The young idealists' strongest arguments against skepticism are their analy-
ses of its possible causes and likely consequences. Turning the middle-aged
man's logic on his own position, the young man reasons that historical relativism may itself be a product of its times, and skepticism an unfounded, if
understandable, response to a period of transition. So Roman intellectuals, he
observes, must have responded to the decline of their empire, mocking the
"naive" Christian idealists who were to replace them. One must, the young
man suggests, be skeptical of skepticism. For if the idealist is inclined to draw
unwarranted conclusions from his period's hopes, the skeptic is likely to draw
them from its fears. Moreover, he tells his companion, the skeptic's assertion
that he alone has faced a difficult truth may, for all its apparent objectivity,
represent but another type of flattering self-deception. No less than faith,
gloom, especially when it passes for wisdom, may be comforting. "Your detachment seems to me suspect," the young man concludes. "It is too like
dead despair, the detachment of a man who has lost, not only hope, but also
lack of hope. It is an unnatural calm" (22). Later, he reproaches his companion for "the comforting conclusion" of skepticism: "to remain in meditative
idleness, paralyzing the heart with the intellect and benevolence with criticism" (96).

If it is truly impossible to know the laws of history, the idealists contend,
then it is better to err on the side of hope. For if hope faces disappointment,
skepticism risks missed opportunities—and in a world of suffering and misery,
they assert, that is unpardonable. "You are a most dangerous sophist, doctor," the young woman declares, "and if I did not know you so well, I should
consider you most immoral" (109). You should consider, the young man answers his friend's irony, that "there are circumstances about which it is wrong
to laugh, however much skepticism there may be in your soul" (73). Perhaps,
the idealists suggest, faith should be feigned when doubt would be selfish: the
higher truth may be silence when truth, as Gonzalo observes, "doth lack . . .
time to speak it in." So their older companions sometimes concede, admitting
that sophistication, as well as naiveté, may be foolish. "For you, doctor, there
remains a humble *a parte* in this tragedy," the young woman warns. "Sterile
criticism and idleness to the end of your days." "It may be, it may well be"
(121), he concedes.

Skepticism of utopian hopes followed by skepticism of skepticism and a qualified re-assertion of hope—that is the pattern of the articles, as well as the dialogues, of *From the Other Shore*. Like the *Marseillaise* as sung by Rachel (the actress Elisa Félix), Herzen writes at the beginning of "After the Storm," the article you are now reading may be compared to "the knell of death toll-, ing at the wedding feast, . . . a reproach, a dread premonition, a moan of despair amidst hope" (43). Do you remember how this woman made her appearance, he asks his readers (44; ellipses in original),

> she moved slowly, with a sombre air and began to sing, in an undertone . . . The agonizing sorrow of that sound came close to despair. She was calling men to battle, but she had no faith that they would go. . . . This was a plea, this was remorse. . . . Then suddenly, out of that weak chest a cry bursts forth . . . a scream—full of fury and passion.
>
> "Aux armes, citoyens,
> Qu'un sang impur abreuve nos sillions"
>
> she adds with the heartlessness of a hangman. Surprised herself at the ecstasy to which she has surrendered, she begins the second verse even more faintly, more despairingly; and once more she calls men to battle, to blood. For a moment the woman in her gains the upper hand; she throws herself on her knees, and the bloody challenge becomes a prayer; love conquers, she cries and presses the banner to her heart. . . . *Amour sacré de la patrie!* But she is suddenly ashamed, she has leapt to her feet and darts away, waving the banner, with the cry: *Aux armes, citoyens!* The crowd did not dare bring her back.
>
> The article that I am giving you is *my* Marseillaise.

Shifting suddenly and frequently from ecstasy to despair, Herzen's work seems poised between doubt and shame at doubt: it calls people to battle, but has no faith they will go. A soliloquy in which the speaker constantly criticizes and modifies his own positions, Herzen's articles are, in effect, vitiated dialogues in which neither "voice" is clearly in the right, neither position authoritative. "We may note that at times the ancient world was right as against Christianity, which undermined it in the name of a utopian and impossible doctrine," Herzen characteristically concludes his inconclusive work (162):

> . . . but what use was it to them to be right? The days of Rome were drawing to a close, the day of the gospel was dawning.
>
> And all these horrors, bloodshed, butcheries and persecution culminated in the famous cry of despair of the most intelligent of revolutionaries, Julian the Apostate, in the cry: "Thou hast conquered, Galilean!"

Re-affirming hope in the words of a skeptic proved wrong, and comparing his ideal to a religion that failed to fulfill its utopian promise, Herzen ends on the deeply ambiguous note characteristic of this work and of its genre.

Ambiguous Framing: Diderot's Supplement to Bougainville's "Voyage"

Both Dostoevsky and Herzen were probably familiar with Diderot's *Supplement*.[12] A conversation between "A" and "B" concerning the ideal "natural order" (219) of Tahiti, Diderot's work contains two embedded utopias—an old Tahitian's farewell to the French visitors and a young Tahitian's dialogue with their chaplain, both fragments ostensibly "suppressed" (193) from Bougainville's work—which B reads aloud to A and which they discuss with a mixture of sympathy and skepticism. The central theme of the two fragments is the contrast between savage "natural laws" and civilized artificial ones, which are, in the Tahitians' view, the cause of European vice and misery. "We have no wish," the old Tahitian laments his endangered paradise, "to barter what you call our ignorance for your useless knowledge" (188)—especially knowledge of "I know not what distinctions between mine and thine" (187) and of a "ferocious" sexuality that is "attended with guilt and terror" (188, 190). The young Tahitian, Orou, also responds with outrage to the chaplain's description of Europe, which, Orou observes, first provokes and then punishes crimes that in Tahiti do not even have a name. With the absolute certainty of utopian delineators, he explains that in order to be happy one need only follow the dictates of "reason," "nature," and "the general order of things" (198). "Would you like to know what is good and what is bad in all times and places?" he asks. "Pay close attention to the nature of things and actions, to your relations with your fellow creatures, to the effect of your behavior on your own well-being and on the general welfare. You are mad if you believe that there is anything in the universe, high or low, that can add or subtract from the laws of nature" (200). To think otherwise, he adds, is "to apply or remove the names of things in a completely arbitrary manner, to associate the ideas of good and evil with certain actions or to dissociate them for no reason save caprice" (201). When you get back to your country, this delineator concludes, "try to teach them how well our method works" (211) so that they, too, might be happy. Instead of converting the savages to Christianity, the chaplain is, like other utopian travelers, himself converted to Tahitian natural religion and "confesses that he was tempted to throw his vestments into the ship and spend the rest of his days with them" (217).

Anthologized or analyzed separately—as they often have been—these two fragments stand as unambiguous utopias.[13] But in the context of the *Supplement*, which describes not only utopian society but also *the reactions of two readers to a description of utopian society*, they function as part of a complex structure that casts a shadow of irony over them. For although both readers—and B in particular—tend to agree that "the civil law should become nothing more than an explicit statement of the laws of nature" (218), they also understand that it may be impossible "to turn back the clock" (219) of history; that the "state of nature, which one may imagine, . . . probably doesn't exist anywhere" (222); and that the very distinction between laws of nature and of civilization may be both untenable and itself a product of civilization. Wryly observing that one can detect "a few European ideas and turns of phrase" (192) in the "Old Man's Farewell," and that Orou's speeches "are cast somewhat in a European mold" (217), A asks how one is to determine which laws are natural and which laws are artificial. The utopian formula, he drily remarks, is "not easy to work out in detail" (218)—especially when one considers that nature itself does not seem to be unambiguously utopian. For example, when A asks if jealousy is natural, B responds (220) that:

> It's the passion of a starved, miserly creature who is afraid of being deprived. In man it is an unjust attitude produced by our false moral standards and the extension of property rights to a free, conscious, thinking being that has a will of its own.
> A. Then, according to you, jealousy has no place in nature?
> B. I didn't say that. Nature includes both vices and virtues along with everything else.

If nature includes both vices and virtues, then it is hard to see how natural law—even if it could be discovered—would be much help in establishing a perfect society. Moreover, as B observes, the very act of establishing a new civil order may be dangerous. "Watch out for the fellow who talks about putting things in order!" he declares. "Putting things in order always means getting other people under your control" (225). The Jesuits' communist society in Paraguay, he cautions, created equality only in bondage.

B concedes, in short, that the choice between Europe and Tahiti is "a difficult choice to make" (226). "So what should we do," A asks, "go back to the state of nature or obey the laws?" (227). B's reply marks the difference between this work and unambiguous utopias. Dividing his loyalty between utopian extravagance and prudent skepticism, B concludes their discussion with the sort of balanced antitheses characteristic of meta-utopias (227-228):

> B. We should speak out against foolish laws until they get reformed, and meanwhile we should obey them as they are. . . . There is less harm to be suffered in being mad among madmen than in being sane all by oneself. We should say to ourselves—and shout incessantly too—that shame, dishonor and penalties have been erroneously attached to actions that are in themselves perfectly harmless. But let us not do those things, because shame, dishonor and penalties are the greatest evils of all. Let us follow the good chaplain's example—be monks in France and savages in Tahiti.
> A. Put on the costume of the country you visit, but keep the suit of clothes you will need to go home in.

But in this complex work's final frame, even this conclusion turns out to be tentative. What do you think would happen, A asks, if we were to "shout incessantly" for reforms in sexual customs—or even if, let us say, we were to read Orou's conversation with the chaplain to the ladies for whom we are presently waiting (228)?

B. What do you suppose they would say if we did?
A. I haven't the faintest notion.
B. Well, what would they think of it?
A. Probably the opposite of what they would say.

More's Utopia: Texts and Readings

The exemplar of meta-utopia, as well as of utopia, is Thomas More's *The Best State of a Commonwealth and the New Island of Utopia: A Truly Golden Handbook, No Less Beneficial than Entertaining.* The father of two contentious children, its patrimony has been frequently disputed. The work has been taken to endorse particular ideologies (e.g., as being unambiguously communist, unambiguously Catholic, and unambiguously liberal)—and to endorse no ideology at all. Responding to tendentious and humorless readings of *Utopia*, C. S. Lewis, for instance, describes it as an entirely playful and essentially apolitical exercise of wit—as "a holiday work, a spontaneous overflow of intellectual high spirits, a revel of debate, paradox, comedy and (above all) of invention, which starts many hares and kills none. It is written by More the translator of Lucian and friend of Erasmus, not More the chancellor or ascetic."[14] Those who read the work this way tend to class it with *Gargantua and Pantagruel* rather than with the *Republic;*[15] they may also cite Beatus Rhenanus' observation that More was "every inch pure jest"[16] and Erasmus' observation that More "loved joking, so that he might seem born for this. . . . Any witty remark he would still enjoy, even were it directed against himself. . . . He especially delighted in composing declamations, and in these liked paradoxical themes, for the reason that this offers keener practice to the wits. This caused him, while still a youth, to compose a dialogue in which he defended Plato's Communism, even to the community of wives."[17] Indeed, writes Erasmus, "he was responsible for my writing the *Praise of Folly*, that is for making the camel dance."[18]

There is also a third school of interpretation which comprehends *Utopia* as the inconclusive dialectic between the dogmatic and the playful, as an essentially ambiguous "seriocomic"[19] work resembling the rhetorical paradox (from which it may have borrowed) and *Don Quixote* and *The Tempest* (which may have borrowed from it). Remarking on the inconsistent views that *Utopia* has been taken to endorse, J. H. Lupton, who prepared the 1895 Latin and English edition of the work, argues that More's political beliefs cannot be identified with those of any of his characters, and that it would be "preposterous" to maintain that "these views are alike seriously propounded or held by [More] himself. . . . Such a notion would be to crystallize what More purposely left in a state of solution."[20] Lupton cites with approval the reading of Sir James Mackintosh, according to whom More regarded his characters' political arguments "with almost every possible degree of approbation and shade of assent; from the frontiers of serious and entire belief, through gradations of descending plausibility, where the lowest are scarcely more than exercises of the ingenuity, and to which some wild paradoxes are appended" (Lupton, *The "Utopia"*, xli). More recently, this interpretation has been defended by David Bevington as consistent with the work's genre, which he describes as "a balanced, two-sided dialogue"[21]—not a one-sided catechism—in which neither Hythloday nor "More" speaks for More. The work, he suggests, dramatizes "a dialogue of the mind with itself" (77). Others have pointed to the ambiguity of the name Raphael ("God has healed") Hythloday ("well-versed in trifles," or "learned in nonsense") itself. To read the text in this way is to take it as what we have been calling a meta-utopia.

* * *

The history of interpretation of *Utopia* is especially interesting because of its close connection with the work's textological history. It seems to be the case that readers who have disagreed about the nature and meaning of *Utopia* may *literally* have read different works. I have before me six English translations of *Utopia* (as well as one Russian version), none of which—even apart from their different renderings of the same passages in the original—agrees with any of the others as to where the work begins and ends and as to what material it contains. In part, this textual variability reflects the fact that More supervised the publication of three editions of his work, each of which contains different framing material; it also apparently reflects the disagreement among later editors as to which, if any, of these frames is properly "part of" the work. Edward Surtz and J. H. Hexter, who prepared the volume of *Utopia* in the Yale *Complete Works of St. Thomas More*, are the only editors to include everything from all three original versions, to describe the composition and order of presentation in each of the three, and to justify the order of their own version (which, because of its very completeness, is not identical to any of More's). Readers of this edition—and of Lupton's slightly briefer one, based on that of March, 1518—are likely to be surprised, as I was, that the framing material occupies as much as one-fifth of the text. Surtz and Hexter include: Erasmus' commendatory letter to the publisher, Froben; Budé's letter to Lupset; the "Map of the Island of *Utopia*" of 1518, and the different map of 1516; the Utopian Alphabet, with the Latin equivalent of each letter; a "Quatrain in the Utopian Vernacular" printed both in "Utopian" and in Latin transliteration; a "Literal Translation of the Above Lines"; "Six Lines on the Island of Utopia by Anemolius, Poet Laureate, Nephew of Hythlodaeus by His Sister"; Giles' letter to Busleyden; Desmarais' letter to Giles; Desmarais' "Poem on the New Island of Utopia"; Gerhard Geldenhauer's verses on "Utopia"; Cornelius de Schrijver's verses "To the Reader"; Busleyden's letter to More; More's first letter to Giles; book 1 of "The Discourse of the Extraordinary Character, Raphael Hythlodaeus"; book 2; More's second letter to Giles; and Beatus Rhenanus' letter to Pirckheimer.[22] More's first letter, book 1, and book 2 contain marginalia, for which Giles claims authorship in the letter to Busleyden but which the 1517 edition attributes to Erasmus.[23] By contrast, Frederic White's frequently reprinted anthology of *Famous Utopias* includes only book 1 and book 2 (without the marginalia), a selection to which Surtz' paperback edition adds only More's first letter to Giles.[24] White gives no indication that any omissions have been made, and although a footnote to Surtz' preface refers the reader to the longer version in the *Complete Works*, he does not describe the shorter text as abridged.

It appears that those who either view *Utopia* as an unambiguous endorsement of a particular ideology or regard the distinction between literary and tractarian works as unimportant tend to offer shorter versions than those who read it as an ironic, playful, and ambiguous literary work.[25] Whereas the editor of the Soviet translation, who explains that Hythloday speaks authoritatively for More,[26] makes the same selection as Father Surtz, the editor of the Penguin edition, who stresses the comic aspects of the work and consequently renders Raphael Hythlodaeus as Raphael Nonsenso, produces a longer text to justify his interpretation. The Penguin editor, Paul Turner, includes: The Utopian Alphabet with Latin equivalents; the sample of Utopian poetry with transliteration and translation; "Lines on the Island of Utopia by the Poet Laureate, Mr. Windbag [i.e., Anemolius] Nonsenso's Sister's Son"; More's first letter to Peter Gilles; Gilles' letter to Busleiden; book 1 and book 2, without the marginalia. Explaining the reasons for this selection, Turner states what many editors leave unstated: namely, that his text reflects his reading. "Of the letters, verses, etc., published with the original text," he observes in the preface, "I have included only those which are part of the practical joke. Among them are lines by Mr. Windbag, which are obviously meant to be silly (though some critics have discovered profound meaning in them), and by their prominent position on the fourth page to establish the April Fool atmosphere right from the start. I flatter myself that my version is quite as silly as the original."[27]

In short, *the hermeneutic circle is linked to a textological one*: reading dictates text, which in turn justifies reading. And as new readers, with different interests and literary experiences, re-interpret the work, its text is likely to change again. The more general point to be made is that the process of continual revision that we expect from works of oral literature sometimes happens—albeit more slowly and by different means—with written works as well, especially when the author has left more than one version or when no authoritative version is extant. In fact, such textually uncertain works are more numerous, and therefore less exceptional, than critics and theorists often assume. Our heritage of ancient literature is largely a heritage of textually reconstructed works; even among modern works, novels as familiar as *War and Peace* (which Tolstoy revised) and *The Possessed* (the missing chapter of which was posthumously discovered) are known and published in more than one version; in medieval literature and Socialist Realism, which are governed by concepts of authorship different from ours, variability is still more rapid and radical (e.g., the re-writing of Socialist Realist novels, by the author or others, to conform to changes in the Party line).[28] If the work is known, as *Utopia* is, primarily in translation, yet another possibility for variation exists

—a variation that is likely to be maximized when the remoteness of the original seems to justify freer versions (to make the text comprehensible at all) or when, as in nineteenth- and twentieth-century Russia, a translation is expected to be not a literal rendition but an "adequate" literary work in its own right. That is, not just differences in languages or in the literary experiences of readerships but also differences in what a translation is expected to accomplish affect particular versions and, therefore, their subsequent interpretations. Whether or not problems of translation are involved, the link between interpretation and textology would seem to support the argument of a number of Russian theorists—who were probably generalizing from their country's own experience as a rapid cultural borrower—that *meaning is not locked "in" the text, but rather derives from the complex and historically changing relationship between readership, interpretative conventions, and a text which may itself not be fixed.* It follows that the aim of textology might better be conceived not as the discovery of an original under layers of error, but as the description of the *entire* "palimpsest," which would be an index to literary and cultural history.[29]

* * *

When *Utopia* is read as a meta-utopia, its margins play on their own marginality. Like the preface to *The Praise of Folly*, the prologues to the books of *Gargantua and Pantagruel*, and the frames of *Don Quixote*—all of which take their own literariness and fictionality as principal themes—the frames of *Utopia* become part of a literary work that self-consciously includes what might otherwise not be taken as part of the work proper. Or to put it differently, *Utopia* represents not merely a political conversation, but rather *an entire book*, from cover to cover, that includes *both* the report of a political conversation *and* supporting advertising, documentation, and "recommended" interpretations. Like the letters from Elsa Triolet in Shklovsky's *Zoo*, these frames, which More solicited and included but did not himself write, become part of a complex literary structure, whose author, in the sense of designer and semantic authority, is not its sole author, in the sense of verbal composer.

Indeed, a number of these letters discuss "More's" role and the nature of the credit he deserves. In his first letter to Giles, "More" himself makes the minimal claim of having done no more than transcribe the conversation as accurately as he could. "Certainly you know," he reminds Giles, "that I was relieved of all the labor of gathering materials for the work and that I had to give no thought at all to their arrangement. I had only to repeat what in your company I heard Raphael relate."[30] Inasmuch as I decided to reproduce Hythloday's "hurried and impromptu" style, as well as his thoughts, as accurately as possible, More continues (39),

> scarcely anything remained for me to do. Otherwise the gathering or the arrangement of the materials could have required a good deal of both time

and application even from a talent neither the meanest nor the most ignorant. If it had been required that the matter be written down not only
accurately but eloquently, I could not have performed the task with any
amount of application. But, as it was, those cares over which I should have
had to perspire so hard had been removed. Since it remained to me only to
write out simply what I had heard, there was no difficulty about it.

In their letters, Desmarais (who refers to "Hythlodaeus' discourse and More's
written account—29) and Busleyden (who describes More's role as "putting
down in writing that afternoon conversation"—33) seem to take More at his
word, but Giles himself, apparently discounting these protestations as either
topoi or the signs of modesty, writes of More's skill in embellishing, not just
reproducing, Hythloday's discourse. "A man of great eloquence," he writes to
Busleyden, "has represented, painted, and set it before our eyes in such a
way that, as often as I read it, I think I see far more than when, being as
much a part of the conversation as More himself, I heard Raphael Hythlodaeus' own words sounding in my ears" (21). Budé agrees (13; italics mine):

> beyond question it is More who has adorned the island and its holy institu-
> tions by his style and eloquence . . . and who has added all these touches
> that bring grace and beauty and impressiveness to the magnificent work —
> *although in the help which he has given he has claimed for himself only
> the role of an arranger of the materials.*
>
> Manifestly it was a point of conscience with him not to arrogate to him-
> self the major part in the work. Otherwise Hythlodaeus could rightly com-
> plain that, if he ever would decide to commit his own experiences to
> paper, More had left him a prematurely plucked and deflowered glory.

One irony here is that, in a sense, More's most important role *is* the "arranger
of the materials"—including this very letter.

Like the *Quixote, Utopia* is centrally concerned with the nature of literature and, especially, of fictionality. The framing letters of Giles and More, for
instance, refer to the conversation with Hythloday as an actual event, thus
playing both on the fictionality of the work and on their own ambiguous
status. Inasmuch as some may doubt the existence of Utopia, "Giles" explains to "Busleyden," he has taken care to document the report. For this
reason, he writes, "I have caused to be added to the book" the poem in the
Utopian vernacular and Utopian alphabet "which, after More's departure,
Hythlodaeus happened to show me" (23). Moreover, Giles observes, he himself can vouch for Hythloday's evident sincerity and More's accuracy. "As to
More's difficulty about the geographical position of the island" he continues
(23),

> Raphael did not fail to mention even that, but in very few words and as it
> were in passing, as if reserving the topic for another place. But, somehow
> or other, an unlucky accident caused us both to fail to catch what he said.
> While Raphael was speaking on the topic, one of More's servants had come
> up to him to whisper something or other in his ear. I was therefore listen-

ing all the more intently when one of our company who had, I suppose, caught cold on shipboard, coughed so loudly that I lost some pharases of what Raphael said. I shall not rest, however, till I have full information on this point so that I shall be able to tell you exactly not only the location of the island but even the longitude and latitude—provided our friend Hythlodaeus be alive and safe.

But the best evidence for the truth of everything in this book, he writes, is Thomas More's word: "what is the use of finding arguments to make the account more credible when we have the distinguished More himself to vouch for it?" (25).

By not making the distinction between fiction and falsehood, More and Giles call attention to it. Itself fictional, More's first letter asks Giles to correct any factual errors in his work: "If there is doubt about anything, I shall rather tell an objective falsehood than an intentional lie—for I would rather be honest than wise" (42). Giles' marginal comment on this passage—"Note the Theological Distinction between an Intentional Lie and an Objective Falsehood" (41)—may be taken as an allusion to the analogous distinction between a *fiction* and an "objective falsehood." More urges Giles to "ask Raphael himself by word of mouth or by letter" (41) the precise length of the bridge over Utopia's Anydrus [i.e., "Waterless"] River and to discover "in what part of the new world Utopia lies. I am sorry that point was omitted, and I would be willing to pay a considerable sum to purchase that information" (43). He foresees, More writes further, that many will doubt the veracity of his report or make "wrongheaded" (45) judgments regarding it, so, he confesses (as Dostoevsky's underground man was to declare in his self-referential work), he may decide not to publish it at all. "Very many men are ignorant of learning; many despise it," he describes his future readers. "This fellow is so grim that he will not hear of a joke; that fellow is so insipid that he cannot endure wit. Some are so dull-minded that they fear all satire as much as a man bitten by a mad dog fears water" (45). Giles notes, "More Calls Men without a Satiric Sense Dull-Minded" (45).

More's second letter to Giles, which was included only in the work's second edition, describes an "actual" reader's response. "I was extremely delighted, my dearest Peter, with a criticism already known to you, made by an unusually sharp person who put this dilemma about our *Utopia*: If the facts are reported as true, I see some rather absurd elements in them, but if as fictitious, then I find More's finished judgment wanting in some matters" (249). To be sure, More continues, this reader "shows plainly how highly he thinks of me when he complains of being cheated of his hope whenever he read something not precise enough, whereas for me it would be more than I could hope if I happened to be able to write at least a few things—even among so many—that were not altogether absurd" (249). Nevertheless, More observes in a passage often cited by those who stress the irony and playfulness of the work (25),

when he doubts whether Utopia is real or fictitious, then I find his finished judgment wanting. I do not pretend that if I had determined to write about the commonwealth and had remembered such a story as I have recounted, I should have perhaps shrunk from a fiction. . . . But I should certainly have tempered the fiction so that, if I wanted to abuse the ignorance of common folk, I should have prefixed some indications at least for the more learned to see through our purpose.

Thus, if I had done nothing else than impose names on ruler, river, city, and island such as might suggest to the more learned that the island was nowhere, the city a phantom, the river without water, and the ruler without a people, it would not have been hard to do and would have been much wittier than what I actually did. Unless the faithfulness of a historian had been binding on me, I am not so stupid as to have preferred to use those barbarous and meaningless names, Utopia, Anydrus, Amaurotum, and Ademus.

These names are, of course, the self-cancelling paradoxes he mentions, and this very letter is one of the "indications for the more learned" of the work's fictionality. Like its generic successors, More's meta-utopia sorts out its readers.

If Beatus Rhenanus' letter to Pirckheimer is read as a part of the work, then his description of the work's reception bares its metafictional devices most conspicuously. "Listen, by the Muses, to a good story," Beatus Rhenanus recalls (253; italics used to indicate Greek in original):

. . . when the *Utopia* was mentioned here recently at a certain gathering of a few responsible men and when I praised it, a certain dolt insisted that no more thanks were due to More than to any recording secretary who merely records the opinions of others at a council . . . in that all More said was taken from the mouth of Hythlodaeus and merely written down by More. Therefore, he said, More deserved praise for no reason other than that he had recorded these matters well—and there were some present who approved the fellow's opinion as that of a man of very sound perception. *Do you not, then, welcome this elegant wit of More, who can impose upon such men as these, no ordinary men but widely respected and theologians at that?*

This passage recalls More's first letter, which asks Giles to discover Utopia's exact location because "there are several among us, and one in particular, a devout man and a theologian by profession, burning with an extraordinary desire to visit Utopia" (43). Hoping to promote Christianity among the Utopians, More explains, this holy man "has made up his mind to arrange to be sent by the pope and, what is more, to be named Bishop for the Utopians. He is in no way deterred by any scruple that he must sue for this prelacy, for he considers it a holy suit which proceeds not from any consideration of honor or gain but from motives of piety" (43).

A central theme of More's work is, in short, its likely reception by the "dull-minded," dogmatic, and humorless—that is, by those who either believe

Utopia to be real or, less literally but perhaps no more wisely, believe it to be unreal but realizable. *Utopia* parodies utopia in advance. One such reader is "Budé," who, though not entirely sure of the existence of Utopia, does believe that if Europe were to copy the institutions Hythloday describes then "beyond the shadow of a doubt, avarice, the vice which perverts and ruins so many minds otherwise extraordinary and lofty, would depart hence once and for all, and the golden age of Saturn would return" (11). Busleyden also contends that "our commonwealths one and all will easily escape [all calamities] provided that they organize themselves exactly on the one pattern of the Utopian commonwealth and do not depart from it, as they say, by a hair's breadth" (37). Most interesting of all are Giles' marginal notes, which not only gloss difficult passages and summarize key points, but also *interpret* the text and advocate the adoption of Hythloday's suggestions. Giles often contrasts the morality of the pagan Utopians with the immorality of Christians— "Today [in Europe] Scarcely the Monks Observe This Custom" (145); "Yet Now [Among Us] Dicing Is the Amusement of Kings" (129); "How Much Wiser the Utopians Are than the Common Run of Christians!" (157)—and urges Europeans to learn a Utopian lesson: "O Holy Commonwealth—and Worthy of Imitation Even by Christians!" (147). When Hythloday concludes with a vehement condemnation of private property, Giles instructs: "Reader, Take Notice of These Words" (241). And like many later scholars, he warns against misinterpretation: "Evidently This Passage Is Satiric" (159).

Those who take Utopia as ultimately inconclusive do not seem to regard "Giles' " and "Busleyden's" reading as entirely mistaken, but rather as simplistic and overly enthusiastic. That is, although they deny that the work unambiguously endorses any particular ideology, they nevertheless do not find it void of political content or, indeed, lacking in considerable sympathy for some of Hythloday's positions. For example, Bevington, who cites Lupton and Mackintosh with approval, argues that "whenever we find an agreement between the two principals [i.e., More and Hythloday] we are surely safe in assuming the author's concurrence."[31] Robert Elliott also sees *Utopia* as a complex, but not entirely unnegotiable, labyrinth, and, like Bevington, takes a number of satiric passages in book 1—for example, Hythloday's attacks on enclosures and on capital punishment for theft—as authoritative. Although Elliott regards book 2, in which Utopia is described, as more problematic than book 1, he reads "More's" foolish final objection to communism— namely, that it would deprive the court of wealth and splendor, the commonwealth's "true glories and ornaments" (More, *Utopia*, 245)—as a fairly clear indication that, on this point, the author's namesake is not his mouthpiece. Whatever More "in his many conflicting roles of philosopher, moralist, religious polemicist, man of great affairs" may have believed about communism, Elliott writes, More the author of *Utopia* approved of egalitarianism. "Thus the shape of *Utopia* is finished off, enigmatically but firmly, in the terms Hythloday provides."[32]

Elliott interprets *Utopia* in much the same way that I interpreted *From the Other Shore*: as a work which expresses sympathy for utopian or socialist ideals, but which also conveys considerable doubt as to both the likelihood of their realization and the reasonableness of their advocates. One might add to his reading that Hythloday often seems to resemble a number of other characters in the work who embrace new ideas too enthusiastically or who lack a sense of self-irony: for example, the theologian who sues to be bishop of the Utopians or the New World sailors for whom the gift of the magnetic needle proved a mixed blessing. "Now, trusting to the magnet, they do not fear wintry weather, being dangerously confident. Thus, there is a risk that what was thought to be a great benefit to them may, through their imprudence, cause them great mischief" (53). It is a passage that may be taken as an allegory of utopian ideology itself. We may also think of Hythloday's conversion to Utopianism when he describes a Utopian convert to Christianity. No sooner was he baptized than this new believer violated the laws of King Utopus (who "made the whole matter of religion an open question and left each one free to choose what he should believe"—221) by speaking publicly (219)

> of Christ's religion with more zeal than discretion. He began to grow so
> warm in his preaching that not only did he prefer our worship to any
> other but he condemned all the rest. He proclaimed them to be profane
> in themselves and their followers to be impious and sacrilegious and wor-
> thy of everlasting fire. When he had long been preaching in this style, they
> arrested him, tried him, and convicted him not for despising their religion
> but for stirring up a riot among the people.

It is possible to be, in Milton's phrase, a "heretic in the truth."

As Hythloday regards the convert, so "More," in the work's concluding lines, regards Hythloday. "When Raphael had finished his story," More recalls, "many things came to my mind which seemed very absurdly established in the customs and laws of the people described. . . . I knew, however, that he was wearied with his tale, and I was not quite certain that he could brook any opposition to his views. . . . I therefore praised their way of life and his speech and, taking him by the hand, led him in to supper" (245). In keeping silent where Hythloday would brook no opposition, More tacitly alludes to their earlier disagreement as to whether the higher truth sometimes demands silence or even the partial expression of untruths—a disagreement which, as we have seen, was to become a generic *topos* of meta-utopia. When, in book 1, Hythloday refuses to take Giles' and More's advice that he become a counselor to kings on the grounds that kings would not listen to his uncompromising condemnation of their behavior, More replies that he did not mean to recommend that "such ideas should be thrust on people, or such advice given as you are positive will never be listened to" (99). One must, More argues, consider the capacity and predisposition of one's audience: to speak the truth, More explains, is not a simple act of stating what one believes to be the case. It is, rather, a highly complex process that involves estimating what is most likely to convince one's listeners of the closest possible approximation to one's beliefs. It is not true, More tells Hythloday (99), that everything is suitable to every place. But there is another philosophy, more practical for statesmen, which knows its stage, adapts itself to the play in hand, and performs its role neatly and appropriately. . . . If you cannot pluck up wrongheaded opinions by the root, if you cannot cure according to your heart's desire vices of long standing, you must not on that account desert the commonwealth. You must not abandon the ship in a storm because you cannot control the winds.

These lines once again look forward to the end of book 2, where More, after pretending to agree with Hythloday, expresses his reservations directly to the reader. Despite Hythloday's great learning, he concludes his account, "I cannot agree with all that he said. But I readily admit that there are many features in the Utopian commonwealth which it is easier for me to wish for in our countries than to have any hope of seeing realized" (245–247). More—or is it just "More"?—here seems to close his work with approval of some of Hythloday's political recommendations, but also with considerable doubt of both their practicality and the efficacy of Hythloday's uncompromising defense of them. But even *this* uncertain and balanced ending is not free from the possibility of irony. For although "More" reserves the last word for himself, he never answers—at least, not to the satisfaction of some readers (e.g., Elliott, *Shape of Utopia*, 38)—Hythloday's objections to prudence, compromise, and the "indirect approach." If we were to take your position seriously, Hythloday argues (101),

> we must dissemble almost all the doctrines of Christ. Yet He forbade us to dissemble them to the extent that what He had whispered in the ears of his disciples He commanded to be preached openly from the housetops. . . . But preachers . . . following I suppose your advice, accommodated his teaching to men's morals as if it were a rule of soft lead that at least in some way or other the two might be made to correspond. By this method I cannot see what they have gained, except that men may be bad in greater comfort.

* * *

I have offered here not another reading, but rather what might be called a *metareading* of *Utopia*: that is, an account of, and an accounting for, its complex interpretive history. Much of the controversy regarding More's work is, in effect, controversy as to its *genre*. That is, the meaning of *Utopia*—like the meaning of all literary works—depends on the reader's assumptions about (1) the appropriate conventions for interpreting the work, and (2) the literary tradition in which it is placed. Those who read the work as a utopia take Hythloday as the delineator and class it with the *Republic* (to which it often refers) and *Looking Backward*. When interpreted as a play of pure wit, *Utopia* is compared to Lucian's *True History*. (Lucian, whom More translated, is a favorite author of the Utopians.) The seriocomic relatives of More's work are generally taken to be *Don Quixote* and *The Praise of Folly*. It is often observed that the connections between *The Praise of Folly* and the praise of Noplace are especially close. Written in More's house, the *Encomium Moriae* is dedicated to the friend on whose name it puns: *The Praise of Folly*—ambiguous and ironic as it is—is also a praise of More. Furthermore, Erasmus supervised the publication of *Utopia*; wrote one of the framing letters and, at More's request, solicited others; and is credited in one edition with the authorship of the marginalia. The third edition of *Utopia* was published in a volume that also contained More's and Erasmus' *Epigrammatica* (as well as Beatus Rhenanus' letter). And as Folly was born in the Fortunate Isles, the Utopians "are very fond of fools. . . . If anyone is so stern and morose that he is not amused with anything they either do or say, they do not trust him with the care of a fool. They fear that he may not treat him with sufficient indulgence since he would find in him neither use nor amusement, which is his sole faculty" (193).

Utopia, in short, is exemplary of the complex issues involved in literary interpretation. It is therefore somewhat surprising that in *New Literary History* J. H. Hexter, hoping to "impose some salutary restrictions on the free flight of fancy of interpreting scholars,"[33] should have used *Utopia* to argue for the relative clarity and simplicity of those issues. Summarizing his previous conclusions in *More's "Utopia": The Biography of an Idea*, Hexter contends that the meaning of *Utopia* is both unambiguous and clearly demonstrable by a method he calls "exhaustive contextual analysis." If meaning is not identified with authorial intention, he argues in a perfect circle, false interpretations may result—false in that they are not compatible with authorial intention. Perhaps because of his tendency as a historian to look for historically determinate meanings, Hexter does not seem to consider that a work's meaning may include the various interpretations which different periods have ascribed to it and which mediate the text for successive generations of readers: for him, its "biography" ends, rather than begins, with publication. Nor does Hexter seem to consider that even if meaning *is* identified with authorial intention, it might be appropriate to take into account the author's intention regarding the *kind* of work he is writing—an omission that leaves Hexter blind to (or impatient with) ambiguity and deaf to irony. It leads him, in particular, to a fallacious or question-begging argument that is especially noteworthy when advanced by an editor of the Yale *Utopia* (in the *Complete Works*). Although that edition includes the framing letters as part of the text and indicates that More himself was responsible for their original inclusion, Hexter cites the defense of Utopian institutions in Budé's and Busleyden's letters as proof that More's first readers and closest friends interpreted the work as Hexter does—which is to say, he relies, without qualification, on the framing letters as *external* evidence! Indeed, for Hexter, the fact that More allowed the letters to appear shows that he must have agreed with them. If contrary interpretations of *Utopia* are allowed, he writes, "then Erasmus, Busleyden, and Budé are wrong in their interpretation of More's intent. And if More allowed the marginal notes and letters to appear in the Basel edition without corrections at the appropriate points, he was certainly lending a measure of confirmation and official status to that error" (*Biography of an Idea*, 47–48). There are, Hexter concludes, only two alternatives: either More deliberately allowed "what was bound to be construed as the stamp of his approval placed on a complete misinterpretation of his ideas; or there was no misinterpretation, his friends understood his intent quite well, and his third thought what his first and second had been. As between these two alternatives I do not find it difficult to choose" (48). The fact that Budé and Busleyden refer to Hythloday as a real person and Utopia as an actual place does not seem to suggest a third alternative to Hexter: namely, that the letters were regarded both by their authors and by More as ironic. Hexter notably does *not* cite as evidence for his reading More's second letter to Giles or the line from Beatus Rhenanus' letter which, in the Yale edition, closes the work: *"Do you not, then, welcome this elegant wit of More, who can impose upon men such as these, no ordinary men but widely respected and theologians at that?"* (253).

The Diary: *Generic Risks*

Chapter One. 1. Instead of a Preface about the Great and the Small Bears, about the Prayer of the Great Goethe, and, Generally, about Bad Habits.

2. The Future Novel. Again, an "Accidental Family."

3. The Christmas Tree at the Artists' Club. Thinking Children and Spoiled Children. "Gluttonous Youth." "Oui-Girls." Jostling Raw Youths. The Hurrying Moscow Captain.

4. The Golden Age in the Pocket.

Chapter Two. 1. The Boy with an Outstretched Hand.

2. The Boy at Christ's Christmas Party.

3. The Colony of Juvenile Delinquents. Gloomy People. The Transformation of Depraved Souls into Pure Ones. Means Acknowledged as the Very Best for Doing So. Small and Insolent Friends of Mankind.

Chapter Three. 1. Russian Society for the Prevention of Cruelty to Animals. Courier. Green Liquor. The Itch for Debauchery and Vorobiev. From the End, or from the Beginning?

2. Spiritualism. The Extraordinary Shrewdness of Devils, If Only They Are Devils.

3. A Word Apropos of My Biography.

4. A Turkish Proverb.

Announcement.

—January, 1876

Any meta-utopia runs the risks of its genre: namely, that its heterogeneity will be perceived as chaos, that its multiple points of view will be seen as incoherence or reduced to singularity, and that the network of allusions and repetitions which link its parts will be taken as no more than recurrent concerns. That, indeed, is also true of other formally anomalous works, such as

Utopia and *The Praise of Folly*, and members of other threshold genres, such as menippean satire. These works are likely to be regarded by some readers as formless or even as nonliterary, and to be defended by others, as Shklovsky defended *Tristram Shandy*, as deliberate inversions of received formal conventions. One man's "loose and baggy monster" may be another man's systematic generic parody.[34] When readers encounter a disputed or disputable work of this type, they may consider (1) the evidence for design and intended membership in a generic tradition, and (2) the likelihood that the work will reward reading in a tradition of similar works whether or not it was designed to be so read. Even if they decide that the work's hermeneutic ambivalence is the product of design, they may still conclude that the price paid for it—weakening the effectiveness of either interpretation—was too great.[35] The readers' answers to these questions will depend on a number of factors, including the nature of their prior literary experience and their reasons for being interested in the work in the first place. As we have seen throughout this study, the classification, evaluation, and interpretation of such works characteristically varies from group to group and period to period—a variability that may itself constitute important evidence about the predispositions and assumptions of different readerships.

There is considerable evidence suggesting that the *Diary* was the product of aesthetic purpose, and that Dostoevsky designed it to be read in the tradition of earlier meta-utopian and metaparodic works. Or to state more precisely the relation of innovative authors to a generic tradition, the development of Dostoevsky's thinking about social and aesthetic questions led him to experiment with the formal features, topics, and attitudes characteristic of a tradition of works with which he was familiar, the tradition that I have called meta-utopia. That is not to say, however, that for contemporary readers the work is likely to (or "should") appear a *successful* innovation in this, or other, generic traditions. On the contrary, it may well be that the ideological and temperamental ambivalences that attracted Dostoevsky to the genre also left him unable to master it. Although some of the *Diary* (e.g., the January, 1876, issue) can be seen as the product of careful planning—present in Dostoevsky's notebooks and reflected in the intricate interweaving of recurrent themes and motifs[36]—much seems to be the product of personal obsession as well. It may also be that the particular innovations Dostoevsky made in that already heterogeneous genre—especially publication in periodical form—rendered the *Diary* too fragmented and too lengthy to reward reading as an integral work. For most readers, Dostoevsky's experiment has failed; and the *Diary* has seemed more interesting for its parts than for its overall design. That, too, is a risk of heterogeneous and encyclopedic genres, whose traditions characteristically contain a number of works that are, at best, of "partial" interest.[37]

The Diary: Belief in the Incredible

> "What do people generally say [about ghosts] ? " muttered Svidrigailov, as though speaking to himself, looking aside and bowing his head: "They say, 'You are ill, so what appears to you is only unreal fantasy.' But that's not strictly logical. I agree that ghosts only appear to the sick, but that only proves that they are unable to appear except to the sick, not that they don't exist. . . . If you believe in a future life, you could believe in that, too."—*Crime and Punishment*[38]

> "You have no tenderness, nothing but truth, and so you judge unjustly."—Aglaia, in *The Idiot*[39]

Like its generic relatives, the *Diary* invites interpretation as a "dialogue of the mind with itself," an "adventure of the soul among Utopian inquiries." It regards those inquiries, and the reader is expected to regard them, "with almost every possible degree of approbation and shade of assent; from the frontiers of serious and entire belief, through gradations of descending plausibility . . . and to which some wild paradoxes are appended." In it, as in More's *Utopia*, utopianism predominates, but that predominance is precarious; and "serious and entire belief" is ever threatened by an uncertain shadow of irony. In part, that shadow is cast by the *Diary*'s playful, metaliterary passages, passages which, for reasons discussed above, have no place in unambiguous utopias and which therefore suggest the possibility of parody. The antitheses of metaliterary play and dogmatic assertion produce meta-utopian ambivalence—that is, not a synthesis, but an intensified dialectic of utopian "pro" and anti-utopian "contra." That dialectic is, in turn, the reflection of Dostoevsky's deepest ambivalence toward what he regarded as the most fundamental moral, religious, and political issues.

Dostoevsky's complex attitude toward his own utopianism recalls Prince Myshkin's attitude toward the ecstatic visions of universal harmony that he experiences during his epileptic fits. Just before the fit, Myshkin explains to himself (*The Idiot*, 213–214),

> His mind and his heart were flooded with extraordinary light; all his uneasiness, all his doubts, all his anxieties were relieved at once. . . . But these moments, these flashes were only the prelude of that final second (it was never more than a second) with which the fit itself began. . . . Thinking of that moment later, when he was all right again, he often said to himself that all these gleams and flashes of the highest self-awareness and self-consciousness, and therefore also of the "highest form of existence," were nothing but disease, the interruption of the normal condition; and if so, it was not at all the highest form of being, but on the contrary must be reckoned the lowest. And yet, all the same, he came at last to an extremely paradoxical conclusion. "What if it *is* a disease? " he decided at last. "What does it matter that it is an abnormal intensity, if the

result, if the minute of sensation, remembered and analyzed afterwards in health, turns out to be the acme of harmony and beauty, and gives a feeling, unknown and undivined till then, of completeness, of proportion, of reconciliation, and of ecstatic devotional merging with the highest synthesis of life?"

In the *Diary*, the ridiculous man also asks what it matters that his vision may have been an impossible dream, if that dream "announced to me a different life, renewed, grand, and full of power!" (ch. 2). In part, the identification of such visions as "the interruption of the normal condition" reflects the fact that they are necessarily experienced alone—*idio*syncratically—and can scarcely be communicated.[40] The ridiculous man's recognition that he "lost the words" to describe the "live image" (ch. 5) possessing his soul is comparable to the Idiot's regret that his visions are ultimately beyond language and therefore beyond sharing. Reflecting on the words he has used to describe them to himself, he continues (214),

> These vague expressions seemed to him very comprehensible, though too weak. That it really was "beauty and worship," that it really was "the highest synthesis of life" he could not doubt, and could not admit the possibility of doubt. It was not as though he saw abnormal and unreal visions of some sort at that moment, as from hashish, opium, or wine, destroying the reason and distorting the soul. . . . These moments were only an extraordinary quickening of self-consciousness—if the condition was to be expressed in one word—and at the same time of self-awareness in the highest degree of immediacy. Since at that second, that is, at the very last conscious moment before the fit, he had time to say to himself clearly and consciously, "Yes, for this moment one might give one's whole life!" then without doubt that moment was really worth the whole of life. He did not insist on the dialectical part of his argument, however. Stupefaction, spiritual darkness, idiocy stood before him conspicuously as the consequence of these "higher moments"; seriously, of course, he could not have disputed it. There was undoubtedly a mistake in his conclusion—that is, in his estimate of that minute, but the reality of the sensation somewhat perplexed him. What, indeed, was he to make of that reality?

The direct sensation of existence which is nevertheless a disease, the height which is also the abyss, the threat of idiocy which reveals the highest wisdom —all these contradictions, already implicit in its ambivalent title, are developed and intensified in this extraordinary novel. The Idiot himself is a direct literary descendant of the wise fool so often and so ambiguously praised in Renaissance literature, especially of the fool to whom he is so often compared, Don Quixote. When Aglaia compares him to this and other quixotic figures, the prince, wondering at her frequent shifts from "genuine and noble feeling" to "unmistakable . . . mockery" (239), cannot decide "whether she was in earnest or laughing" (236).

Don Quixote is also a central figure in the self-consciously quixotic *Diary*, where he plays a complex—multiple and inconsistent—role. In some articles, for example, in "The Metternichs and the Don Quixotes" (February, 77, I, 4), the type exemplified by Cervantes' hero turns out not to *be* ridiculous, but only to be called such by scoffers who are themselves, like their counterparts in most utopias, ridiculous. These scoffers, maintains Dostoevsky, who in his pre-Siberian days was himself given the mocking epithet "Knight of the Mournful Countenance,"[41] fail to understand that in the Last Days the most practical policies are the most idealistic, while the most machiavellian strategies are the most likely to fail. "Believe me," he concludes, "Don Quixote also knows an advantage and is able to calculate." But in other articles (e.g., "A Lie Is Saved by a Lie," September, 77, II, 1), Don Quixote is alluded to as truly foolish, both because he takes fiction for nonfiction and because, like the dreamers of Dostoevsky's early stories, he will not recognize or acknowledge unpoetic fact. These contradictions are similar to those of the diarist himself. At times, he portrays himself as the only one to understand apocalyptic politics, and, therefore, as the greatest realist. At other times, however, he portrays himself as a somewhat ludicrous and harmless flâneur, imagining an impossible golden age when pompous generals and their wives have become "cleverer than Voltaire, more sensitive than Rousseau, incomparably more seductive than Alcibiades, Don Juan, the Lucreces, the Juliets, and the Beatrices! . . . And can it be, can it really be, that the golden age exists only on porcelain cups?" ("The Golden Age in the Pocket," January, 76, I, 4). It is especially interesting that when, in the well-known digression from an article on "The Beginning of the End," the diarist interprets *Don Quixote*, his understanding of Cervantes' work seems to correspond to the import of his own (March, 76, II, 1; italics and ellipsis in original):

> Someone, possibly Heine, related how, while reading *Don Quixote* as a child, he had cried profusely when he reached the part where the contemptible and sensible barber Samson Carasco defeated him. In the whole world, there is nothing more profound or more powerful than this *fiction*. This is still the last and greatest word of human thought, this is the bitterest irony man could express; and if the world were to end, and there, somewhere, they should ask people: "Did you understand your life on earth, and what have you concluded about it?"—man could silently present *Don Quixote*: "This is my conclusion about life; can you condemn me for it?" I am not asserting he would be right to say so, but . . .

Here Dostoevsky interrupts his own prediction of a millenarian end to history to suggest an image of a very different Last Judgment, one of the "bitterest irony," with which he sadly agrees—for a moment. Characteristically, even this contradictory evaluation of the human condition is itself almost contradicted by a final qualification, which is, in turn, qualified by the final ellipsis . . .

The diarist seems to react with a similar mixture of irony and agreement in his assessments of the *Diary*'s other quixotic figures, especially the "paradoxicalist" and a second paradoxicalist, the "witty bureaucrat." These wise and foolish figures speak in exemplary rhetorical paradoxes, praising the unprais-able and advising the unadvisable. Their contradictions seem to epitomize those of the *Diary* itself, and to point to its generic roots. When the paradox-icalist praises war, for instance, it is hard to tell whether to take the article as a satire on European conflicts and their apologists, or—in view of the fact that Dostoevsky himself advances quite similar arguments in "War Is Not Always a Scourge, Sometimes It Is Salvation" and other apparently un-ironic articles— as quite the opposite, that is, as a call to arms. Is the paradoxicalist's enco-mium to hypocritical politeness as the closest approximation to the golden age to be taken as an oblique endorsement of Dostoevsky's plans for a genuine utopia—plans to which the paradoxicalist is eventually converted—or, on the contrary, as a wry satire on "a man whom absolutely no one knows" but a type whom everyone knows: "he is a *dreamer*" (April, 76, II, 2). Or is he per-haps not an impractical dreamer, but only called such (as the diarist implies at the end of one article) by those who do not wish to consider his arguments? When he is at last converted to the diarist's political program, in what light, or shadow, is that program placed?

And is the ridiculous man really ridiculous or only called ridiculous? We may observe that the interpretive history of this story repeats that of More's *Utopia* (and parallels that of Dostoevsky's Grand Inquisitor legend). Whereas most readers have taken the "Dream" as an unambiguous utopia, and the nar-rator's conversion as his genuine salvation, a number have interpreted the story in the opposite way. "The Golden Age, like every other important con-cept in Dostoevsky's world, is a dialectical concept: it can be sacrament or blasphemy, the vision of regeneration in Christ or the vision of degeneration in the imitation of Christ," Edward Wasiolek has observed. *"The Dream of a Ridiculous Man* is blasphemy, and yet it has been taken universally by Dosto-evsky's interpreters as *sacrament."*[42] This school of interpretation usually argues that the story's narrator converts not from solipsistic atheism to the true faith, but rather from nihilistic egoism to monomaniacal egoism. The solipsist, it is contended, is recognizable in his religious rebirth, especially in his conviction that he alone knows the Truth: he is, in short, another one of *The Possessed.*

Each proponent of this reading discovers in the ridiculous man's sermons what I called earlier an "irony of origins." That is, his beliefs are discredited as the product of his personality and biography and therefore, if not neces-sarily false, at least compromised in their advocacy. According to Wasiolek (145-147),

> The dream of the Ridiculous Man is *his dream*, and it is as good as his
> motives, and his motives are self-interested. Dostoevsky has presented in
> his story what he has presented so often: he has placed some cherished
> truth in the mouth and being of a self-interested person. . . . Dostoevsky
> criticism will always go wrong when it separates Dostoevsky's ideas from
> those characters who carry the ideas. . . . What we must not forget is that
> the dream is the Ridiculous Man's dream. Psychology has taught us that

we are all the actors in our dreams. . . . He corrupts the truth by making it his. . . .

By contrast, those who take the story as an unambiguous utopia implicitly or explicitly rule out psychological readings as inappropriate. They compare the story not to psychological novels or stories, but rather to the lives of the saints (such as the embedded Life of Zossima in *Karamazov*) or to religious narratives of conversion (sometimes citing the conversion of Markel in *Karamazov* or of Raskolnikov in the epilogue to *Crime and Punishment*). In the story of Markel, it may be recalled, the doctor regards the dying man's conversion as evidence that "he is going insane because of the disease" (344—pt. 2, bk. 6, ch. 1). But this crude psychology, like that of other "psychologists" in *Karamazov*, seems to be an example of self-serving narrow-mindedness, a complacent refusal to accept the possibility of a Truth reached not by personal need, motive, or experience, but by grace: a Truth, that is, which is inexplicable solely in terms of biography.

There are, in other words, works in which one will go wrong to "separate . . . ideas from those characters who carry the ideas" and those in which one will go wrong if one does *not* so separate them. In novels or novelistic short stories one must understand ideas as *someone's* ideas; in utopias, saints' lives, certain philosophical parables (such as Voltaire's), or medieval dream-visions, one must not. *The question, in short, is one of genre*; and unless that question is addressed, arguments are bound to be circular or at cross purposes. One cannot *show* the story to be anti-utopian by means of psychology, because it is precisely this method of interpretation which is in question. Conversely, one cannot demonstrate it to be an unambiguous utopia (or an account of a genuine conversion) by identifying the hero's views with the author's, because the appropriateness of such an identification is what needs to be proved. One can only show that *if* one takes the story to be of this kind, *then* certain readings are implausible. But *whether* to take it one way would seem to be a question about which sophisticated readers may and do disagree. "The Dream," in other words, is what we have been calling here a boundary work— that is, one which has come to be interpreted according to contradictory generic conventions.

No one, to my knowledge, has tried to resolve these contradictions by reading the story in the context of the *Diary*—that is, by taking it not as a self-sufficient but as an embedded work. But even this contextual interpretation ultimately fails to resolve them. When I first tried to read "The Dream" in this way, the story seemed to be an unambiguous utopia.[43] Appearing in the same issue of the *Diary* in which Dostoevsky proclaims that the Eastern War is the "exception" to history, that "War Is Not Always a Scourge, Sometimes It Is Salvation," and that Russia has taken "the first step toward the achievement of that eternal peace in which we are fortunate to believe—toward the achievement *in truth* of international unity and *in truth* of philanthropic prosperity!" (April, 77, I, 2)—appearing in this context, the story seemed to be a fictional exemplification of those beliefs. But as I read further, and re-read earlier passages of the *Diary*, I discovered ambiguity. The story's immediate context was undoubtedly utopian, I reasoned, but it also seemed to allude to more distant sections that are not. Is the ridiculous man, perhaps, another paradoxicalist? Are we expected to think of the diarist's warnings against "false Christs" and his psychological studies of those who, convinced that they alone know the way to brotherhood, are themselves the most extreme example of unbrotherly "Dissociation" (March, 76, I, 3)? Does his dream, we may ask, resemble the saving visions of "The Peasant Marey" (February, 76, I, 3) and "Vlas" (1873) or, on the contrary, the insane one of "Bobok"? And does the narrative's subtitle, "A Fantastic Story," indicate that it is not a psychological story, or is it rather designed to recall the *Diary*'s earlier study of monomaniacal egoism with the same subtitle, "The Meek One"?

The *Diary*, in short, is itself an ambiguous context, and the story appears to be not only a boundary work—that is, one that has been interpreted according to contradictory generic conventions—but also a threshold work, that is, one *designed* to resonate between opposing genres and interpretations. Or to put it differently, *the "Dream" is a meta-utopia embedded in a meta-utopia*, an epitome of the larger work's genre *and* of its ambivalence. If one chooses to take it this way, the passage that will be foregrounded is the one immediately before the ending in which the ridiculous man, admitting his vision to be impossible, still refuses to surrender it. "I'll go further," he writes, "let this never be realized, and let paradise never come (this much I already understand!)—well, all the same, I will go on preaching it." Those who read *Utopia* as a meta-utopia may recall the concluding lines of book 2, in which "More"—or is it More?—observes that "I cannot agree with all that he [Hythloday] said. But I readily admit that there are many features in the Utopian commonwealth which it is easier for me to wish for in our countries than to have any hope of seeing realized" (245–247). When the "Dream" is read in this ambiguous way, its import seems closest neither to *The Possessed* nor to the epilogue of *Crime and Punishment*, but to *The Idiot*; and its title—like that of *The Idiot*—seems to invite the contradictory readings it has in fact received.

* * *

The diarist's utopian sermons and the ridiculous man's advocacy of an admittedly impossible utopia may be interpreted as entering into dialogue with a number of the *Diary*'s articles about other movements or beliefs that ostentatiously defy common sense. In a series of three articles on the spread of spiritualism in Russia (and in a number of others which allude to these three), Dostoevsky investigates the sociological and psychological causes that might have led people to join this, and similar, movements. He discovers a "law of human nature, common to everyone, and precisely concerning faith and disbelief in general"—that is, concerning all faith, including his own. The etiology of spiritualism turns out to be an etiology of utopianism as well—or so Dostoevsky seems to imply when he wryly observes that friends have discerned in my account "*something* that seems to be favorable to spiritualism, despite all my denials" (April, 76, II, 3). Placed among his uncompromising predictions of an imminent end to history, these seriocomic and deeply ambivalent articles cast an additional shadow of irony on the work's utopianism. Conversely, the work's dialectic of utopianism and anti-utopianism, like the similar dialectic in one of its models, *From the Other Shore*, becomes emblematic of all encounters of faith with doubt, and of hope with disillusionment.

The central theme of these articles on psychic phenomena is, characteristically, a paradoxical one: belief in the incredible. Dostoevsky chooses to examine the nature of such beliefs by considering the kinds of arguments raised in favor of and in opposition to them; and he concludes that such arguments are necessarily inconclusive and at cross purposes. For if the beliefs are truly incredible, Dostoevsky reasons, then they cannot be proved. And if they are accepted in spite of (or because of) their incredibility, then it is equally pointless to try to disprove them. It is, therefore, with considerable irony that Dostoevsky discusses the efforts of the Committee for the Investigation of Spiritualistic Phenomena, and of its chairman, the chemist Dmitri Mendeleev, to "crush spiritualism" by disproving it on scientific grounds. For in the first place, Dostoevsky observes, one cannot refute a rejection of science by showing it to be unscientific; and, in the second place, for such an investigation to be meaningful even on scientific grounds "it would be necessary that at least one of the scientists on the committee should be capable of admitting the existence of devils, if only hypothetically." "However," Dostoevsky continues drily, "you could hardly find one of them who believes in the devil, despite the fact that terribly many people who do not believe in God believe readily and with pleasure in the devil. Therefore, the committee is incompetent in this matter" (January, 76, III, 2).

On the other hand, Dostoevsky continues, the spiritualists will never convince their opponents of the existence of a nonmaterial world because any evidence they might offer would necessarily be material. "Writing to Moscow from the other world, Gogol affirmed that these are devils," he gives a sample of such evidence. "I have read the letter, it's his style" (January, 76, III, 2). The devil in *Karamazov* discusses the spiritualists in a similar vein: "just imagine," he remarks to Ivan, "they imagine that they are serving the cause of religion, because the devils show them their horns from the other world. That, they say, is a material proof, so to speak, of the existence of another world. The other world and material proofs, what next!" (774).

Yet another reason one cannot demonstrate either the truth or falsity of such beliefs, according to Dostoevsky, is that the very same "evidence" that is disproof for one side may be the surest proof for the other. For example, Dostoevsky writes in his article on "The Extraordinary Shrewdness of Devils, If Only They Are Devils," the opponents of spiritualism have argued that if these really were devils, they would surely reveal some new scientific truth or create some awesome invention and so banish all doubt of their existence; since they have performed only the most trivial tricks, the skeptics conclude, they would have to be very stupid devils indeed—and therefore cannot be devils at all. But it would be possible to argue, Dostoevsky answers, that this very refusal to prove their existence is the surest sign of both their existence and their intelligence. "This time people are attacking them though they aren't guilty," he remarks, "and are considering them foolish" when they are not. For what would happen if the devils "were to invent the electric telegraph (that is, if it had not already been invented)" or to shower humanity with material blessings beyond the dreams of the most ecstatic utopian? People would, of course, at first be sure that "only now has the higher life begun" and would fall down and worship the Beast; but, Dostoevsky predicts, "it is doubtful that these raptures would be enough for a single generation! Suddenly people would see that they had no more life . . . that life had been taken from them in exchange for bread, for 'stones turned to bread' . . . and that *happiness is not in happiness, but only in the attaining of happiness.* Boredom and ennui would ensue" and, in the end, people would reject the devils forever. "No," he concludes, "the devils will not commit such an important political mistake. They are shrewd politicians, and are advancing to their goal by the subtlest and most sensible way (that is, again, if they really are devils!)" (January, 76, III, 2; italics in original).

It is even possible, Dostoevsky suggests, that Mendeleev himself is playing into the hands of the devils and acting according to their plan. For they doubtless understand, as Mendeleev and his committee apparently do not, that not evidence but vanity confirms mystical belief, from which it follows that ridicule and accusations of fraud will encourage, not crush, spiritualism. Mystical movements *need* scoffers, and "mystical ideas love persecution, they are created by it. Every such persecuted thought resembles that petroleum which the incendiaries poured over the floors and walls of the Tuileries before the fire. . . . Oh, the devils know the power of a forbidden belief. . . . " (January, 76, III, 2). Still more, Dostoevsky reasons, if the committee should somehow induce a moment of doubt in the spiritualists, that very doubt would (according to the "law" governing such beliefs) soon lead them to still more fanatic expressions of belief and to actions so compromising to their vanity and worldly position that all possibility of a change of heart would be lost forever. Ivan's devil makes a similar point in *Karamazov*: in matters of faith and doubt, he explains (784),

> Homeopathic doses perhaps are the strongest. . . . hesitation, suspense, conflict between belief and disbelief—is sometimes such torture to a conscientious man, such as you are, that it's better to hang oneself at once. Knowing that you are inclined to believe in me, I administered some disbelief by telling you that anecdote. I lead you to belief and disbelief by turns, and I have my motive in it. It's the new method.

The diarist's "eternal law of human nature" is, in short, that for all such "mystical" beliefs "even the most mathematical proofs mean absolutely nothing. . . . Faith and mathematical proofs are two incompatible things. He who wishes to believe cannot be stopped" (March, 76, II, 3). In a number of passages, the diarist seems to acknowledge the applicability of that law to his own mystical beliefs, and to his tendency to reaffirm them all the more strongly as disconfirmations accumulate and ridicule grows sharper. For example, in one of his articles on Don Quixote, his central symbol of idealism and Russia's mission, he explains why, for a madman, disconfirmation is in principle impossible: because he can always save one "lie" (i.e., illusion) with another, still more fantastic one. Indeed, Dostoevsky concludes, this self-protective process leads even sane people to self-deception regarding cherished ideas—though, of course, in that case, doubt will recur, "tease your mind, roam about in your soul, and prevent you from living in peace with your beloved fancy" (September, 77, II, 1). Most interesting of all, at the close of one of his prophetic articles Dostoevsky unexpectedly considers the psychology of prophecy itself, and concludes with a reformulation of his "eternal law": "We always see reality almost exactly the way we *wish* to see it, the way we desire *in advance* to interpret it to ourselves. . . . This is not at all unusual, and at times, I swear, we sooner believe in a miracle and in an impossibility than in a reality or in a truth *which we do not want to see*. And so it always is on earth, in this is the whole history of mankind" (May–June, 77, I, 1).

* * *

Self-reflection—the ability to make an object of one's deepest feeling, to set it before oneself, to bow down to it, and perhaps immediately after, to ridicule it—was developed in him [Herzen] to the highest degree. ("Old People," 1873)

That same self-reflection is exemplified in the *Diary*'s own resonance between utopia and its parodies, and, more generally, between all faith and doubt. For the *Diary* is shaped as a literary work by Dostoevsky's complex and tortured quest for faith. He once described that quest in a letter from exile: There are moments, he wrote (*Pis'ma*, I, 142), when

one thirsts for faith like "parched grass" . . . . I will speak for myself: I am a child of the century, a child of disbelief and doubt to this day and even (this I know) to the grave. What terrible torments this thirst to believe has cost me and still costs me; a thirst which grows all the stronger in my soul as opposite proofs increase within me. . . . Still more, even if someone proved to me that Christ was outside the truth, and it *really* were so that the truth is outside of Christ, I would still rather remain with Christ than with the truth.

Notes

All citations from *The Diary of a Writer* are from volumes 11 and 12 of the thirteen-volume complete works of Dostoevsky, ed. B. Tomaševskij and K. Xalabaev (Moscow-Leningrad: Gosizdat, 1926-1930). References are by month, year, chapter, article: for example, "The Boy at Christ's Christmas Party" is January, 76, II, 2. For 1873, reference is by article title and year: for example, "Vlas," 1873. Tomaševskij and Xalabaev have placed the announcement to the January, 1876, issue in the appendix to volume 11, p. 508. All translations from the *Diary* are mine.

For Dostoevsky's articles and feuilletons, I have used volume 13 of Tomaševskij and Xalabaev, henceforth *Stat'i*. For Dostoevsky's letters, I have used the four-volume edition edited by A. S. Dolinin (Moscow-Leningrad: Gosizdat, 1929-1958), henceforth *Pis'ma*. Unless otherwise indicated, translations from the articles and letters are mine.

I have used standard translations (Constance Garnett whenever possible) of Dostoevsky's novels and the *Winter Notes on Summer Impressions*, amended for accuracy when necessary based on the texts in the thirty-volume *Complete Works* of Dostoevsky now in process of publication. Citations from translated versions of other works of Russian literature have also been amended for accuracy when needed.

Only first references appear in the notes; all subsequent references are given in the text.

Preface

1. These points are made, for example, in Boris Tomashevsky, "Literary Genres," *Russian Poetics in Translation*, vol. 5, *Formalism: History, Comparison, Genre*, ed. L. M. O'Toole and Ann Shukman (Colchester: Univ. of Essex, 1978), pp. 52–93; Jan Mukařovsky, *Aesthetic Function, Norm and Value as Social Facts*, tr. Mark E. Suino (Ann Arbor: Dept. of Slavic Languages, Univ. of Michigan, 1970); Mikhail Bakhtin, *Problems of Dostoevsky's Poetics* (especially ch. 4, "Characteristics of Genre and Plot Characteristics in Dostoevsky's Works"), tr. R. W. Rotsel (Ann Arbor: Ardis, 1973); and Claudio Guillén, *Literature as System: Essays toward the Theory of Literary History* (Princeton: Princeton Univ. Press, 1971). For a summary of key issues and approaches in genre theory, see also the chapter on "Literary Genres" in René Wellek and Austin Warren, *Theory of Literature*, 3rd ed. (New York: Harcourt, Brace, 1956), pp. 226-237.

2. Paul Hernadi, *Beyond Genre: New Directions in Literary Classification* (Ithaca: Cornell Univ. Press, 1972), pp. 152–153.
3. Barbara Herrnstein Smith, review of *Beyond Genre* by Paul Hernadi, *Journal of Aesthetics and Art Criticism*, 32, no. 2 (1973): 296–298.
4. The best consideration of genre in relation to the purposes of classifiers is Dan Ben-Amos, "Introduction" and "Analytical Categories and Ethnic Genres," *Folklore Genres*, ed. Dan Ben-Amos (Austin: Univ. of Texas Press, 1976) pp. ix–xlv, 215–242. See also the book's excellent bibliography on genre theory.
5. An excellent recent study on lyric forms of discourse is Sharon Cameron, *Lyric Time: Dickinson and the Limits of Genre* (Baltimore: Johns Hopkins Univ. Press, 1979).
6. On the origins and development of the Soviet Socialist Realist "novel," see Katerina Clark, *Ritual Form in the Soviet Novel: Socialist Realism in Its Cultural Context* (forthcoming).
7. One can, of course, reasonably demand that terms be used consistently in any given discussion.
8. For a Formalist account of that projected science, see Boris M. Ejxenbaum, "The Theory of the Formal Method," *Readings in Russian Poetics: Formalist and Structuralist Views*, ed. Ladislav Matejka and Krystyna Pomorska (Cambridge, Mass.: M.I.T. Press, 1971), pp. 3–37. The Russian word "nauka," it should be noted, has different connotations than the English "science"; but it may also be observed that in Formalist usage, the meaning of the Russian word comes relatively close to that of the English.
9. A recent metareading (i.e., a reading of readings) of Dostoevsky's Grand Inquisitor legend is Robert L. Belknap, "The Rhetoric of an Ideological Novel," in *Literature and Society in Imperial Russia, 1800–1914*, ed. William Mills Todd III (Stanford: Stanford Univ. Press, 1978), pp. 173–201.

1. Dostoevsky's Icon of Chaos

1. Pt. 3, ch. 6; Constance Garnett translates the line: "Can anything that has no shape appear in a shape?"—*The Idiot* (New York: Random, Modern Library Giant, 1935), p. 389.

   For a consideration of the relation of Ippolit's question to Dostoevsky's own aesthetics, see Robert Louis Jackson, "Two Kinds of Beauty," *Dostoevsky's Quest for Form: A Study of His Philosophy of Art* (New Haven: Yale Univ. Press, 1966), pp. 40–70.
2. Herman Melville, *Moby-Dick or, The Whale*, ed. Charles Feidelson, Jr. (Indianapolis: Bobbs-Merrill, 1964), pp. 35–36.
3. For information on the *Diary*'s circulation, see the editorial notes to volume 12 of the Tomaševskij and Xalabaev *Complete Works*, p. 460. The most popular issue sold 8,000 copies.

4. Leo Tolstoy, "Some Words about *War and Peace*," in *War and Peace*, ed. George Gibian (New York: Norton, 1966), p. 1366.
5. I. L. Volgin, "'Dnevnik pisatelja': tekst i kontekst," in *Dostoevskij: Materialy i issledovanija*, vol. 3, ed. G. M. Fridlender (Leningrad: Nauka, 1978), pp. 151-158. See also Volgin's earlier article, "Dostoevskij i carskaja cenzura (k istorii izdanija 'Dnevnika pisatelja')," *Russkaja literatura*, no. 4 (1970): 106-120. The best study of the *Diary* as a literary work is V. A. Tunimanov's programmatic article, "Publicistika Dostoevskogo. 'Dnevnik pisatelja,'" in *Dostoevskij–xudožnik i myslitel': Sbornik statej* (Moscow: Xudožestvennaja literatura, 1972), pp. 165-209. Other studies of the *Diary* as a literary work include L. S. Dmitrieva, "O žanrovom svoeobrazii 'Dnevnika pisatelja' F. M Dostoevskogo (k probleme tipologii žurnala)," *Vestnik Moskovskogo universiteta*, serija 11, "Žurnalistika," no. 6 (1969): 23-25; V. A. Desnickij, "Publicistika i literatura v 'Dnevnika pisatelja' F. M. Dostoevskogo," the introduction to volume 12 of the 1926-1930 edition of Dostoevsky's works; and V. A. Sidorov's pioneering article, "O Dnevnike pisatelja," in *Dostoevskij: Stat'i i materialy (sbornik vtoroj)*, ed. A. S. Dolinin (Leningrad-Moscow: Mysl', 1924), vol. 2, pp. 109-116.

I first discussed the *Diary* as a literary work in my doctoral dissertation: "Dostoevsky's *Diary of a Writer*: Threshold Art" (Yale 1974), which despite some similarity in terminology with the present study, overlaps it in only a few places. An article based on that dissertation, "Dostoevskij's *Writer's Diary* as Literature of Process," appeared in *Russian Literature*, 4-1 (1976): 1-14. The last portion of chapter 2 of the present study draws on my article "Reading between the Genres: Dostoevsky's *Writer's Diary* as Metafiction," *Yale Review* (Winter 1979): 224-234.
6. "From all twelve issues (for January, February, March, etc.) a book will be composed" ("Announcement," January, 76).
7. Mikhail Bakhtin, *Problems of Dostoevsky's Poetics*, tr. R. W. Rotsel (Ann Arbor: Ardis, 1973), p. 97. References in text are to *PDP*.
8. The best study of the poetics and traditions of menippean satire is Philip Hoyt Holland, "Robert Burton's *Anatomy of Melancholy* and Menippean Satire, Humanist and English," dissertation (Univ. of London, 1979).
9. "Dejstvitel'nost' stremitsja k razdrobleniju" (Reality strives toward fragmentation), *Notes from the House of the Dead*, pt. 2, ch. 7.
10. The two quotations are from Ivan Gončarov, *Sobranie sočienenij v 8 tomax*, vol. 8 (Moscow, 1955), pp. 212-213 and 457, respectively, as cited in Jackson, *Dostoevsky's Quest*, pp. 109-111. I follow Jackson's discussion of these passages.
11. *F. M. Dostoevskij v rabote nad romanom "Podrostok": Tvorčeskie rukopisi*, ed. I. I. Anisimov et al., Literaturnoe nasledstvo, 77 (Moscow: Nauka, 1965), pp. 342-343.
12. Fyodor Dostoevsky, *"Notes from Underground" and "The Grand Inquisitor," with Relevant Works by Chernyshevsky, Shchedrin and Dostoevsky*, tr. Ralph E. Matlaw (New York: Dutton, 1960), p. 3.
13. *The House of the Dead*, tr. Constance Garnett (New York: Dell, 1959), pp. 32-35.

14. *A Raw Youth*, tr. Constance Garnett (New York: Dell, 1959), p. 26.
15. The translation of this paragraph is Constance Garnett's, amended for accuracy and punctuation, in *The Short Stories of Dostoevsky*, ed. William Phillips (New York: Dial, 1946), p. 545.
16. Jean-Paul Sartre, *Nausea*, tr. Lloyd Alexander (New York: New Directions, 1964), pp. 39–40.
17. V. G. Belinskij, *Polnoe sobranie sočinenij*, vol. 10 (Moscow, 1956), p. 318, as cited in E. I. Žurbina, *Teorija i praktika xudožestvenno-publicističeskix žanrov: Očerk, Fel'eton* (Moscow: Mysl', 1969), p. 32.
18. Žurbina, *Teorija i praktika*, p. 6. My discussion of the feuilleton also draws on *Fel'etony sorokovyx godov: Žurnal'naja i gazetnaja proza I. A. Gončarova, F. M. Dostoevskogo, I. S. Turgeneva*, ed. Ju. G. Oksman (Moscow-Leningrad: Academia, 1930); Donald Fanger, "The Most Fantastic City: Approaches to a Myth," *Dostoevsky and Romantic Realism: A Study of Dostoevsky in Relation to Balzac, Dickens, and Gogol* (Chicago: Univ. of Chicago Press, 1965); and Joseph Frank, "The Petersburg Feuilletons," *Dostoevsky: The Seeds of Revolt, 1821–1849* (Princeton: Princeton Univ. Press, 1976).
19. Cited by Žurbina, *Teorija i praktika*, p. 56, from vol. 30 of Gorky's collected works, 1956.
20. V. G. Korolenko, *Sobranie sočinenij v desjati tomax*, vol. 8 (Moscow, 1955), p. 15, as cited in Žurbina, *Teorija i praktika*, p. 70.
21. Montaigne, "Of Friendship," in *Selected Essays*, ed. Blanchard Bates (New York: Random, 1949), p. 59.
22. On "Aesopian language" in Dostoevsky's feuilletons, see Frank, "The Petersburg Feuilletons."
23. Cited by Frank, ibid., p. 219.
24. In Russia, the *term* "feuilleton" later came to be applied to a class of politically dogmatic texts (see Žurbina, *Teorija i praktika*, part 2). In the present study we are concerned only with the "whimsical" type. For an excellent example of a feuilleton rich in metaliterary play, see Druzhinin's "Dramatic Feuilleton about the Feuilleton and about Feuilletonists," in *Russkij fel'ton*, ed. A. V. Zapadov and E. P. Proxorov (Moscow: Gosizdat pol. lit., 1958), pp. 122–128.
25. Viktor Šklovskij, *Gamburgskij Ščet [The Hamburg Score]* (1928; rpt. Ann Arbor: Xerox/Univ. Microfilms, 1968), p. 63.
26. From the June 1 feuilleton, translated from *Stat'i*. All translations from the June 1 feuilleton are mine; translations from the other three feuilletons are from David Magarshack (trans.), *Dostoevsky's Occasional Writings* (New York: Random, 1963), amended for accuracy when necessary. Magarshack gives April 22 as the date for the April 27 feuilleton (in *Stat'i*) and, in addition to omitting the feuilleton for June 1, includes another which, in fact, was not written by Dostoevsky. References to feuilletons are by date, according to *Stat'i*.
27. *The Short Stories of Dostoevsky*, pp. 61–62.
28. The contents of each issue of *Time* and *Epoch* may be found in the

appendix to V. S. Nečaeva, *Žurnal M. M. i F. M. Dostoevskix "Epoxa,"* *1864-65* (Moscow: Nauka, 1975), pp. 233-260.

29. For a discussion of the relation of the "Petersburg Visions" to "A Weak Heart," see Fanger, "The Most Fantastic City."

30. F. Dostoevsky, *Winter Notes on Summer Impressions*, tr. Richard Lee Renfield (New York: Criterion, 1955), p. 35.

31. According to Tunimanov, D. V. Averkiev suggested, in his own *Diary of a Writer* (1885), that Addison may have been a model for Dostoevsky's experiment: Tunimanov, "Publicistika Dostoevskogo," p. 166, note 1.

32. Charles Dickens, *The Old Curiosity Shop*, ed. Angus Easson (Harmondsworth: Penguin, 1972), p. 678. Citations from the *Clock* are to the appendix of this edition, henceforth *OCS*. For information on the *Clock*'s publication, I also draw on Malcolm Andrews' introduction.

33. As cited in John Forster, *The Life of Charles Dickens*, ed. J. W. T. Ley (London: Cecil Palmer, 1928), p. 140.

34. Shklovsky's observations are cited in chapter 2, p. 57.

35. Fyodor Dostoevsky, *The Possessed*, tr. Constance Garnett (New York: Random, 1936), pp. 127-128.

36. Anna Dostoevsky, *Dostoevsky: Reminiscences*, tr. and ed. Beatrice Stillman (New York: Liveright, 1977), pp. 212-213 (italics mine).

37. V. V. Vinogradov, *Problema avtorstva i teorija stilej* (Moscow: Xudožestvennaya literatura, 1961), p. 467.

38. Apparently excluding the 1873 *Diary*, the close of the 1877 *Diary* refers to the two, not three, years of the work's publication; and the 1880 *Diary* was designated the "third" year of publication—not the fourth, as it would have been if the columns in the *Citizen* were included.

39. "Various Varieties" is the title of a feuilleton that appeared in Dostoevsky's journal *Time*, issue no. 2, February, 1861.

40. I owe the term "algorithm" in this sense to a coversation with Robert L. Belknap, and to subsequent conversations with Aron Katsenelinboigen.

41. *The Unpublished Dostoevsky, Diaries and Notebooks (1860-81)*, vol. 2, tr. Arline Boyer and Carl Proffer (Ann Arbor: Ardis, 1976), p. 87. The Russian text may be found in *Neizdannyj Dostoevskij: Zapisnye knižki i tetradi, 1860-1881*, ed. V. R. Ščerbina et al., Literaturnoe nasledstvo, 83, (Moscow: Nauka, 1971), p. 390.

42. On the "structure of inherent relationships" in *Karamazov*, see Robert L. Belknap, *The Structure of "The Brothers Karamazov"* (The Hague: Mouton, 1967). In the *Diary* this kind of structure is used not only as a principle of artistic unity, but also as an illustration of Dostoevsky's theory of "synchronicity"—that is, his idea that in certain periods, and especially when history is drawing to its apocalyptic close, there may be significant, even occult links, between simultaneous events that have no causal connection. This theory of "synchronism," as Dostoevsky calls it, is first outlined in "Diplomacy in the Face of Worldwide Questions" (May–June, 77, II, 2); I discuss the theory in my dissertation, "Dostoevsky's *Diary of a Writer*," pp. 126-127.

43. V. A. Sidorov, "O Dnevnike pisatelja."
44. *The Unpublished Dostoevsky*, vol. 1 (1973), pp. 40-41. For the Russian text, see *Neizdannyj Dostoevskij*, pp. 174-175.
45. V. V. Timofeeva (O. Počinkovskaja), "God raboty s znamenitym pisatelem," in *F. M. Dostoevskij v vospominanijax sovremennikov*, ed. A. S. Dolinin, 2 vols. (n.p.: Xudožestvennaja literatura, 1964), vol. 2, p. 170.

2. Threshold Art

1. My discussion of literature is close to that of John M. Ellis in his recent study, *The Theory of Literary Criticism: A Logical Analysis* (Berkeley: Univ. of Calif. Press, 1974), chapter 2. "Literary texts," writes Ellis, "are defined as those that are used by the society in such a way that *the text is not taken as specifically relevant to the immediate context of its origin*" (p. 44; italics in original). I differ from Ellis in two important respects. First, Ellis's "literature" is an evaluative as well as a semiotic concept— "the category is that of the texts that are considered worth treating in the way that literary texts are treated" and so "the definition of literature must . . . bring into a definition in a very central way the notion of value" (p. 51). Second, I am not concerned, as Ellis is, with the definition of a term or with the "circumstances . . . appropriate to the use of the word 'literature'" (p. 31), but with the identification and characterization of a class of texts.
2. On the distinction between evidentiary and exemplificative use of a text, see Barbara Herrnstein Smith, *On the Margins of Discourse: The Relation of Literature to Language* (Chicago: Univ. of Chicago Press, 1978). See especially the discussion of "found poetry" and the "re-authoring" of texts, in the book's title essay, pp. 41-75.
3. Tynyanov uses this and related examples in his essays "Literaturnyj fakt" and "O literaturnoj evolucii." All citations from Ju. N. Tynjanov, *Poètika, istorija literatury, kino* (Moscow: Nauka, 1977); citations in the text are to *Poètika*. An English translation of "On Literary Evolution" appears in *Readings in Russian Poetics: Formalist and Structuralist Views* (henceforth *Readings*), pp. 66-78. On the familiar letter, see William Mills Todd III, *The Familiar Letter as a Literary Genre in the Age of Pushkin* (Princeton: Princeton Univ. Press, 1976).
4. The point is made in Smith, "The Ethics of Interpretation," *Margins of Discourse*, pp. 133-154.
5. Nikolaj S. Trubetskoj, "Afanasij Nikitin's *Journey beyond the Three Seas* as a Work of Literature [kak literaturnyj pamjatnik]," *Readings*, pp. 199-219.
6. Tynjanov, *Poètika*, p. 261.
7. For an excellent study of glosses and margins, see Lawrence Lipking, "The Marginal Gloss: Notes and Asides on Poe, Valery, 'The Ancient Mariner,' The Ordeal of the Margin, *Storiella as She Is Syung*, Versions of Leonardo,

and the Plight of Modern Criticism," *Critical Inquiry*, 3 (Summer 1977): 609-655. My discussion of boundary cases is also indebted to Smith, "On the Margins of Discourse," *Margins of Discourse*.

8. The difference is discussed by Tynjanov, *Poètika*, pp. 256-257.

9. Martin Price, "The Irrelevant Detail and the Emergence of Form," in *Aspects of Narrative: Selected Papers from the English Institute*, ed. J. Hillis Miller (New York: Columbia Univ. Press, 1971), p. 91

10. From the well-known letter to Strakhov, April 23-26, 1876, in the ninety-volume (Jubilee) edition of his works: *Polnoe sobranie sočinenij* (Moscow: Xudožestvennaja literatura, 1935-1958), vol. 62, pp. 268-270. All cited translations from Tolstoy have been checked with this edition and amended for accuracy when necessary. The translation cited here is Magarshack's, as it appears in Price, *Aspects*, pp. 78-79.

11. Leo Tolstoy, *Short Stories*, ed. Ernest J. Simmons (New York: Random, 1964), p. 175. The translation is by Louise and Aylmer Maude.

12. On the metacommunicative message "this is play," see Gregory Bateson, "A Theory of Play and Fantasy," in *Steps to an Ecology of Mind* (New York: Ballantine, 1972), pp. 177-193. See also the development of Bateson's ideas in Erving Goffman, *Frame Analysis: An Essay on the Organization of Experience* (New York: Harper, 1974).

13. See Martin Price, "The Fictional Contract," in *Literary Theory and Structure: Essays in Honor of William K. Wimsatt*, ed. Frank Brady, John Palmer, and Martin Price (New Haven: Yale Univ. Press, 1973), pp. 151-178, for a development of ideas in "The Irrelevant Detail."

14. Smith, *Margins of Discourse*, pp. 28-30.

15. Leo Tolstoy, "Some Words about *War and Peace*," in *War and Peace*, ed. George Gibian (New York: Norton, 1966), p. 1371.

16. Marc Slonim, taking the preface as nonfictional, speaks of Alyosha's "mature life" in his introduction to Fyodor Dostoevsky, *The Brothers Karamazov*, tr. Constance Garnett (New York: Random, 1950), p. xiii. Pagination according to Modern Language college edition; citations from *Karamazov* in the text are to this edition.

17. "From the Author," *Karamazov*, p. xviii [*sic*]. Robert L. Belknap has argued for the fictionality of the preface in *The Structure of "The Brothers Karamazov"* (The Hague: Mouton, 1967), pp. 106-109.

18. Northrop Frye, *Anatomy of Criticism: Four Essays* (Princeton: Princeton Univ. Press, 1957), p. 304.

19. As Barbara Herrnstein Smith observes, when a linguist gives as an example of a possible sentence "The carpenter hit the nail with the hammer" or a logician offers the sample proposition "All swans are white" they are representing, not making, statements, and the statements are therefore fictional—or, in her terms, "fictive." One could not refute the logician by pointing to a black swan. Nevertheless, as she points out, these statements are still not artworks (Smith, *Margins of Discourse*, pp. 50-54).

20. Boris M. Ejxenbaum, "Kak sdelana 'Šinel'' Gogolja," in *Skvoz' literaturu: Sbornik statej* (1924; rpt. Wurzburg: Journalfranz, 1972), p. 194.

An English translation of "How Gogol's 'Overcoat' Is Made" appears in *Gogol from the Twentieth Century*, ed. and tr. Robert A. Maguire (Princeton: Princeton Univ. Press, 1974), pp. 267–291.

21. On the connection between "The Nose" and *Tristram Shandy*, see V. V. Vinogradov, "Naturaličeskij grotesk (Sjužet i komposicija povesti Gogolja 'Nos')," *Evolucija russkogo naturalizma: Gogol' i Dostoevskij* (Leningrad: Academia, 1929), pp. 7–88.

22. "Some Words about *War and Peace.*"

23. "This is not a fiction," Tolstoy writes at the end of the narrative section of "Lucerne," "but a positive fact, which can be verified by anyone who likes from the permanent residents at the Hotel Schweizerhof, after ascertaining from the papers who the foreigners were who were staying at the Schweizerhof on the 7th of July" (*Short Stories*, p. 328).

24. *Art and Illusion: A Study in the Psychology of Pictorial Representation*, 1st paperback ed., Bollingen Series 35, 5 (Princeton: Princeton Univ. Press, 1969).

25. Viktor Šklovskij, "Prostranstvo v živopisi i suprematisty," *Xod konja: Sbornik statej* [*The Knight's Move: A Collection of Articles*] (1923; rpt. Ann Arbor: Xerox/Univ. Microfilms, 1974), p. 97.

26. Cited in Viktor Šklovskij, "Iskusstvo, kak priem," *O teorii prozy* [*On the Theory of Prose*] (Moscow: Federacija, 1929), p. 13. Shklovsky identifies the citation as from Tolstoy's diary of February 29, 1897 [*sic*] —another defamiliarization?

27. Viktor Shklovsky, *Zoo or Letters Not about Love*, tr. and ed. Richard Sheldon (Ithaca: Cornell Univ. Press, 1971), p. 79. Citations in text are to this edition. For the Russian text, I have used the first edition (Berlin: Gelikon, 1923).

28. Tynjanov, "Literaturnoe segodnja," *Poètika* p. 166. Sheldon translates a portion of this essay in the introduction to *Zoo*, p. xxxi.

29. Viktor Šklovskij, *Gamburgskij Ščet*, p. 108.

30. "Pervoe predislovie," *Xod konja*, p. 9 (ellipsis in original).

31. Not only Shklovsky, but other Formalist critics as well have often been treated in a humorless or one-sided way. A recent example is Mary Louise Pratt, *Toward a Speech Act Theory of Literary Discourse* (Bloomington: Indiana Univ. Press, 1977). I present an alternative picture of Russian Formalism in "The Heresiarch of *Meta*," *PTL*, 3 (1978): 407–427.

32. Tynjanov, "Žurnal, kritik, čitatel' i pisatel'," *Poètika*, p. 149.

33. V. A. Sidorov's article on the *Diary* as a literary form appeared posthumously.

34. Boris M. Ejxenbaum, *Moj vremmenik: Slovesnost', nauka, kritika, smes'* (Leningrad: Izdatel'stvo pisatelej, 1929), p. 5.

35. Konstantin Mochulsky, *Dostoevsky: His Life and Work*, tr. Michael A. Minihan (Princeton: Princeton Univ. Press, 1967), p. 535.

36. The notebooks for the *Diary* may be found in *The Unpublished Dostoevsky*, vol. 2, p. 63 ff. (in Russian in *Neizdannyj Dostoevskij*, p. 366 ff.):

see, for instance, the plan for the article "A Turkish Proverb," English version, vol. 2, p. 117; Russian, p. 417.

37. In his preface to the 1925 translation of the *Dostoevsky* lectures, Arnold Bennet quotes Gide as saying that "everything that Dostoevsky ever wrote is worth reading and must be read. Nothing can safely be omitted." Bennet specifically regrets that "Dostoevsky's important *Journal d'un Écrivain* exists in French but not in English," André Gide, *Dostoevsky* (Norfolk, Conn.: New Directions, 1961), p. xviii.

38. Harry Levin, *James Joyce* (Norfolk, Conn., 1941), p. 42; as cited in M. H. Abrams, *Natural Supernaturalism: Tradition and Revolution in Romantic Literature* (New York: Norton, 1971), p. 130.

39. André Gide, *"The Counterfeiters" with Journal of "The Counterfeiters"*, tr. Dorothy Bussy (novel) and Justin O'Brien (journal) (New York: Modern Library, 1955), p. 187.

40. It is unclear whether Gide believed that Dostoevsky had intended the *Diary* as a metaliterary work of this kind or whether, regardless of Dostoevsky's intentions, Gide found it interesting to take it that way. Judging from some comments in the *Dostoevsky* lectures, the second possibility seems more likely. In 1927, Gide published *Journal des Faux-Monnayeurs*, that is, the journal of a novel in the form of a diary of a novelist who . . .

41. The notebooks for the January, 1876, *Diary* specifically refer to the prefatory "dedication" to *Don Juan*, *Neizdannyj Dostoevskij*, p. 377.

42. "Otvet Russkomu vestniku," *Stat'i*, p. 213. This article also contains Dostoevsky's discussion (especially interesting in light of his later work on the *Diary*) of Pushkin's "Egyptian Nights" as a work that takes the *form* of a fragment in order to depict a "single moment" from the current of Roman life, pp. 211–212.

43. See the version in *The Short Stories of Dostoevsky*.

44. *Pis'ma*, II, 59. See the discussion of this letter in Jackson, "The Creative Process," *Dostoevsky's Quest*, p. 164.

3. Utopia as a Literary Genre

1. A notable exception to these criticisms is Robert Elliott, *The Shape of Utopia: Studies in a Literary Genre* (Chicago: Univ. of Chicago Press, 1970). See in particular the chapters on "Saturnalia, Satire and Utopia," pp. 3–24, and on "The Aesthetics of Utopia," pp. 102–128. Parts of Elliott's earlier study, *The Power of Satire: Magic, Ritual, Art* (Princeton: Princeton Univ. Press, 1960), contributed to my understanding of utopia as a didactic genre.

While completing the present study, I have come across Darko Suvin's interesting *Metamorphoses of Science Fiction: On the Poetics and History of a Literary Genre* (New Haven: Yale Univ. Press, 1979), which also considers the problems of "imperialist" definitions—though Suvin's class of utopias is considerably broader than mine.

2. *The Story of Utopias* (1922; rpt. New York: Viking, 1962).
3. *More's "Utopia": The Biography of an Idea* (1952; rpt. New York: Harper, 1965). Hexter is one of those who describe the fictionality of *Utopia* as a way of increasing the "sense of reality" of the descriptions, p. 29.
4. For a sample of the process by which Hexter uses his history of the work's composition to defend his view of its meaning, see ibid., pp. 33–35.
5. *Utopian Fantasy: A Study of English Utopian Fiction since the End of the Nineteenth Century*, 2nd ed. (New York: McGraw-Hill, 1973).
6. Ibid., p. ix. Strictly speaking, this passage describes how the second portion of the list (1951–1971) was compiled.
7. For example, in the chapter on "Literary Achievement," Gerber writes: "A limited amount of fantasy and the prevalence of social ideas in a utopian novel cannot be avoided and should be accepted as a distinctive feature of the utopian genre . . . " (ibid., p. 122).
8. On the emergence of genres, see Claudio Guillén, "Genre and Counter-genre: The Discovery of the Picaresque," *Literature as System*, pp. 135–158.
9. The phrase occurs in the title of More's work: "The Best State of a Commonwealth and the New Island of Utopia." Unless otherwise indicated, all citations from *Utopia* are from *The Complete Works of Thomas More*, vol. 4 (*Utopia*), ed. Edward Surtz, S.J., and J. H. Hexter (New Haven: Yale Univ. Press, 1965).
10. *The Republic of Plato*, tr. Francis Macdonald Cornford (New York: Oxford Univ. Press, 1945), p. 110.
11. Edward Bellamy, *Looking Backward, 2000–1887* (New York: Signet, 1960). All citations are to this edition, which, following Bellamy's second edition, includes the postscript.
12. Fictionality is not a criterion of literary utopias; but is understandable that literary works which describe an unreal society should be entirely or mostly fictional.
13. The delineator of B. F. Skinner's *Walden Two* is explicitly compared to Virgil and Beatrice in chapter 8. As a rule, Skinner is quite conscious of, and often discusses, generic conventions and precedents.
14. Here again, I am not engaged in defining or accounting for the usage of the *word* "novel," but rather in identifying a class of texts in the way that all genres are identified in the present study, that is, by their semiotic nature. Thus, I am describing as interpretive conventions what are more commonly described as characteristics of the works themselves, that is, as "formal realism" (my first convention) and psychology (my second convention). This distinction will become important when we discuss narratives which may be interpreted either as novels or as utopias—that is, boundary works, in which the same text changes in meaning depending on which generic conventions are considered appropriate. The class of texts which will be called novels in this study are identified without reference to length—which is to say, it includes short stories, as well as long narratives, that are appropriately interpreted according to the two specified conventions.

15. On the use of language in the novel, see Mikhail Bakhtin, "Slovo v romane," in *Voprosy literatury i èstetiki: Issledovanija raznyx let* (Moscow: Xudožestvennaja literatura, 1975), pp. 72–233, and my discussion of Bakhtin's theories, "The Heresiarch of *Meta*." For an English translation of "Slovo v romane," see Mikhail Bakhtin, *The Dialogic Imagination: Four Essays in the Philosophy of Language and Theory of the Novel*, tr. Caryl Emerson and Michael Holquist (Austin: Univ. of Texas Press, 1981).

16. Leo Tolstoy, *War and Peace*, tr. Ann Dunnigan (New York: Signet, 1968), p. 1409 (first epilogue, ch. 16).

17. Readers whose expectations of prose fiction have been formed by novels are likely to be disappointed by utopias and to judge as a particular work's aesthetic flaws and its author's intellectual limitations what are in fact the genre's basic conventions and assumptions. It is possible that utopias written in dialogue form do not encourage the expectations of novels and therefore prove less disappointing. I suspect as well that readerships familiar with non-novelistic—which is to say, nonrealistic and nonpsychological—forms of prose fiction are also more receptive to utopias. That is probably the case in the Soviet Union, where the dominant mode of narrative fiction, Socialist Realism, derives in part from such utopias as Chernyshevsky's *What Is to Be Done?* and makes use of a fully authoritative speaker. (A series of Russian translations of Western utopias is published under the title *Forerunners of Scientific Socialism*.) On the Russian sources of the Socialist Realist hero, see Rufus W. Mathewson, Jr., *The Positive Hero in Russian Literature*, 2nd ed. (Stanford: Stanford Univ. Press, 1975); and Katerina Clark's *Ritual Form in the Soviet Novel*. On the implications of Socialist Realism for the theory of literature and art, see my "Socialist Realism and Literary Theory," *Journal of Aesthetics and Art Criticism*, 38, no. 2 (Winter 1979): 121–133.

18. A recently reprinted American feminist utopia is Charlotte Perkins Gilman, *Herland* (New York: Pantheon, 1979). *Herland* was written in 1915 and serialized in Gilman's monthly magazine, *The Forerunner*.

19. B. F. Skinner, *Walden Two* (New York: Macmillan, 1948), p. 63.

20. William Morris, *News from Nowhere, or An Epoch of Rest, Being Some Chapters from a Utopian Romance* (New York: Longmans, 1910), p. 66. *News from Nowhere* was first published serially in 1890.

21. Alexander Herzen, *My Past and Thoughts: The Memoirs of Alexander Herzen*, tr. Constance Garnett, revised by Humphrey Higgens (New York: Knopf, 1968), vol. 2, p. 823. See the entire discussion of Proudhon and the family, vol. 2, pp. 805–832.

22. *Under Western Eyes* (Garden City: Doubleday-Anchor, 1963). Originally published in 1911.

23. Eugene Zamiatin, *We*, tr. Gregory Zilboorg (New York: Dutton, n.d.: translation originally published 1924), p. 41. Citations are to this edition, with translations amended for accuracy with reference to the Russian text of *My* (New York: Inter-Language Literary Associates, 1967).

24. My discussion of "wisdom" literature follows Michael Holquist, "Puzzle

and Mystery, The Narrative Poles of Knowing: *Crime and Punishment*,"
Dostoevsky and the Novel (Princeton: Princeton Univ. Press, 1977), pp.
75-101; and his article, "Whodunit and Other Questions: Metaphysical
Detective Stories in Post-War Fiction," *New Literary History*, 3, no. 1
(Autumn 1971): 135-156.

25. Felix Emil Held, "Johann Valentin Andreae's *Christianopolis*: An Ideal
State of the Seventeenth Century," dissertation (Univ. of Illinois, 1914),
pp. 142-143. The second half of the dissertation is a translation of *Christianopolis*, which I cite henceforth in the text.

26. William Dean Howells, *A Traveler from Altruria* (New York: Hill and
Wang, 1957), p. 34.

27. Edward Bellamy, *Equality* (1897; rpt. New York: AMS Press, 1970),
p. viii.

28. *A Modern Utopia* (Lincoln: Univ. of Nebraska Press, 1967), p. xxxi.

29. An interesting consideration of these nonfictional sections of literary
utopias may be found in Elliott, *The Shape of Utopia*, pp. 110-128; the
discussion of Mercier and Cabet is on p. 112.

30. For an example of how other, nongeneric, expectations can be used for
didactic purposes, see Stanley Eugene Fish, *Surprised by Sin: The Reader
in "Paradise Lost"* (New York: St. Martin's Press, 1967) and *Self-Consuming Artifacts: The Experience of Seventeenth-Century Literature* (Berkeley: Univ. of Calif. Press, 1972). For the use of similar strategies in satire,
see Henry W. Sams, "Swift's Satire of the Second Person" (1959), in
*Twentieth Century Interpretations of "Gulliver's Travels": A Collection
of Critical Essays*, ed. Frank Brady (Englewood Cliffs, N.J.: Prentice-Hall, 1968), pp. 35-40.

31. *Oeuvres d'Étienne Cabet*, vol. 1, *Voyage en Icarie* (Paris: Anthropos,
1970), p. vi.

32. Gregory Bateson, *Steps to an Ecology of Mind*, pp. 201-279.

33. On the verbal duels of Ivan and Smerdyakov, see my article "Verbal
Pollution in *The Brothers Karamazov*," *PTL*, 3 (1978): 223-233.

34. For a more detailed discussion of this topic, see my article "The Reader
as Voyeur: Tolstoi and the Poetics of Didactic Fiction," *Canadian-American Slavic Studies*, 12, no. 4 (Winter 1978): 465-480.

35. *Great Short Works of Leo Tolstoy*, tr. Louise and Aylmer Maude (New
York: Harper, 1967), p. 411.

36. On the origins of satire in magic, see Elliott, *The Power of Satire*; on
magical functions of Soviet journalism, see Herbert Marcuse, *Soviet Marxism: A Critical Analysis* (New York: Columbia Univ. Press, 1958).

37. The term "false listening" derives from Smith (*Margins of Discourse*,
pp. 100-101, 114, 119), who uses it in a different sense.

38. Denis Diderot, *"Rameau's Nephew" and Other Works*, tr. Jacques Barzun
and Ralph H. Bowen (Indianapolis: Bobbs-Merrill, 1956), p. 202.

39. N. G. Černyševskij, *Sobranie sočinenij v pjati tomax*, vol. 1, *Čto delat'?
Iz rasskazov o novyx ljudjax* (Moscow: Ogonek, 1974), pp. 12-14. Translation mine.

40. On the poetics and implied readers of literary and nonliterary apocalypses, see Joseph Anthony Wittreich, *Visionary Poetics: Milton's Tradition and His Legacy* (San Marino, Calif.: Huntington Library, 1979). On closure in apocalyptic models of history and in literary narratives, see Frank Kermode, *The Sense of an Ending: Studies in the Theory of Fiction* (New York: Oxford Univ. Press, 1967).

41. Victor Shklovsky, "Art as Technique," in *Russian Formalist Criticism: Four Essays*, ed. Lee T. Lemon and Marion J. Reis (Lincoln: Univ. of Nebraska Press, 1965), pp. 18–21.

42. D. S. Mirsky, *Pushkin* (New York: Dutton, 1963), p. 77.

43. For an account of the composition and publication of Chernyshevsky's work, see the chapter on him in E. Lampert, *Sons against Fathers: Studies in Russian Radicalism and Revolution* (Oxford: Clarendon Press, 1965), pp. 94–225.

44. For an account of the reception and textology of *Looking Backward*, see the introduction and textual note to Robert C. Elliott (ed.), *Looking Backward, 2000–1887* (New York: Houghton Mifflin, 1966). Elliott notes that Tolstoy arranged for the first Russian translation of Bellamy's work, which by 1918 had been translated nine more times into various languages of the Russian empire (p. viii). Erich Fromm's preface to the edition cited in this study is one that enthusiastically traces the progress of the world and the work, with whose "open" text it almost seems to merge.

4. Recontextualizations

Part 1: Theory of Parody

1. The significance and dynamics of the "environment" in which literature is written and read are discussed in Boris M. Ejxenbaum, "Literary Environment," in *Readings*.

2. See especially Bakhtin, *PDP*, pp. 150–227, and V. N. Vološinov, *Marxism and the Philosophy of Language* (henceforth *Marxism*), tr. Ladislav Matejka and I. R. Titunik (New York: Seminar, 1973), pp. 109–159. I discuss their model of intertextuality in "The Heresiarch of *Meta*."

3. On imitation in the broader sense, and its relation to other forms of intertextuality, see Thomas M. Greene, "Imitation and Discovery in the Renaissance" and "The Falling Leaf: Etiology and Literary History" (unpublished manuscripts).

An interesting case of intertextuality is Pushkin's play *The Covetous Knight (Scenes from Chenstone's Tragi-comedy "The Covetous Knight")* —the subtitle in English in the original—a work which does not, on closer inspection, appear to be the imitation it claims to be. Assuming that Chenstone is William Shenstone, scholars have been unable to locate any Shenstone play by that title; and a number have concluded that Pushkin was deliberately engaging in "mystification," as the Soviet editors of the

Jubilee edition (Moscow: Academia, 1936; vol. 3, p. 464) put it. They suspect an attempt to forestall interpretation of the play as a fictionalization of Pushkin's miserly father; Pushkin's characteristic metaliterary playfulness, it seems to me, may also be involved. A sort of inverse forgery, Pushkin's play does not pretend, as a forgery does, to be original when it is not, but rather to be *un*original when it is not.

4. Here again, I am identifying a class, not defining a word: the *word* "parody," it might be noted, also has a history of usage that does *not* entail discrediting an original (e.g., in music).

5. For example, Gilbert Highet defines parody as "imitation which, through distortion and exaggeration, evokes amusement, derision, and sometimes scorn" (*The Anatomy of Satire* [Princeton: Princeton Univ. Press, 1962], p. 69). *The Princeton Encyclopedia of Poetics* (ed. Alex Preminger, 2nd ed. [Princeton: Princeton Univ. Press, 1974]) first distinguishes between "comic p., which is close to burlesque, and literary or critical p., which follows more closely a given author's style or a particular work of art. . . . Critical p. has been defined as the exaggerated imitation of a work of art." An essay that just appeared in *Poetics Today* (Ziva Ben-Porat, "Method in *Madness*," *PT*, 1, no. 1-2) defines parody as an "alleged representation, usually comic, of a literary text or other artistic object—i.e. a representation of a 'modelled reality,' which is itself already a particular representation of an original 'reality'" (p. 247).

Neither Christopher Stone (*Parody* [London: Martin Secker, n.d.]), nor Leonard Feinberg (*An Introduction to Satire* [Ames, Iowa: Iowa State Univ. Press, 1967]), nor Dwight Macdonald (in the appendix to *Parodies: An Anthology from Chaucer to Beerbohm—and After*, ed. Dwight Macdonald [New York: Random House, 1960]) defines parody, but all seem to agree that it is a form of satire and that a good definition "at least brings in humor" (Macdonald, *Parodies*, 557).

Russian Formalists (Shklovsky, Tynyanov, and some of their successors) have tended to waffle between definitions in terms of textual features—"devices" and devices that bare devices—and characterizations in terms of social function, the approach of the present study. Sander L. Gilman (*The Parodic Sermon in European Perspective: Aspects of Liturgical Parody from the Middle Ages to the Twentieth Century* [Wiesbaden: Franz Steiner, 1974]), who defines parody as "a literary form which is created by incorporating elements of an already existing form in a manner creating a conscious contrast," insists that features present in the text itself—the objective "description of form" rather than necessarily subjective interpretations of "motivation" or reception—must be the basis of a definition: ". . . parody can not be defined by the ends which it is thought to achieve. . . . As a workable literary term it can only be limited by a factual description of the means employed by the author" (pp. 2-3). I much prefer Dr. Johnson's definition: "a kind of writing in which the words of an author or his thoughts are taken and by a slight change adapted to some new purpose" (cited by Macdonald, *Parodies*, p. 557), which does not mention literariness or humor and does mention purpose.

6. As cited in Louis L. Martz, *The Poetry of Meditation: A Study of English Religious Literature of the Seventeenth Century*, 2nd ed. (New Haven: Yale Univ. Press, 1962), p. 179. See the discussion of sacred parody, pp. 184-193.
7. Henry Fielding, *"Joseph Andrews" and "Shamela"*, ed. Martin Battestin (Boston: Houghton Mifflin, 1961), from the preface to *Joseph Andrews*, p. 12.
8. Tynyanov's most extensive considerations of parody and its relation to literary evolution are "Dostoevskij i Gogol' (k teorii parodii)" and "O parodii," in *Poètika*, pp. 198-226, 284-309.
9. Macdonald also includes a section of "unconscious self-parodies."
10. Leo N. Tolstoy, *What Is Art?*, tr. Aylmer Maude (New York: Bobbs-Merrill, 1960), p. 162.
11. For example, in Highet, *Anatomy of Satire*, p. 69.

Part 2: Anti-utopia as a Parodic Genre

1. Although I shall be primarily concerned with literary anti-genres, it should be noted that there are nonliterary anti-genres as well. Moreover, it is possible for a target genre to be nonliterary and its parody to be literary (or the reverse); and either may be literary in one period and nonliterary in another. In principle, all combinations are possible. To take a few examples, both mock-epic and epic are literary; medieval parodic grammars and liturgies and their targets would seem to have been nonliterary; the parodic sermon has, like its target, changed its status, perhaps more than once. It should also be noted that the generalizations I offer regarding "classic texts" and "exemplars" in a *written* literary tradition would probably have to be modified for *oral* literary anti-genres.

    On medieval parodic grammars and liturgies, see Mikhail Bakhtin, *Rabelais and His World*, tr. Helene Iswolsky (Cambridge, Mass: MIT Press, 1968), pp. 84-86. On the parodic sermon, see Gilman, *The Parodic Sermon*.
2. *The Portable Swift*, ed. Carl Van Doren (New York: Viking, 1948), p. 403.
3. On the themes of anti-utopianism and "novelness" in Dostoevsky, see Michael Holquist, *Dostoevsky and the Novel*.
4. Bakhtin links these parodies to parodic social rituals, especially carnival, in *Rabelais*.
5. Ambrose Bierce, *The Devil's Dictionary* (New York: Dover, 1958).
6. Samuel Johnson, *Rasselas, Poems, and Selected Prose*, ed. Bertrand H. Bronson (New York: Holt Rinehart, 1958), pp. 212-216.
7. Mikhail Bakhtin, "Forms of Time and of the Chronotope in the Novel," *The Dialogic Imagination*.
8. Pushkin, vol. 2, p. 208 (*Ruslan i Ljudmila*, vol. 1, pp. 460-461).

9. Evgenij Zamjatin, "O literature, revoljucii i èntropii," in *Lica* (New York: Inter-Language Literary Associates, 1967), p. 253.

10. Francis Bacon, *New Atlantis*, in *"The Advancement of Learning" and "New Atlantis"*, ed. Arthur Johnston (Oxford: Clarendon Press, 1974), p. 239.

11. Bakhtin, "Epic and Novel," *The Dialogic Imagination*.

12. For a translation of the full text of the famous note, see Mochulsky, *Dostoevsky*, p. 544. Although Dostoevsky recorded this note during his preparation for *Karamazov*—that is, long after *Notes* had been written—it may be taken as an indication of the great importance of *Candide* in his thinking: Dostoevsky was, in effect, constantly writing (and re-writing) "the Russian *Candide*."

13. *The Portable Voltaire*, ed. Ben Ray Redman (New York: Viking, 1963), p. 270.

14. V. Garshin, *The Scarlet Flower* (Moscow: Foreign Languages, n.d.), p. 166.

15. Jorge Luis Borges, *Labyrinths: Selected Stories and Other Writings*, ed. Donald A. Yates and James E. Irby, 2nd ed. (New York: New Directions, 1964), p. 7.

16. Aldous Huxley, *Brave New World* (New York: Harper-Perennial, 1969), p. 154.

17. *The Stoic and Epicurean Philosophers: The Complete Extant Writings of Epicurus, Epictetus, Lucretius, Marcus Aurelius*, ed. Whitney J. Oates (New York: Modern Library, 1940), p. 224.

18. Michael Bakunin, *Selected Writings*, ed. Arthur Lehning, tr. Steven Cox and Olive Stevens (New York: Grove, 1974), p. 114.

19. Abram Tertz [pseudonym of Andrey Sinyavsky], *The Makepeace Experiment*, tr. Manya Harari (London: Collins and Harvill, 1965), p. 56. Translations have been amended for accuracy with reference to the edition of the novel in *Fantastičeskij mir Abrama Terca* (New York: Inter-Language Literary Associates, 1967).

20. Richard Sheldon's English translation of "Bundle" appears in *The Serapion Brothers: A Critical Anthology*, ed. Gary Kern and Christopher Collins (Ann Arbor: Ardis, 1975), pp. 129–130.

21. On the terms and texts of that debate, see William Nelson, *Fact and Fiction: The Dilemma of the Renaissance Storyteller* (Cambridge, Mass.: Harvard Univ. Press, 1973); on the "extraordinary voyage," see Philip Babcock Gove, *The Imaginary Voyage in Prose Fiction: A History of Its Criticism and a Guide for Its Study, with an Annotated Check List of 215 Imaginary Voyages from 1700 to 1800* (New York: Columbia Univ. Press, 1941).

22. "Ja bojus'" (I Am Afraid), in *Lica*, p. 190.

   We has a complex textual history. Because it could not be published in the Soviet Union, it was first published in English translation (1924); the first edition in Russian, also published abroad, falsely purported to be a re-translation back into Russian from a Czech translation (with errors deliberately inserted to make the claim plausible), a ruse vainly intended to spare the author accusations of having conspired in a foreign edition. It is risky, therefore, to guess Zamyatin's intentions regarding the final editing of his work for the press; but given the work's frequent self-referential play and the author's familiarity with the Formalists and their literature, it seems possible that he would have had the work printed so that when D-503 refers to writing a particular page of his manuscript, the reader would be on the same page of the book. For further information on the history of the publication of *We*, see Marc Slonim's introduction to the Dutton edition.

Part 3: Meta-utopia

1. *A Hero of Our Time*, tr. Martin Parker (Moscow: Foreign Languages, n.d.), p. 66.
2. V. Šklovskij, "Evgenij Onegin (Puškin i Stern)," in *Očerki po poètike Puškina* (Berlin: Epoxa, 1923), pp. 197–220.
3. My interpretation of the rhetorical paradox and of *The Praise of Folly* follows Walter Kaiser, *Praisers of Folly: Erasmus, Rabelais, Shakespeare* (Cambridge, Mass.: Harvard Univ. Press, 1963); and Rosalie L. Colie, *Paradoxia Epidemica: The Renaissance Tradition of Paradox* (Princeton: Princeton Univ. Press, 1966).
4. Desiderius Erasmus, *Moriae Encomium or The Praise of Folly*, tr. Harry Carter (New York: Heritage, n.d.), pp. 5–6.
5. I discuss the role of the rhetorical paradox in Dostoevsky's novel in "Verbal Pollution in *The Brothers Karamazov*."
6. The paradoxicalist of *The Possessed*, Kirillov, argues that the free individual is *bound* to show his or her self-will, that only the extremes of denial and atheism can be evidence of true faith, and that life only makes sense after a senseless act of suicide—that is, by an act of self-destruction that repeats the self-cancelling logic of paradox.
7. *A Modern Utopia*, pp. v–vi. Taking Wells' work as a utopia, Hillegas includes the sort of preface often added to utopias of another era—compare with Fromm's preface to *Looking Backward*.
8. *We*, p. 8. Himself the author of an essay on Wells, Zamyatin here may be alluding to *A Modern Utopia*.
9. The "seriocomic" tone of meta-utopia probably reflects its generic debt to menippean satire. On utopian themes in menippean satire, see Holland, *Robert Burton's "Anatomy of Melancholy" and Menippean Satire*, and Bakhtin, *PDP* (ch. 4).
10. William Shakespeare, *The Tempest*, ed. Robert Langbaum (New York: Signet, 1964), act II, scene i, ll. 148–174.
11. Alexander Herzen, *"From the Other Shore" and "The Russian People and Socialism: An Open Letter to Jules Michelet"*, intro. Isaiah Berlin (New York: George Braziller, 1956), p. 27. For the complex textual history of this work, see the bibliographical note, pp. xxiv–xxv.

12. Dostoevsky, of course, was quite familiar with the works of Diderot. "To our great joy," his wife described their stay in Italy in 1868, "the city of Florence had an excellent library . . . and my husband went there every day to read for a while after dinner. He borrowed from the library the works of Voltaire and Diderot, which he knew fluently in French, and read them at home all winter" (Anna Dostoevsky, *Dostoevsky: Reminiscences*, p. 153). Russian authors no doubt were aware of Diderot's own Russian connection: his library, purchased (as a form of subsidy) by Catherine the Great, reverted to Russia after his death, and so Russia thereby came into possession of the manuscripts of a number of his still unpublished works (e.g., *D'Alembert's Dream*).

13. Orou's conversation with the chaplain appears in *French Utopias: An Anthology of Ideal Societies*, ed. and trans. Frank E. Manuel and Fritzie P. Manuel (New York: Schocken, 1971); the "Old Man's Farewell" is anthologized in *The Anarchists*, ed. Irving Louis Horowitz (New York: Dell, 1964). Neither anthology mentions the ironic framing of these utopian passages in the *Supplement*.

14. C. S. Lewis, "A Play of Wit," in *Twentieth Century Interpretations of "Utopia": A Collection of Critical Essays* (Englewood Cliffs, N.J.: Prentice-Hall, 1968), p. 68.

15. "Its place on our shelves," writes Lewis, "is . . . within reasonable distance of *Rabelais*, a long way from the *Republic*" (ibid., p. 68). T. S. Dorsch cites Lewis' reading with approval: "Following his method in arranging the books on my shelves, I should place *Utopia* next to my copy of the works of Lucian. . . . " ("A Detestable State," in *Twentieth Century Interpretations of "Utopia"*, p. 88). Note both critics' defense of an interpretation by a classification.

16. Cited in Elliott, *The Shape of Utopia*, p. 36, from Thomas More, *Latin Epigrams*, tr. Leicester Bradner and Charles A. Lynch (Chicago: Univ. of Chicago Press, 1953), p. 126.

17. Johan Huizinga, *Erasmus and the Age of Reformation, with a Selection from the Letters of Erasmus*, tr. F. Hopman (text) and Barbara Flower (letters) (New York: Harper, 1957), pp. 234-238.

18. Ibid., p. 234.

19. On the "seriocomic" aspects and antecedents of *Utopia*, see Holland, *Robert Burton's "Anatomy of Melancholy"*, and Nelson's introduction to *Twentieth Century Interpretations of "Utopia"*. See also the references to *Utopia* in Nelson's *Fact or Fiction: The Dilemma of the Renaissance Storyteller*.

20. J. H. Lupton (ed.), *The "Utopia" of Sir Thomas More* (Oxford: Clarendon Press, 1895), p. xli.

21. David Bevington, "The Divided Mind," in *Twentieth Century Interpretations of "Utopia"*, p. 78.

22. Surtz and Hexter note that the prefatory letter by Beatus Rhenanus, which was included in the edition containing both *Utopia* and the *Epigrammatica* of More and Erasmus, "apparently was intended as introduc-

tory to both *Utopia* and the *Epigrammatica* but . . . never fell into its right position and came to serve as prefatory only to the *Epigrammatica*" (*Utopia*, cxcii). Surtz and Hexter include only the "pertinent passage'" from this preface—which is to say, the passage dealing with *Utopia* and its reception—in their edition, placing it at the work's close. In other words, both the specific text and the placing of the preface is their choice, not More's; and it would also seem to be possible that its very inclusion as part of *Utopia* is not authoritative. Unless otherwise stated, my information regarding the composition of the editions of *Utopia* published during More's lifetime is from Surtz and Hexter; useful textological data may also be found in Lupton, *The "Utopia"*.

23. In the letter to Busleyden, Giles writes: "I have appended also some brief annotations in the margins" (*Utopia*, p. 23). Surtz and Hexter note, however, that on the title page of the 1517 edition Lupset attributes the annotations to Erasmus (ibid., pp. 280–281).

24. The two editions are: Frederic R. White (ed.), *Famous Utopias of the Renaissance* (New York: Hendricks House, 1955; originally Packard, 1946); and Edward Surtz, S.J. (ed.), *Utopia* by St. Thomas More (New Haven: Yale Univ. Press, 1964). Another edition, Mildred Campbell (ed.), *The Utopia of Sir Thomas More* (Roslyn, N.Y.: Black, 1947), seems to confuse the framing material of Robynson's translation with that of More's original editions: Campbell describes not only More's and Giles' letters, but also the note from the Printer to the Reader of the Robynson translation (which explains why the Utopian alphabet was not included) as "part of the mechanism designed to lend reality to the tale" (p. 3).

25. The notable exception to this generalization is the Surtz and Hexter edition; Hexter's interpretation of the text is discussed below.

26. A. I. Malein, *Utopija* (Moscow-Leningrad: Akademija nauk, 1947), p. 239. "In the mouth of Hythloday," Malein notes, "More out of caution places his own thoughts in what follows, and, out of fear of the censor, himself plays the role of his opponent."

27. Paul Turner (ed. and trans.), *Utopia* by Thomas More (Harmondsworth, England: Penguin, 1965), p. 22. Somewhat inconsistently, Turner nevertheless states elsewhere in his introduction that "I am simple minded enough to believe, with certain qualifications, that the book means what it says. . . . that *Utopia* is what it appears to be, a blueprint, however provisionally, for a perfect society" (pp. 12–13). I am unable to decide whether Turner intended the ironic implications of this edition's cover illustration, a detail from the painting "The Construction of the Tower of Babel" attributed to Hendrick van Cleve III.

28. On the actual operation of this re-authoring, see Katerina Clark, *Ritual Form in the Soviet Novel*.

29. This argument regarding the aims of textology is advanced in D. S. Lixačev, *Tekstologija, na materiale Russkoj literatury X–XVIII vv.* (Moscow-Leningrad: Adakemija nauk, 1962).

30. *The Complete Works of St. Thomas More*, vol. 4, p. 239. Citations in the following discussion are to this edition.
31. Bevington, "The Divided Mind," p. 80.
32. Elliott, *The Shape of Utopia*, pp. 47-48.
33. J. H. Hexter, "Intention, Words, and Meaning: The Case of More's *Utopia*," *New Literary History*, 6, no. 3 (Spring 1975): 541.
34. So Henry James' and Percy Lubbock's characterization of the novels of Tolstoy and Dostoevsky as formless has been answered by a number of critics who, instead, see those novels as governed by an aesthetic (or anti-aesthetic) different from, or systematically defiant of, the norms of nineteenth-century Western novels.
35. On the cost of this kind of ambivalence, see Wayne C. Booth, *The Rhetoric of Fiction* (Chicago: Univ. of Chicago Press, 1961), pp. 354-364; and Booth, *A Rhetoric of Irony* (Chicago: Univ. of Chicago Press, 1974), pp. 127-128.
36. For example, the sketch, feuilleton, and short story that comprise the second chapter of the January, 1876, issue contain a number of allusions and references to each other, and to the chapter's overarching theme of the suffering of children. That chapter as a whole seems to echo and be echoed by the discussions of utopia—that is, of the possibility of eliminating such suffering—in a number of the issue's other articles, especially "The Golden Age in the Pocket" and "Russian Society for the Prevention of Cruelty to Animals"; and those articles, in turn, seem to enter into dialogue with the issue's anti-utopian sketch, "The Extraordinary Shrewdness of Devils." Here, as elsewhere in the *Diary*, the theme of the transformation of reality into utopia (and of "Depraved Souls into Pure Ones") is paralleled, and perhaps parodied, by the metaliterary theme of the transformation of reality into art—a process both discussed and dramatized in that very issue.
37. An interesting consequence of such failures may be that in some cases an abridged edition, which has been constructed to foreground the author's intended overall design for the work, may create a better impression of that design than the work in its entirety. Speaking more generally, one function that abridged editions may serve is to make unusual works, and works from remote times and cultures, "similar" enough to known works to be "assimilated." It is also common for translations to assimilate works in this way.
38. Fyodor Dostoevsky, *Crime and Punishment*, tr. Constance Garnett (New York: Modern Library, 1950), p. 283 (pt. 4, ch. 1).
39. Fyodor Dostoevsky, *The Idiot*, p. 406 (pt. 3, ch. 8).
40. On the etymological significance of the novel's title, see Michael Holquist, "The Gaps in Christology: *The Idiot*," *Dostoevsky and the Novel*, pp. 102-123.
41. For an account of this incident, see Frank, *Dostoevsky: The Seeds of Revolt, 1821-1849*, p. 168.
42. Edward Wasiolek, *Dostoevsky: The Major Fiction* (Cambridge, Mass.: M.I.T. Press, 1964), p. 145. The most interesting recent interpretation of

the "Dream" as anti-utopia is Holquist, "The Either/Or of Duels and Dreams: *A Gentle Creature* and *Dream of a Ridiculous Man*," *Dostoevsky and the Novel*, pp. 148–164.

43. So I argued in my review of Holquist's *Dostoevsky and the Novel*: "State of the Field: A Review Article," *Slavic and East European Journal*, 22, no. 2 (Summer 1978): 203–207.

Index